The Industrial Revolution

Patrick N. Allitt, Ph.D.

THE
GREAT
COURSES®

Smithsonian®

PUBLISHED BY:

THE GREAT COURSES
Corporate Headquarters
4840 Westfields Boulevard, Suite 500
Chantilly, Virginia 20151-2299
Phone: 1-800-832-2412
Fax: 703-378-3819
www.thegreatcourses.com

Patrick N. Allitt, Ph.D.
Cahoon Family Professor
of American History
Emory University

Professor Patrick N. Allitt was born in 1956 and raised in Mickleover, England. He attended John Port School in the Derbyshire village of Etwall and was an undergraduate at Hertford College, University of Oxford, from 1974 to 1977. He studied American History at the University of California, Berkeley, where he earned his Ph.D. in 1986. Between 1985 and 1988, he was a Henry Luce Postdoctoral Fellow at Harvard Divinity School, where he specialized in American Religious History. Since then, he has been on the history faculty of Emory University, except for one year (1992–1993) as a fellow at the Princeton University Center for the Study of Religion. He was the director of Emory's Center for Teaching and Curriculum from 2004 to 2009 and has been the Cahoon Family Professor of American History since 2009.

Professor Allitt is the author of five scholarly books: *A Climate of Crisis: America in the Age of Environmentalism*; *The Conservatives: Ideas and Personalities throughout American History*; *Religion in America Since 1945: A History*; *Catholic Converts: British and American Intellectuals Turn to Rome*; and *Catholic Intellectuals and Conservative Politics in America, 1950–1985*. In addition, he is the editor of *Major Problems in American Religious History* and author of a memoir about his life as a college professor, *I'm the Teacher, You're the Student: A Semester in the University Classroom*. He has written numerous articles and reviews for academic and popular journals, including recent book reviews in *The Spectator* and *The Weekly Standard*.

Professor Allitt has made seven other Great Courses: *The Rise and Fall of the British Empire*; *The Conservative Tradition*; *American Religious History*; *Victorian Britain*; *The History of the United States, 2nd Edition* (with

Professors Allen C. Guelzo and Gary W. Gallagher); *The American Identity*; and *The Art of Teaching: Best Practices from a Master Educator*.

Professor Allitt's wife, Toni, is a Michigan native. They have one daughter, Frances. ■

About Smithsonian

Founded in 1846, the Smithsonian Institution is the world's largest museum and research complex, consisting of 19 museums and galleries, the National Zoological Park, and 9 research facilities. The total number of artifacts, works of art, and specimens in the Smithsonian's collections is estimated at 137 million. These collections represent America's rich heritage, art from across the globe, and the immense diversity of the natural and cultural world.

In support of its mission—the increase and diffusion of knowledge—the Smithsonian focuses on four Grand Challenges that describe its areas of study, collaboration, and exhibition: Unlocking the Mysteries of the Universe, Understanding and Sustaining a Biodiverse Planet, Valuing World Cultures, and Understanding the American Experience. The Smithsonian's partnership with The Great Courses is an opportunity to encourage continuous exploration by learners of all ages across these areas of study.

This course, *The Industrial Revolution*, covers the emergence of the Industrial Revolution in 18th-century Britain and the spread of its inventions and ideas to the fledgling United States, seeking to show how and why this great modern transformation occurred. From the steam engine to the horseless carriage, the rise of the factory to the role of immigrant labor, the course provides insight not only into the historical period but also into the birth of modern life and work as we know it. ■

Table of Contents

INTRODUCTION

Professor Biography i
Course Scope 1

LECTURE GUIDES

LECTURE 1
Industrialization Is Good for You 4

LECTURE 2
Why Was Britain First? 21

LECTURE 3
The Agricultural Revolution 38

LECTURE 4
Cities and Manufacturing Traditions 57

LECTURE 5
The Royal Shipyards 76

LECTURE 6
The Textile Industry 95

LECTURE 7
Coal Mining—Powering the Revolution 113

LECTURE 8
Iron—Coking and Puddling 132

LECTURE 9
Wedgwood and the Pottery Business 149

LECTURE 10
Building Britain's Canals 168

Table of Contents

LECTURE 11
Steam Technology and the First Railways........................188

LECTURE 12
The Railway Revolution...206

LECTURE 13
Isambard Kingdom Brunel—Master Engineer.................226

LECTURE 14
The Machine-Tool Makers 245

LECTURE 15
The Worker's-Eye View...264

LECTURE 16
Poets, Novelists, and Factories.....................................283

LECTURE 17
How Industry Changed Politics......................................302

LECTURE 18
Dismal Science—The Economists 321

SUPPLEMENTAL MATERIAL

Bibliography...340

The Industrial Revolution

Scope:

Throughout most of world history, nearly everyone has been poor, life expectancy has been short, and famine has been a frequent visitor. Today, many parts of the world are so wealthy that they regard poverty not as normal but as a special problem that ought to be eliminated. The single great cause of this increase in wealth has been industrialization. We know now beyond question that industrial societies generate wealth, which eventually spreads widely to benefit all their people, even though inequalities increase and even though the early stages of industrialization are often dirty, exploitative, and painful. No other way out of collective poverty has yet been discovered.

Britain was the first country to undertake industrialization. It began in the mid-18th century, by which time Britain had achieved political stability, acquired a colonial and commercial empire, founded banks and insurance systems, and discovered ways to increase its food output so that fewer farmers could feed more people than ever before. First in the cotton textile industry, then with improvements in coal mining, pottery manufacture, and iron smelting, new methods began to catch on, including the application of water and steam power to machinery, the concentration of large work forces in factories and mines, and the division of labor. When the economist Adam Smith wrote his classic work *An Inquiry into the Causes of the Wealth of Nations* (1776), all these processes were just getting underway. Part of Smith's genius was to recognize that they were not of merely local significance but had potentially world-changing implications.

Industrialization also required good transport and good communications. In the late 18th century, British entrepreneurs began to build a canal system to link up the country's navigable rivers and to connect all its major cities so that bulk goods could be carried economically between them. No sooner was the canal network complete, by about 1830, than a newer and faster technology, railways, began to displace it. Trains exploited improvements in steam-engine technology, which had been undertaken a century earlier to pump water out of flooded coal mines; when miniaturized, this technology proved adaptable to locomotives that could achieve high speeds running on smooth metal rails.

This course of 36 lectures asks why Britain was the first country to industrialize, why the United States and many parts of Europe caught up in the 19th century, and how these changes affected the course of world history. The initiative had shifted to the United States by the later decades of the 19th century. Carnegie in steel and Rockefeller in oil built near-monopoly corporations of unprecedented size as they came to dominate entire industries. Henry Ford, borrowing from the bicycle and meat-packing industries, worked out how to mass-produce motor cars on a moving assembly line from fully interchangeable component parts. Orville and Wilbur Wright then achieved what had been regarded throughout most of world history as the impossible—they made machines capable of controlled and sustained flight.

Industrialization victimized some people even as it benefited others. This course will examine the lives of early industrial workers who suffered terrible working conditions in horribly polluted cities, frequent industrial accidents, reduced life expectancy, and the shattering of traditional ways of life. These were the conditions in which socialism drew the interest of such intellectuals as Karl Marx, who could simultaneously admire industry and deplore capitalism, the economic system to which it was linked. Industrial societies specialize in constant innovation, which can also mean constant insecurity for people trapped in its coils. Among the themes we will cover is the way industry changed the distribution of political power both within nations and between them. Warfare, once mechanized and industrialized, became more destructive and hideous than ever before, as the two world wars attested in the first half of the 20th century.

The course ends with a survey of the globalization of industry; the Asian Tigers are now catching up with their Western rivals. One lecture late in the course considers the computer revolution and the phenomenal increase in knowledge-related technologies, all of which have been accompanied by great feats of miniaturization. Another considers the environmental costs of the Industrial Revolution. By the end of this series, you will be better placed to understand the processes that have enabled you to anticipate a long life of unprecedented comfort, surrounded by convenient devices, user-friendly technologies, and the prospect that more such conveniences will arise to help you and your descendants in the coming decades. ■

Industrialization Is Good for You
Lecture 1

The Industrial Revolution, which transformed the world over the past two and a half centuries, was the most profound and beneficial event in human history since the Neolithic Revolution—the discovery some 12,000 years ago that plants and animals could be domesticated. Industrialization has created, on balance, a much safer world and one that supports larger populations with greater life expectancy than ever before. Over the course of these 36 lectures, we'll explore how humanity has learned to make and distribute devices of increasing complexity, whose collective effect has been to make life longer, richer, safer, and more varied for us than for nearly all our predecessors on the planet.

An Anti-Traditional Phenomenon

- Beginning in the 1700s, in central England, an ingenious group of men began experimenting with the business of making things and discovered that traditional methods could be improved, accelerated, and made more efficient. Their advances began in woolen and cotton textiles but soon spread to pottery, coal mining, iron making, and transport.

- The basic insight that it was possible to make things more quickly and efficiently led to new methods of transportation and new ways those items might be sold and traded. Those insights, in turn, led to new ideas about how a society involved in such manufacturing and trading should be reorganized. The result was a new distribution of status and wealth.

- A new era of critical thinking began. Industrialization depends on the idea that tradition should not always constrain us and that careful thought can enable us to do what our ancestors never even attempted. In this sense, industrialization has immense anti-traditional implications.

Steam engines were one of the great technologies of the first industrial era, and steam-powered locomotives survived on Britain's railways until 1968.

- By now, industrialization has been institutionalized to such a degree that we expect to see new inventions and methods introduced every year and to watch old ones fall into obsolescence. Although the process is benign overall, that doesn't mean that everyone profits from it. The nature of social change is that it produces winners and losers. Each time a technology is made obsolete, some people may lose their livelihoods or drop out of the workforce altogether.

- Still, although industrialization has caused constant upheavals and dislocations, in the long run, it has created a higher standard of living for more people than ever before, greater longevity, and greater opportunities.

- The overall effect of industrialization has been liberating; in fact, democracy correlates closely with industrialization, as does the presence of mass literacy, widespread higher education, and respect for human rights.

Connotations of *Industry*

- The word *industry* tends to conjure negative associations, perhaps in part because of certain odd characteristics that we nearly all share. First, humans are capable of an incredible depth of ingratitude. Most of us never think about the debt we owe to our industrial predecessors—except when the things they gave us are suddenly taken away.
    - Think about electrical power. We're so familiar with electricity that we never think about it when it's working; we think about it only when it suddenly stops working. Of course, most people in world history have had to manage without electricity. We have it as part of the legacy of the Industrial Revolution.

    - The great iron and steel manufacturer Andrew Carnegie once said that capitalism was all about turning luxuries into necessities. In other words, new inventions that once caused a sensation gradually become familiar and feel normal, until we reach the point of wondering how we ever got along without them. Then, we forget how useful they are until we're forced to do without them again.

- In addition, most of us think more about the future than the past. We take what the world gives us as our starting point.
    - The gifts of the past are present all around us and are too familiar to induce a sense of awe and wonder. The future, by contrast, is a zone of speculation where we can imagine marvelous improvements over our current condition.

    - If we do think about the past, it's often nostalgically; we're likely to daydream about either the simple contentment of the "good old days" or the pageantry of aristocratic life we see in costume dramas. Factories and commerce seem like intruders into that world, rather than sources of improvement.

- The third reason the Industrial Revolution has negative associations is that there is much to dislike about it. The people who brought it about were trying to make themselves rich and were rarely motivated by a sense of benevolence toward others. Many of them were ruthless employers; the successful ones made themselves rich while leaving their employees poor.

- A long moral and literary tradition has condemned rather than celebrated the industrialist. The great novelist Charles Dickens lived in the midst of the Industrial Revolution and was unsparing in describing its ugliness, squalor, and human cost.

- In real life, John D. Rockefeller, the pioneer of the modern American oil industry, who made himself one of the richest men in the world, was widely hated as a grasping, unscrupulous monopolist who destroyed other people's livelihoods and drove his workers hard and mercilessly.

- Industry has also caused many of the environmental problems we face today. The Industrial Revolution began by burning coal in massive quantities, then went on to burn oil in even greater amounts. As we know, extracting fossil fuels from the earth is dangerous and dirty, and burning them causes pollution.

- Finally, the Industrial Revolution made warfare much more horrific, with mass killing by means of machine guns, high-explosive bombs, and industrial gas. Worse still, it brought us nuclear weapons, the ultimate indiscriminate killing machine, capable of destroying everything.

Embracing the Paradox

- It might seem paradoxical to celebrate a process that shattered traditional ways of life, increased economic inequality, exploited workers, fouled the atmosphere, and exponentially increased the horrors of war. Nevertheless, the basic principle of this course is that we should embrace the paradox and be grateful for the Industrial Revolution.

- Most people in traditional societies are powerless, and the accident of birth decides irrevocably what they will do in life. These are ways of life that tend to be short, oppressive, and exhausting. To be a hunter-gatherer or a peasant—the fate of tens of millions throughout world history—is to live a life of constant drudgery, completely devoid of choice.

- Although the inequality of industrial societies is real, it's an inequality where the poorest are far less poor than their ancestors. It's true that the gap between the richest and the poorest often increases with industrialization, but it's also true that the poorest people in advanced industrial societies are in many ways richer than the richest people in a traditional society.

- It would be pointless to deny that the exploitation of industrial workers has been severe at many times and places throughout the Industrial Revolution.
  - The Marxists, who presented the most powerful challenge to industrial capitalism from the mid-1800s to the late 1900s, regarded exploitation as inseparable from capitalism and aimed to destroy it.

  - Karl Marx himself believed that as the rich got richer, the poor would get poorer until, finally, they would rise up in rebellion against the wealthy minority. What Marx was seeking was industrialization without exploitation—that is, industrialization without capitalism.

  - But what actually happened in the early 20th century is that the rich realized they could continue getting richer only by making the poor richer. They recognized that their capacity to make things had outstripped their pool of consumers; thus, it was necessary to turn the makers into consumers, too.

  - The first employer to apply this principle in a significant way was Henry Ford, who overnight raised the average worker's pay at his auto assembly line factories from about $1.50 per day to $5. The raise kept the workers on the job and had the effect of turning them into buyers and drivers of Ford cars.

- Some economic historians believe that one of the reasons for the severity of the Great Depression was that wages, although they had been rising rapidly in the last 20 to 30 years, had not risen fast enough to keep up with increases in output during the 1920s. In other words, wages needed to be higher still.

- There were also widespread fears during World War II that as soon as the demand created by the war ended, depression conditions would return. With the scarcity of labor during the war, however, wages rose sharply, creating the enlarged buying power that could sustain the economy when the fighting ended.

- Environmentally, the early stages of the Industrial Revolution were filthy, with appalling levels of smog and smoke. Marx's colleague Friedrich Engels wrote that rivers in certain parts of England were open sewers, full of human waste and industrial effluent. As late as the 1960s, American rivers were often contaminated with high levels of detergent, phosphorous compounds, oil sludge, and other effluent.
  - That's not true today, however; the rivers of Britain and America are incomparably cleaner now than they were half a century ago, even though productivity has continued to rise. The environmental movement mobilized citizens to protest against pollution, at which point democratic governments passed legislation to restrict it and to clean up the long legacy of industrial pollution. Environmental remediation became a new entrepreneurial opportunity, and inventors hastened to supply the demand.

  - Ironically, the way to correct a problem caused by industrialization was with *more* industrialization. Historians recognize that there's a close correlation between a society's wealth and its ability to clean up the environment.

- The horribly destructive weapons made possible through industrialization remain with us. Even here, however, there are a few offsetting factors to consider. The maturing of industrial societies has led to a steady fall in violence.

o Psychologist Steven Pinker has demonstrated convincingly that war and violence are far less common than they used to be.

o Three principal reasons for this, he says, are the rise of international commerce; the rise of the nation-state, which has advanced legal systems and a monopoly of force; and the rise of mass education, which encourages people to be more reasonable and restrained—in other words, industrial society.

• It seems reasonable, then, to claim that industrialization has created, on balance, a much safer world. It's certainly one that supports larger populations with greater life expectancy than ever before.

Suggested Reading

Dickens, *Hard Times*.

Engels, *The Condition of the Working Class in England*.

Pinker, *The Better Angels of Our Nature*.

Questions to Consider

1. Why do you think the functioning of democracy correlates so closely with industrialization?

2. Do you agree or disagree with the claim that industrialization has created a safer world?

Industrialization Is Good for You
Lecture 1—Transcript

Welcome to this series of lectures on the history of the Industrial Revolution. My name is Patrick Allitt, and this is my eighth lecture series with The Great Courses. I was born and raised in England, as you can tell from my voice, but I've lived nearly all my adult life in the United States and recently became a United States citizen.

The fact that I can speak to you without seeing you, and that you can listen to me or watch me at a time different from the time I'm doing it, in places hundreds or thousands of miles away from where I now stand in Fairfax County, Virginia, is the result of a series of advanced industrial technologies. Why do these technologies exist? Who invented them, and who found ways to mass produce them at affordable prices? Over the course of these 36 lectures, I'll explain how humanity has learned to make and distribute ever-more complex devices, whose collective effect has been to make life longer, richer, safer, and more varied for us than for nearly all our predecessors on the planet.

The word *industry* doesn't sound thrilling in most peoples' ears; it probably sounds grimly utilitarian. Perhaps it makes you think of factories with smoke pouring from their chimneys and men in overalls toiling beside noisy machines. Or, since factories like that are already a thing of the past in most parts of America, perhaps it makes you think of antiseptic tile and glass environments, where men and women in white lab coats supervise robots as they assemble microscopically small devices. By now, we use the word more broadly, speaking of "the tourism industry," or else we might say, "Higher education has become an industry in its own right," just meaning that these are activities that employ thousands of people and involve large sums of money. Follow the word back a few hundred years and you'll find it used to mean "hard work." An American Puritan might say "Brother William's industry is equal to his piety," meaning simply that he keeps going at whatever work is given to him, and is careful to do it well. A sense of that meaning persists in our adjective *industrious*, whose meaning is very different from that of *industrial*, despite their common origin.

If the word *industry* doesn't thrill you, the historical process for which it stands really should. The Industrial Revolution, which has transformed the world over the past two and a half centuries, is the most profound and beneficial event in human history since the Neolithic Revolution, the discovery some 12,000 years ago that plants and animals could be domesticated. Beginning in the 1700s in central England, very near to my own hometown of Derby, ingenious and businesslike men began experimenting with how to make things, and they discovered that traditional methods could be improved, accelerated, and made more efficient. It started in woolen and cotton textiles, but it soon spread to pottery, coal mining, iron, and transport. The basic insight that it was possible to make things more quickly and more efficiently led to new inventions as to how things might be carried, and how they might be sold, advertised, traded. Those insights, in turn, eventually led to new ideas about how a society involved in such manufacturing and trading should be reorganized. It led to a new distribution of status and wealth, and had very great political consequences.

As the rate of new inventions continued to increase into the 19th century, it gave a lift to an ideal of critical thinking. Industrialization depended on the idea that tradition shouldn't always constrain us, and that careful thought can enable us to do things that our ancestors never even attempted. In this sense, industrialization has immense anti-traditional implications. By now, it's been institutionalized to such a degree that we expect to see new inventions, gadgets, and methods introduced every year and to watch old ones fall by the wayside. For example, throughout most of world history, the idea that men could fly was almost the definition of the impossible; of course men can't fly. The Wright brothers turned it into a practical reality, and the astonishing progress of flight since then has demonstrated repeated reapplications of the same principle.

If the process of industrialization is benign overall, that doesn't mean that everyone profits from it; certainly that they don't profit from it equally. The nature of social change is that it produces winners and losers. Each time a technology has been made obsolete, people who lived by using it have lost their livelihood and been forced to switch over to the new one, or else to drop out of the workforce altogether. Probably everyone watching or listening to this lecture can think of new inventions that they deplore rather than welcome. In fact, inability to keep up with the new ones is one of the sure signs of aging today. Still, although industrialization has caused constant upheavals and dislocations, in the long run it's created higher standards of living for more people than ever before, greater longevity, and greater opportunities. I certainly believe its overall effect has been liberating. The presence and functioning of democracy correlates very closely with industrialization. So does the presence of mass literacy, widespread higher education, and respect for human rights.

It's an incredible story, and even the 18 hours of this course aren't going to be long enough for me to do more than sketch it in outline while encouraging you to read more and also to visit some of the best-preserved sites of industrial history. Luckily, there are a lot of these sites, and the Western democracies in particular have done a very good job of preserving them for posterity.

England, where the Industrial Revolution began, is full of places to explore this heritage. There are old iron works; an entire valley in Shropshire has now been dedicated to the history of the iron industry. There are old coal mines that can be visited underground. There's a magnificent place called "The Big Pit" in South Wales where you can actually go and live out, for a moment, the lives of the old coal miners. There are wonderful textile factories like Quarry Bank Mill in Cheshire, where machines 150 years old—some of the very first devices of the Industrial Revolution—have been brought back into service, and you can walk through, stage by stage, the various processes of the textile industry. Best of all, dozens of steam railways are thriving all across Britain. Steam engines were one of the great technologies of the first industrial era, and steam-powered locomotives survived on Britain's railways until 1968, when I was 12 years old. Their withdrawal was met with such widespread dismay that several hundred of the locomotives were rescued from the scrapyards, renovated, and set to work on stretches of previously abandoned lines. Thousands of hobbyists have run these steam railways ever since, enabling visitors to enjoy the clouds of smoke and steam, the distinctive smell of burning coal and hot metal, and the link that such trains give to earlier days. Even the kids who never grew up with them in the way that I did seem to love the steam engines just as much, as there's something instinctively very fascinating about them and plenty of opportunities still to see them.

To revert to a point I was making previously, the reason you might not be thrilled when you hear the word *industry* is because of certain odd human characteristics that we nearly all share. The first of these characteristics is that we have an incredible talent for ingratitude. Evolutionary biologists somewhere can perhaps explain how ingratitude is an adaptive trait that's helped us to survive. By ingratitude, I mean simply that most of us never think about what incredible debts of gratitude we owe to our industrial predecessors, except when the things they gave us are suddenly taken away. Think about power cuts. We're so familiar with electricity that we virtually never think about it when it's working; we only stop to think about it when it stops working. Remember how irritable you got last time the lights suddenly all went out, or the refrigerator stopped working, or the air conditioning went silent and it was 90 degrees outside? Only the absence of electricity can give us the shock of recognition about how much we rely on this invisible, colorless, odorless, and inexpensive stuff, and the recognition that generations of ingenious people learned how to utilize it for our comfort and convenience. Most people in world history had to manage without electricity. We have it as part of the legacy of the Industrial Revolution.

The great iron and steel manufacturer Andrew Carnegie, who started his life in Scotland as a poor boy and came to America where he built a great fortune in iron and steel in the Pittsburgh area, once said that capitalism was all about turning luxuries into necessities. In other words, new inventions that once caused a sensation gradually became familiar and started to feel normal, until we reach the point of wondering how we ever got along without them. Then we almost forget about them completely, or at least we forget how useful they are until we're forced to do without them once again. Anyone who's over 35 today will remember a world with no internet and no cell phones. Back in 1980, when we didn't have them, we didn't feel deprived. But try taking away the internet and the cell phones now. Many of us would feel completely at a loss about how to deal with everyday life in the most elementary matters, because we've come to depend upon them so much.

A second reason we're not thrilled by the idea of industry, in addition to our propensity for ingratitude, is that most of us think more about the future than about the past. We take what the world gives us as our starting point. It's present all around us as a sheer matter of fact, and it's too familiar to induce a sense of awe and wonder. The future, by contrast, is a zone of speculation where we can imagine marvelous improvements over our current condition. If we do think about the past, it's often nostalgically, where we're more likely to daydream about either the simple contentment of the good old days or the pageantry of aristocratic life as we see it presented to us in costume dramas like *Downton Abbey*. In that world, factories and commerce seem like intruders into an idyll rather than as sources of improvement.

The third reason we're not thrilled is because there's so much to dislike about the Industrial Revolution. The men who brought it about were trying to make themselves rich, and they were very rarely motivated by a sense of benevolence toward their fellow man. Many of them were ruthless employers; humorless, miserly. The successful ones made themselves rich while leaving their employees poor, and a long moral and literary tradition has condemned them rather than celebrated them. One of the very best places to look for examples of this is in the fiction of Charles Dickens. Characters like Mr. Bounderby and Mr. Gradgrind in Charles Dickens's *Hard Times*; an unimaginative industrialist and his disciple who believe that all the joy in life should be squeezed out, leaving nothing but the harsh facts, and they make a cult of the facts. Bounderby, a pompous, complacent, self-made man turns out to be a scoundrel; the kind of man every reader loves to hate. Charles Dickens, one of the most popular novelists of his time, lived in the midst of the Industrial Revolution, in the middle decades of the 19th century. He was unsparing in describing its ugliness, its squalor, and its very, very high human cost. In real life, similarly, on this side of the Atlantic, John D. Rockefeller, the pioneer of the modern American oil industry who made himself one of the richest men in the world, was widely hated as a grasping, unscrupulous monopolist who destroyed other men's livelihoods and drove his workers hard and mercilessly.

A fourth reason we're not thrilled is because industry has caused most of the environmental problems that we're concerned about today. The Industrial Revolution began by burning coal in massive quantities, and then it went on to burn oil in even greater amounts. Extracting fossil fuels from the earth is dangerous and dirty—probably the most dangerous jobs still today is to be a coal miner—while burning them causes pollution. We're involved in a costly and difficult cleanup process that's far from complete, and we worry now about industrially-produced greenhouse gases that can actually affect the world's entire climate.

A fifth reason we're not excited by the idea of industry is because it's made warfare so much more terrible. Men hacking at each other with swords and axes is bad enough, but by 20th-century standards that seems almost restrained. The industrial world brought us mass killing by means of machine guns, high-explosive bombs, and industrial gas on the battlefield and in the gas chamber. Worse still, it brought nuclear weapons, the ultimate indiscriminate weapon that kills everyone and destroys everything. After the First World War in which he participated, Winston Churchill wrote that since scientists had become involved in making weapons, war had become worse than ever before in history. Churchill wrote, "War, which used to be cruel and magnificent, has now become cruel and squalid." For anyone who wants to denounce industrialization, its consequences for warfare make a logical place to start.

It may seem paradoxical to say that we should celebrate a process that shattered traditional ways of life, increased economic inequality, exploited workers, fouled the atmosphere, and exponentially increased the horrors of war. Nevertheless, the basic principle of this course is that we should embrace the paradox and we should be grateful for the Industrial Revolution. Now let me try to explain why.

First of all, the question of tradition: It's much easier to enjoy tradition from a distance than it is to live with it close up. Most people in traditional societies are powerless, and the accident of birth decides irrevocably what they'll do in their lives. These are ways of life that tend to be short, oppressive, and exhausting. Although we like to grumble about the characteristic woes of modern life, most of them are far more bearable than the woes of antiquity. To be hunters and gatherers, or to be peasants, the fate of tens of millions of people throughout world history, is to live a life of constant drudgery, completely devoid of choice. When a mother today says to her child, "Work hard and you can have any job you want. You could even become President," she's perhaps being a little bit optimistic, but essentially what she says is true. For hunters and gatherers or for peasant women to say such things to their children would've been outright lies. I think the issue is that we tend to expect that if we'd lived in the past and if we sentimentalized tradition, we expect that we'd have some of the most interesting positions in traditional societies; we'd enjoy the lives of kings rather than the lives of peasants or the lives of hunters and gatherers. It's hard for us to know much about them, and it's difficult for us to feel the misery of traditional life for most ordinary people.

Second, although the inequality of industrial societies is real, it's an inequality where the poorest are far less poor than their ancestors. It's true that the gap between the richest and the poorest increases with industrialization, but it's also true that the poorest people in advanced industrial societies are in many ways richer than the richest people in a traditional society. That sounds a little bit paradoxical, so let me give you an example if I can. Even the poorest people in America today have access to motor vehicles, telephones, electricity, radio, television, basic medical care, and foods from all over the world. It doesn't mean they have easy access to them, but at times in their lives they'll encounter all of these things. Even kings 500 years ago had none of those things. Their travel was slower and much more uncomfortable; their ability to communicate was more limited; their sources of entertainment were restricted; and their diets, especially at certain seasons of the year, the winter above all, was monotonous and dull. Their privileged status brought them no exemption from epidemics or from a wide array of illnesses and sources of pain that we can now remedy. The poorest American today would feel a real sense of grievance at having to live a king's life from five centuries ago.

Third, it would be pointless to deny that the exploitation of industrial workers has been severe at many times and places throughout the industrial centuries. The Marxists, who presented the most powerful challenge to industrial capitalism from the mid-1800s to the late 1900s, a trend that finally expired along with the Soviet Union at the end of the 1980s, regarded exploitation as inseparable from capitalism and they wanted to destroy it. Marx himself believed that as the rich got richer, the poor would get poorer, until finally they'd rise up in rebellion against the wealthy minority. Marx himself, incidentally, was very much in favor of industrialization; he was never sentimental about rural life. What he was looking for was industrialization without exploitation; that is, industrialization without capitalism.

But what actually happened is that in the early 20th century, the rich realized that they could only carry on getting richer by making the poor richer, at which point they did exactly that. They recognized that their capacity to make things had outstripped their pool of consumers, so now it was necessary to turn the makers into consumers, too. The first employer to apply this principle in a large way was Henry Ford, the great car manufacturer, who overnight raised the average worker's pay at his auto assembly line factories from about $1.50 per day to $5 a day, far more than a 100 percent pay raise. The $5 day at Ford's factories—this was just before the beginning of the First World War—had the effect of keeping the men at a terribly monotonous job that previously they'd quit in droves. People would come to work at Ford, but the job was so boring that very quickly they'd leave it again. But once they were being paid $5 a day, it was simply too good to resist, so they tended to stay at work and that tended to mean that the work got done better and the cars got made more efficiently, and it meant that Ford himself, the boss, had suddenly gotten a much greater pool of potential buyers, because now the thousands of men who were making them were also becoming the buyers and drivers of Ford cars.

Of course, you could take the view that it's still exploitation in the sense that the men don't get paid the full value of their work since the employer is still making a profit. Ford was shrewd enough to understand the mechanics of this perfectly well. On the other hand, this is surely a situation where everyone is better off than they were before. That is, it's a plus-sum game: There's more wealth and it's being distributed more widely than previously.

Some economic historians believe that one of the reasons for the severity of the Great Depression was that wages, although they'd been rising rapidly in the last 20–30 years, hadn't risen fast enough to keep up with increases in output during the 1920s. In other words, wages needed to be higher still. There were also widespread fears during the Second World War that as soon as the demand created by the war ended, depression conditions would return. It's interesting to read American writers during World War II. In the foreground is the imperative necessity of defeating Germany and Japan. But then in the background is this fear: When the war ends, will the depression come back? Many reasonable and reputable people thought it might. But it didn't happen because wages rose so sharply during the war when labor was scarce, creating the enlarged buying power that could sustain the economy when the fighting ended.

What about the environmental issue? I think there's room for optimism even here. Again, there's no denying that the early stages of the Industrial Revolution were very dirty indeed. Descriptions of early industrial cities— like Manchester in England in the 1840s, or for that matter many cities in China, India, and Mexico today—include appalling levels of smog and smoke, places where it's difficult to breathe, leading to a high incidence of lung diseases and chronic bronchial ailments. Karl Marx's friend Friedrich Engels, in his classic book *The Condition of the Working Class in England*, published in 1845, described the rivers as open sewers, full of human waste and industrial effluent, filthy, stinking, and lifeless. As late as the 1960s, American rivers were often contaminated with high levels of detergent, phosphorous compounds, oil sludge, and other effluent, resulting in periodic mass die-offs among the fish.

But that's not true today. The rivers of Britain and America are incomparably cleaner now than they were half a century ago or a century ago, even though productivity has continued to increase. Why is that? It's because the environmental movement, starting in the 1960s, mobilized citizens to protest against pollution, at which point democratic governments passed legislation to restrict it and to clean up the long legacy of industrial pollution. Environmental remediation became a new entrepreneurial activity, an opportunity for inventors, and the inventors themselves and the businesspeople hastened to supply the demand. As a result, the cleanup has been impressive. Factories, mines, and oil refineries are far more efficient than they were 50 years ago. Their waste streams have shrunk, and safe disposal has become a social imperative, widely shared as a wide social consensus on the importance of a clean environment.

Ironically, the way to correct this problem caused by industrialization wasn't by getting rid of the industry as some people suggested, but with more industrialization; more and better. Historians now recognize, too, that there's a very close correlation between a society's wealth and its ability to clean up. Countries that are still struggling to get industry under way, like India and China today, may not yet devote as many resources to limiting pollution as they will, probably, a few decades from now. Once they've met basic consumer demand for food, shelter, housing, elementary education, then they'll turn to remedying the nasty byproducts of the process. Wealthier societies are the ones that tend to clean up.

Of the objections I suggested before, the question of war is a much tougher one to answer so cheerfully. The horribly destructive weapons made possible through industrialization remain with us today. Even here, however, there are a few offsetting factors to consider.

The maturing of industrial societies has led to a steady fall in violence. Steven Pinker's book, *The Better Angels of Our Nature*, published in 2011, demonstrates convincingly that war and violence are far less common than they used to be. The three principal reasons he gives are the rise of international commerce; the rise of the nation state, which has advanced legal systems and a monopoly of force; and the rise of mass education, which encourages people to be far more reasonable and restrained than their distant ancestors. In other words: industrial society. I don't want to push this claim too far, but I still think it's reasonable to claim that industrialization has created, on balance, a much safer world. It's certainly one that supports bigger populations with greater life expectancy than ever before.

All of these are big claims. The next 34 lectures will be an attempt to back them up; not with big generalizations of the kind I've offered here, but with plenty of details and specifics, showing exactly who did what, where, when, and why—the five big Ws—and to make possible the Industrial Revolution itself. At the very end, I'll review these claims again and I hope convince you that they're right. With luck, I'll also have convinced you by then that it's right to feel grateful for the Industrial Revolution.

Why Was Britain First?
Lecture 2

For a century, historians have debated what factors in British life enabled Britain to begin industrialization earlier than any other nation. In this lecture, we'll discuss those factors, which include the growth of political stability, the development of sophisticated financial institutions, a surplus population available to work, the habits of hard work and self-discipline on which industrial life depends, intellectual notions of "human capital," a flexible social system, and an aggressive colonial policy.

Growth of Political Stability

- Industrialization—the building and running of factories—required the investment of large sums of money over long periods of time. In Britain, the development of political stability after 1689 made investors willing to risk their money on industrial ventures.

- In the 17th century, Britain was riven by civil war, revolution, and regicide. In 1642, after an escalating series of confrontations related to where ultimate political power lay, King Charles I declared war against Parliament. Over the next four years, the royalist army and the army of Parliament clashed in a succession of sieges and pitched battles. The outcome was a victory for Parliament and defeat for the king.

- Charles I was eventually captured, tried, and executed for treason. In 1653, one of the leaders of Parliament, Oliver Cromwell became the lord protector of England and governed the nation until his death in 1658. At that time, the English aristocracy brought the former king's son back from exile and crowned him Charles II.

- Charles II's brother and successor, James II, antagonized the people whose support he needed and was forced to flee from England in 1688. Parliament did not repeat the mistake of attempting to govern without a king, but it did make clear that from then on, Parliament was supreme and the king ruled on its sufferance.

- These events of 1688–1689, known as the Glorious Revolution, created conditions of political stability that have endured right up to the present, making the constitutional monarchy of Britain one of the most durable in the world.

Emergence of Financial Institutions

- Industrial investment was also facilitated by the development of sophisticated banking and insurance institutions. The Bank of England, established by an act of Parliament in 1694, stabilized the nation's finances.

- The Bank of England was a joint-stock venture, capitalized at £1.2 million, that acted as banker to the government. It was able to lend at the comparatively low interest rate of eight percent. The act creating it also raised a tax on beer, ale, and vinegar, the first £100,000 of which was earmarked each year for interest payment on the national debt.

- Banknotes were introduced as the equivalent of money, and the trustworthiness of the bank enabled paper money to become serviceable in business transactions. "As safe as the Bank of England" soon became a byword, and it began to attract investment from abroad. In the 18th century, lawyers also worked out techniques to limit investors' liability so that the risk of loss was confined to the amount they had invested—a great stimulus to economic growth.

- Economic theorists began to see the national debt as an asset, as well as a liability. Britain's wealthiest merchants, by buying government bonds, were also investing in the future of the state and its ability to keep paying them interest and, eventually, of returning their capital. Insurance supplemented joint-stock ventures, enabling investors to hedge risks.

- The stock market also began in the 1690s, in Jonathan's Coffee House in London. Colonial ventures in sugar, tobacco, slaves, spices, and other high-value commodities all generated surplus wealth that sought reinvestment. Industrialization presupposes great concentrations of capital, and British colonial trade ventures generated it.
  - In the 1500s, British privateers, such as Francis Drake, preyed on Spanish treasure fleets. After the defeat of the Spanish Armada in 1588, Britain got involved in colonizing the Americas. Following establishment of the colonies, Britain began to participate in the slave trade—a high-risk, high-return business.

  - There was a similarly risky but profitable trade in India in high-value silks, spices, and tea. The East India Company, founded in 1600, had a monopoly on British trade beyond the Cape of Good Hope. The East India Company gradually became the key political player in India. Britain moved steadily to dominate the whole subcontinent and, eventually, to unify and rule it.

Surplus Population

- Industrialization would not have been possible in Britain without a surplus population able to work in mills, mines, and factories and to create a swelling domestic market for more goods. Population rose rapidly between the mid-18th and mid-19th centuries. The population of Britain was about 5 million in 1700 and only half a million more by 1750. Then it took off; there were 8.3 million people by 1801 and 16.8 million by 1851.

- Ironically, in 1798, Thomas Malthus cautioned that population growth always outstrips the capacity of the land to feed the people and that the result is bound to be misery, malnutrition, and vice. Malthus reasoned that population increases geometrically, whereas the food supply could only increase arithmetically. That had been true for generations, but Britain was now discovering ways to break out of this vicious circle.

- Since the late 18ᵗʰ century, incredible gains in population have been achieved in the industrial nations, yet people are better fed than ever before. This is one of the most astonishing achievements of the last 250 years.

- Improvements in agriculture and a climatic warming trend both helped. Nutrition improved, as did longevity. In the 1790s, Edward Jenner developed the smallpox inoculation. In the same era, bubonic plague, one of the great killers in the 14ᵗʰ to 17ᵗʰ centuries, began to disappear.

- Britain was first to experience demographic transition, which is characteristic of industrial societies. The term refers to a period of high birth and death rates, followed by a lower death rate and rapid population growth, in turn followed by a lower birth rate. The rate of increase begins to decline toward a new and much higher equilibrium point.

Work Ethic and Self-Discipline

- Industrialization was characterized by certain attitudes toward work and self-discipline, many of which had been nurtured by the Protestant Reformation.

- According to the Weber-Tawney thesis, developed in the early 20ᵗʰ century, the Protestant theory of predestination encouraged stern self-monitoring and a search for clues that one was among God's chosen. The Calvinist idea of predestination led not to fatalism but to intense seriousness, sobriety, and punctuality. The idea of a calling, which was familiar in Protestant life, was the secular equivalent of the old Catholic vocation to the religious life.

- These attitudes partially replaced the older Christian idea that accumulating wealth is sinful with the idea that sober, continuous, and successful hard work is a way of doing the Lord's work. The rise of these attitudes corresponded to industrial development in Britain, the Netherlands, northern Germany, and the United States.

- The Weber-Tawney theory that there is a connection between religion and the rise of capitalism remains controversial, partly because Protestant Scotland was much slower to industrialize than England and partly because Catholic Belgium industrialized earlier than Protestant Holland. The theory isn't a perfect fit, but it remains noteworthy.

- A strikingly large number of the great industrial entrepreneurs of the late 18th century were Nonconformists (Quakers, Presbyterians, Congregationalists, Baptists, and Unitarians). That is, they refused to conform to the state Church of England and insisted on remaining outside it, despite civil penalties. Nonconformists were excluded from the old universities and could not be army officers or magistrates, but they were not barred from any economic activity.

"Human Capital" and Flexibility in Social Systems

- Industrialization also presupposes the existence of "human capital"; an interest in science, technology, and innovation; a willingness to experiment; and a belief that the future might be different from, and better than, the past.
  - Fatalism has been an incredibly powerful source of inertia throughout human history. Industrialization defied the idea that the future

Wind and water power had been used for centuries, but after 1800, they began to be operated in new and more effective ways to speed up the processes of manufacturing.

is bound to be the same as the past and insisted that it can be different and better.

○ Generations of intellectual innovators, such as Robert Boyle, John Locke, and Isaac Newton, along with the Royal Society (founded in 1660), led to increasing secularization of scientific knowledge. In the 17th and early 18th centuries, there was a sharp split between science, considered a gentleman's activity, and technology, the province of mechanics and tinkerers. After 1800, these two disciplines came together, ensuring that the secularization of science would continue.

• Flexibility among the elite and political sympathy for economic growth were also essential to the rise of industrialism.

○ In 18th-century Britain, members of the aristocracy were already interested in coal mining on their lands and in agricultural improvement. By contrast, many of the European aristocracies regarded work as dishonorable or were far more preoccupied with war and disdained economic activity.

○ Although British aristocrats tended to look down on commercial activities, when they saw a great opportunity or when the burden of their debts embarrassed them, they did, in fact, seize the opportunity to restore their estates.

Aggressive Colonial Policy

• In the 18th century, the British government also supported an aggressive colonial policy. Britain conducted five immense wars during this period and emerged on the winning side in four of them, losing only the American Revolutionary War. British success led to overwhelming naval dominance.

• The Royal Navy actively supported merchant navy and colonial trade ventures. That, in turn, created the ideal support for British manufacturers, especially of textiles, to sell abroad, capturing foreign markets and expanding them rapidly. British mercantile policy also made sure that Britain's colonies served British interests.

- The Navigation Acts, which would later be a grievance to American colonists, specified that all trade with Britain and its colonies must be in British ships and that all colonial imports and exports must pass through Britain en route to their ultimate destinations. These laws played a significant role in nurturing an unparalleled British merchant marine.

Suggested Reading

Deane, *The First Industrial Revolution.*

Floud and Johnson, eds., *The Cambridge Economic History of Modern Britain*, vol. 1, *Industrialization, 1700–1860.*

Lane, *The Industrial Revolution.*

Musson, *The Growth of British Industry.*

Questions to Consider

1. How did Britain's vigorous colonial and commercial policies contribute to its eventual industrialization?

2. What factors contributed to Britain's extraordinary political stability after the Glorious Revolution?

Why Was Britain First?
Lecture 2—Transcript

For a century, historians have debated what factors in British life enabled it to begin industrialization earlier than any other nation. Most agree that the important things included political stability, the development of flexible financial institutions, a strong social system, a surplus population available to work, and the habits of hard work and self-discipline on which industrial life depends.

Industrialization, the building and running of factories, required the investment of large sums of money over long periods of time. The development of political stability after 1689 made investors willing to risk their money on industrial ventures. Obviously, if you're not confident that the political system is going to be stable and that upheavals might destroy your investment, you'll be hesitant to do it. But once the society becomes stable, it's more likely that people will do it.

Let me begin by offering a little political historical background: 17th-century Britain, Britain in the 1600s, was riven by civil war, revolution, and regicide, the killing of the king. In 1642, after an escalating series of confrontations relating to where ultimate political power lay, King Charles I declared war against his own Parliament. Over the next four years, his Royalist army and the army of Parliament, which is remembered in popular tradition as the "Roundheads," fought a succession of sieges and pitched battles on fields that can still be visited in England today. The outcome was victory for Parliament and defeat for the king.

Despite being defeated, King Charles I flatly refused to negotiate with the victors, refusing to concede to them the principle of their ultimate sovereignty. He claimed that God himself had appointed him king. He was a great believer in the theory of the divine right of kingship and denied that Parliament had any authority to negotiate questions of power with him. Then he escaped and opened the war again. When he was captured for a second time, one of the Parliamentary leaders, Oliver Cromwell, put him on trial in Parliament, had him convicted of treason, and executed him by beheading in 1649. It was a public execution in Whitehall; the king's head was cut off in public. England then tried to become a republic. It was called the Commonwealth. It didn't work very well, and in 1643, Cromwell himself became the Lord Protector of England—something like a military dictator—and governed England until his death in 1658.

This early experiment made a great impression on later revolutionaries, including the Americans of the 1770s and '80s, to all of whom the name of Cromwell and the knowledge of his deeds were familiar. The problem England encountered in the 1650s was that no one with sufficient civil and military authority could be found to take Cromwell's place and there was no institutional mechanism in place for a smooth succession. So, the English aristocracy brought the old king's son back from exile in France and crowned him as the new king, King Charles II.

Charles II restored the traditions of monarchy but never forgot what had happened to his father. When he died in 1685, his brother and successor, King James II, was less prudent. James II antagonized all the people whose support he needed, and finally he was forced to flee from England at the end of the year 1688. Parliament didn't repeat the mistake of attempting to govern without a king; they recognized that a king was necessary at the top of the system. But it did make clear that from then on, Parliament was supreme and that the king ruled on the sufferance of Parliament.

These events of 1688–1689 are remembered in British history as the "Glorious Revolution"; "glorious" because nobody was killed. A very important constitutional principle was established, and it was done bloodlessly. James II ran away, and Parliament then brought into Britain the stadtholder of the Netherlands, the most senior executive officer of the Netherlands, who became King William III. He was married to the deposed king's daughter, and she became Queen Mary II. It's the only time in British history that two monarchs have ruled jointly. They created the conditions of political stability that have endured right up to the present, making Britain a constitutional monarchy and one of the most durable, if not the most durable, in the world.

The wealthiest and most powerful men in the kingdom had access to power and influence. Although Britain was far from being a democracy in the late

1600s and early 1700s—only about five percent even of the men could vote and none of the women, and you had to be a property owner to be able to vote—still, the ones who counted for most as local leaders and commercial leaders did have access to power.

Investment in industry was facilitated not only by political stability, but also by the development of sophisticated banking and insurance institutions. The Bank of England, established by act of Parliament in 1694, stabilized the nation's finances. The new king, William III, needed to rebuild the Royal Navy to take on the power of King Louis XIV of France. He granted a charter to this bank, the Bank of England, which was itself a copy of the Swedish national bank, founded earlier still in 1668. It was a joint-stock venture, capitalized at 1.2 million pounds, and it acted from then on as banker to the government. It was able to lend money at the comparatively low interest rate of eight percent per year, and this is very unlike the chaotic finances of the Stuart monarchy that had preceded this era, and the chaotic finances of the Bourbon monarchy in France. The French had to pay much, much higher interest rates to their bankers. The act of Parliament creating the Bank of England also raised a tax on beer, ale, and vinegar, the first 100,000 pounds of which each year was earmarked for interest payment on the national debt.

The Bank of England also introduced bank notes as the equivalent of money, and the trustworthiness of the bank enabled paper money to become serviceable in business transactions. "As safe as the Bank of England" soon became a byword, and it began to attract investment from abroad, too, especially from Dutch merchants who could see that it was safe to invest in the Bank of England.

The bank profited from making loans and receiving interest on them. It had an incentive to lend to apparently trustworthy men with industrial and commercial projects inside the kingdom. It was supplemented by local banks throughout the English provinces, usually set up by successful local businessmen who knew the people to whom they were lending and could keep a very shrewd eye on their loans. England, before the Industrial Revolution, England was a face-to-face world where people had extremely strong local traditions and where one's reputation for probity was absolutely essential. In other words, much of the available money, accumulated mostly in trade and in pre-industrial forms of manufacturing, was put to good use in other economic activities rather than being hoarded or being diverted into luxury and display. Many of these businessmen belonged to puritanical Protestant churches that objected to ostentatiousness. They tended to prefer reinvestment, sobriety, and good business practices.

Also in the 18th century, lawyers began to work out techniques to limit investors' liability so that the risk of loss when a business went wrong or a venture failed was confined to the amount they'd invested, rather than drawing on their personal resources. This, of course, is another great stimulus to economic growth. Economic theorists began to see the national debt as an asset as well as a liability. Why was that? Britain's wealthiest merchants, by buying government bonds, were also investing in the future of the state and its ability to keep paying them interest, and eventually, if they wanted, to have their capital returned. These commercial leaders had the strongest possible incentive to support the government against external threats; they want the stability to persist.

Such threats were real, as the old Stuart royal family, the family of King James II, tried to reassert its claim to the throne. There was a Jacobite uprising in 1715—the Jacobites were the descendants of the Stuarts, the followers of King James II—and there was a more serious one in 1745, led by Bonnie Prince Charlie, who's a picturesque romantic figure in Scottish folklore. He was the grandson of King James II. With French help, Bonnie Prince Charlie landed in Scotland, raised an army of Scottish clansmen, and marched south to seize what he believed to be his throne; he was still the legitimate king in his view. His march caused a panic in London. The government was on the brink of flight. But the Scottish Highland Army, out of its element and not realizing how it had terrified the government, became discouraged when it came to the England midlands town of Derby and declined to march any further. At that point, as they turned back towards Scotland, the nation, the government in London, rallied for a brutally effective counter-campaign, culminating at the Battle of Culloden in April of 1746, a decisive defeat for Bonnie Prince Charlie and really the end of the challenge by the Stuart dynasty to the throne of England.

Insurance supplemented joint-stock ventures, enabling investors to hedge their risks. The stock market also began in the 1690s, in Jonathan's Coffee House in London. Colonial ventures in sugar, tobacco, slaves, spices, and other high-value commodities were all generating surplus wealth that sought reinvestment.

Industrialization presupposes great concentrations of capital, and it was colonial trade ventures, in large measure, that generated this capital. In the 1500s, British privateers like Francis Drake had preyed on Spanish treasure fleets. After the defeat of the Spanish Armada in 1588, one of the decisive naval victories of Britain's naval rise to power, Britain became involved in colonizing the Americas directly. It's no coincidence that it's just after that that they sail off to Virginia and Maryland. They hoped for gold; they hoped they'd find gold. But in the event, they found tobacco almost as useful, and that was the basis of the prosperity of the Virginia and Maryland colonies.

After the establishment of colonies, Britain began to participate in the slave trade, a high-risk, high-return business, leaving aside for a moment the humanitarian aspect of it. Merchants in the ports began to accumulate money from the slave trade: London, Glasgow, Liverpool, and Bristol. In 1700, most of the richest people in Britain lived in the countryside and were farmers, but as 18th century progressed, more and more of the richest men came to live in towns as commerce became more dominant.

Similarly, the risky but very profitable India trade was involved in high-value silks, spices, and tea. The East India Company, founded in 1600, had a monopoly of British trade beyond the Cape of Good Hope; that is to say, in the Indian Ocean. Britain's trading position there gradually improved as it forced out its rivals, the Portuguese, the French, and the Dutch. The East India Company gradually became the key political player in India, too. It started out strictly as a trading company, but became more and more politically involved. One of the company's officers, Robert Clive, won a victory at the Battle of Plassey in 1757. This was in Bengal in northeastern India, and it made his army the dominant force in the whole area. From then on, between the 1750s and 1800, Britain moved steadily to dominate the whole subcontinent, and eventually to unify and rule it right through until the 1940s.

Industrialization wouldn't have been possible without surplus population able to work in the mills, the mines, and the factories and to create a swelling domestic market for more goods. Population rose rapidly between the mid-18th century and the mid-19th. It was probably about 5 million in 1700 and only half a million more by 1750. But then it began to take off: It was 8.3 million by 1801, and 16.8 million, more than doubling, by 1851.

Ironically, these were the years of Thomas Malthus's *Essay on Population* from 1798, an influential book that cautioned that population always outstrips the capacity of the land to feed them, and that the result is bound to be misery, malnutrition, and vice. Malthus reasoned like this: The population increases geometrically. Two parents can have four children. Four can easily lead to eight, eight to 16, 16 to 32, and so on, whereas the food supply can only increase arithmetically. Even if more land is being used, it'll rise in a ratio like this: 2, 3, 4, 5. In other words, subsistence would always limit the ability of population to grow, and some people would always be close to starvation. We call Malthusian checks on population growth, famine, plague, disease, and so on. That had been true for generations, but just as Malthus said it, Britain was discovering ways to break out of this iron circle. Since then, incredible gains in population have been achieved in the industrial nations, and yet the people are better fed than ever before. This is one of the most astonishing achievements of the last 250 years.

Improvements in agriculture, which will be the subject of Lecture 3, and a climatic warming trend both helped. We're aware of the hazards of global warming, but as Europe emerged from what historians call the "Little Ice Age" of the preceding centuries, summers became longer, temperatures higher, and harvests better; there was more food available for more people. Nutrition improved, and so did longevity. In the 1790s, Edward Jenner developed smallpox inoculations. He'd noticed that milkmaids didn't suffer from smallpox, which was then one of the great scourges that killed and disfigured thousands. Jenner realized that the milkmaids caught cowpox from the cattle, a related disease, and that it gave them a level of immunity to smallpox. He experimented with deliberately infecting other people with cowpox and succeeded in giving them the same immunity. He's remembered in medical history as the "father of immunology." In the same era, bubonic plague, which had been one of the great killers in the 14th to 17th centuries, began to disappear.

Britain was first to experience demographic transition, which is characteristic of industrial societies. From having a high birth rate and a high death rate, which is characteristic of a preindustrial society, what happens is that more people start to live longer, with the results that the population rises very sharply. Suddenly, the birth rate remains high and the death rate slows down, and that leads to rapid population growth. But eventually, as people became familiar with the fact that most of their children won't die but will live, the birth rate starts to come down. Now the rate of increase begins to decline towards a new and much higher equilibrium point in which you have a lower birth rate, a lower death rate, and a higher overall population. That's a very characteristic thing of industrial societies, known to demographers as "demographic transition."

Industrialization also presupposed certain characteristic attitudes towards work and self-discipline, many of which had been nurtured by the Protestant Reformation. The Weber-Tawney thesis, developed early in the 20th century, retains at least some value. The argument was that the Protestant theory of predestination encouraged stern self-monitoring throughout one's life. The Calvinist idea is that God's already decided, before you're even born, whether you're destined to go to heaven or to hell. You deserve to go to hell, but God in his mercy might have saved you. You could respond to that view fatalistically and say, "In that case it doesn't matter what I do on Earth." What actually happens is that people look for clues that they were, in fact, among God's chosen. It leads not to fatalism, but to intense seriousness, sobriety, and punctuality.

The idea of a calling, which is familiar in Protestant life, was the secular equivalent of the old Catholic vocation for the religious life. It partially replaced the older Christian idea that accumulating wealth is sinful—a sin of cupidity—replacing it with the idea that sober, continuous and successful hard work is a way of doing the Lord's work. It corresponds to the development of industrial society in Britain, the Netherlands, northern Germany, and a little bit later in the United States. But this theory that there's a connection between religion and the rise of capitalism, the theory of Max Weber and Tawney, remains controversial, partly because Protestant Scotland was so much slower to industrialize than England, and because in the Low countries, Catholic Belgium became industrial earlier than Protestant Holland. So it's not a perfect fit, but it's a noteworthy one.

A strikingly large number of the great industrial entrepreneurs of the late 18th century were nonconformists; that is to say, they were Quakers, Presbyterians, Congregationalists, Baptists, and Unitarians. *Nonconformist* simply means that they refused to conform, to belong, to the state Church of England and insisted on remaining outside it, despite the fact that it made them liable to civil penalties. If you were a nonconformist, if you weren't a member of the Church of England, you were excluded from the old universities, Oxford and Cambridge. You couldn't be an army officer. You couldn't be a magistrate. You were a second-class citizen. But on the other hand, nonconformists weren't barred from any economic activity, so it may simply be that their energy was directed in this way.

Industrialization also presupposed the existence of human capital, an interest in science, technology, and innovation; a willingness to experiment; and a belief that the future might be different from and better than the past. That's a point easy to overlook, but one that can hardly be emphasized too strongly. Fatalism has been an incredibly powerful source of inertia throughout human history. Industrialization defies the idea that the future is bound to be the same as the past. It insists that it can be different and better. Generations of intellectual innovators—Robert Boyle, John Locke, Isaac Newton; people like this—coming up with fascinating new theories about the nature of reality. Starting in 1660, the Royal Society, a scientific organization, tried to secularize scientific knowledge and advance it more systematically than ever before.

In 17th and early 18th centuries, there was a sharp split between science as a gentleman's activity and technology, which is the world of the mechanics and the tinkerers, many of them illiterate. When science and technology started to come together, particularly after 1800, then they ensured that the process would be institutionalized and that it would continue. Here's the historian

Eric Hobsbawm, one of the most influential historians of industrialization. He writes:

> The early Industrial Revolution was technically rather primitive, not because no better science and technology was available or because men took no interest in it or could not be persuaded to use it. It was simple because, by and large, the application of simple ideas and devices, often of ideas available for centuries, could produce striking results. The novelty lay not in the innovations, but in the readiness of practical men to put their minds to using the science and technology which had long been available and within reach, and in the wide market which lay open to goods as prices and costs fell rapidly.

The examples he gives are those of wind and water power. They'd been used for centuries in wind mills and water mills, but now they began to be utilized in new and more effective ways to speed up the processes of manufacturing, first in the textile industry and then in many others.

Another quality, which is absolutely essential if industrialization was going to catch on, was flexibility among members of the British political elite and the idea that they should be politically sympathetic towards the objective of economic growth. In the 18th century, the aristocracy (some of them) was already interested in coal mining on their lands or in agricultural improvement. That is, they had a disposition to take an interest in these kinds of activities that were going to enrich Britain. By contrast, many of the European aristocracies regarded work as dishonorable. For example, in Spain, you can only enjoy the honorific Don, like Don Quixote, so long as you don't do lucrative work. To work is to be dishonored and to lose your status as a gentleman. Or, aristocracies elsewhere were far more preoccupied with war. This is true, for example, of the elites in Prussia. They disdained economic activity. They despised it and looked down on it and regarded it as beneath their notice; beneath contempt, in fact. British aristocrats also tended to look down on commercial activities; they certainly didn't think highly of shopkeepers. But when they saw a great opportunity, or when the burden of their debts embarrassed them, they did in fact seize the opportunity to do lucrative work and to restore their estates.

In the 18th century, the British government also supported an aggressive colonial policy. Britain fought five immense wars against France in the 18th century, and Britain emerged on the winning side in four out of those five. The only one they lost decisively was the war of the American Revolution. As they did so, they achieved overwhelming naval dominance; control of the seas. The Royal Navy actively supported merchant navy and Britain's colonial trade ventures, which spanned the world by the middle of the 18th century. That, in turn, created perfect support for British manufacturers, especially of textiles, to sell them abroad, capturing foreign markets and expanding them rapidly, particularly the cotton trade, which required the mass importation of raw cotton and the mass export of finished cloth to Europe, India, and Africa. British mercantile policy was set up to make sure that the colonies served Britain's own interests.

The Navigation Acts, which were later on going to be a grievance to the American colonists, one of the precipitating factors of the American Revolutionary War, specified that all trade with Britain and its colonies must take place in British ships, and that all colonial imports and exports must pass through Britain en route to their ultimate destination. This was a source of annoyance to the Americans because they would've liked to trade directly with their ultimate customers but were forced by British law to send their trade to England; it was narrowing from the American point of view. But these laws had a very large role to play in the nurturing an unparalleled British merchant marine.

To conclude, in this lecture I've suggested that many of the factors that made 18th-century Britain a conducive place for industrialization were germinating. Among the most important were political stability, the existence and development of sound financial institutions, population growth, a government sympathetic to commercial and colonial ventures, and an adaptable population.

In the next lecture, I'll turn from here to look at British agriculture, to show how improvements in food production created the surpluses of food that made it possible for large numbers of people to leave the land and turn to manufacturing instead.

The Agricultural Revolution
Lecture 3

Brit</sup>ritish agriculture became increasingly productive in the century after 1700, freeing up thousands of people to leave the land and move into manufacturing work. A combination of factors made these improvements possible, including new forms of land tenure and use, enhanced crops, improvements in animal breeding, and innovations in farm machinery. Some historians call these processes, collectively, the Agricultural Revolution. Population was growing rapidly after 1750, but food production more than kept pace, so that the ancient specter of famine receded ever farther into the distance.

The Shift to Enclosure

- The shift from the traditional open-field system to enclosure was a necessary first step for the Agricultural Revolution in Britain. Traditionally, open fields had been broken into strips, on which different farmers grew their own crops side by side. The system was inefficient because each farmer's strips of land were scattered. Diligent farmers were at the mercy of lazy ones whose land sprouted weeds. The unfenced common land in the village was open to all, for wood gathering and the grazing of sheep, pigs, cows, and geese.

- Enclosure was the consolidation of these strips into single fields that could then be fenced. Enclosure had begun in the Tudor era, continued through the 17th century, and accelerated in the 18th century.

- The usual method was for the major local landowners to introduce a bill into Parliament for enclosure of the village. Lands would be surveyed and then shared out in consolidated parcels to all who had legal title to them. Wealthier farmers gained from this process, whereas landless men, denied their ancient commons rights, were the losers.

- Holders of traditional rights to graze or collect firewood on common land or to live in cottages on the common often found that if they could not document these traditions, they would be excluded. At that point, they either left the land completely, becoming part of the first generation of industrial workers, or became landless farm laborers.

Increases in Cultivated Land

- The enclosure and farming of previously common land increased the total volume of land under cultivation, while the average size of farms also grew. Average farm size increased from about 65 acres of scattered land in 1700 to a concentrated farm area of about 150 acres in certain counties.

- The total amount of land under cultivation went up from 21 million acres in 1700 to about 29 million in 1800. Wasteland was cleared and seeded, often for the first time. Swamplands were drained to create fertile new farmland.

- A common pattern by 1800 was that tenant farmers rented from large landowners, while themselves hiring landless farm laborers—a three-tiered rural population. Increasingly, rural laborers were men as the number of women and children doing farm work declined.

- Farming gradually shifted from subsistence to a market orientation. As growing numbers of British people made their living from nonfarm activities, farmers concentrated on looking for profitable ways to grow the food needed by others.

- In the 1720s, Daniel Defoe noted the beginning of what we now call sales in farm produce futures. Although Defoe suspected that farmers were being defrauded, this development suggests the maturation of a business model that offered farmers cash or credit at times other than once a year when the harvest went to market.

Enhancements in Crop Yields

- New crops and new forms of rotation led to increases in productivity. Ever since the discovery of America, new food crops had become available to supplement the traditional wheat, oats, barley, and vegetables of the English diet.

- Potatoes were among the most important of these new crops. Potatoes provide three or four times as much nutrition per acre as cereal crops, as well as vitamin C. They were vital to the Irish food supply (where population was growing quickly) but less so in England, where they were regarded as poor people's food.

- The introduction of root crops, such as turnips, rutabagas, and field beets, and of clover increased the food supply for people and animals and had a beneficial nitrogen-fixing effect. A system of growing clover and turnips instead of leaving fields fallow was introduced from the Netherlands in the mid-1600s and caught on throughout much of England. Clover, in particular, was highly effective in maintaining nitrogen levels in the soil.

- "Turnip" Townshend (1674–1738), a politician and aristocrat interested in agricultural improvements, was a pioneer of this method. He established the four-year crop rotation in this sequence: wheat, turnips, barley, clover. The clover and turnips were used as animal fodder, which increased the farm's production of manure that could itself be used on the fields to improve fertility.

- At this time, farmers were also learning to set aside grains from the strongest and most disease-resistant plants as seeds for the following year—an early form of selective farming that led to yield increases.

Improvements in Animal Breeding
- Fencing facilitated improvements in animal breeding. Although we take fences, walls, and hedges entirely for granted, they had important effects by demarcating land, keeping animals off cropland, and making selective breeding effective. Breeders began to cultivate animals for specific characteristics—notably, sheep for wool and meat and cows for milk, leather, and meat.

Darwin's arguments concerning natural selection were based in part on the process of domestic selection, that is, the modification of animals to better meet human needs.

- The best of the breeders was Robert Bakewell (1725–1795), who created the New Leicester sheep breed, which was made to grow rapidly, producing tasty mutton. Bakewell also joined up with Robert Fowler to produce a fast-growing cow that was ideal for beef production. Another sheep breeder, John Ellman, bred the Southdown sheep, which produced wool that was easy to card and spin.

- By 1850, British cows and sheep were completely different— stronger and more useful than their predecessors of the 1700s. Farmers replaced oxen with bigger, stronger, and faster horses as their principal draft animals.

Innovations in Farm Machinery
- Early mechanization of farming also increased productivity. Seed drills improved the regularity of plant distribution in fields. The traditional method was *broadcasting*, but it was deficient in even distribution and depth and vulnerable to birds and other scavengers.

- The seed drill was invented by an eccentric farmer and theorist, Jethro Tull (1674–1741), a contemporary of "Turnip" Townshend. Tull's seed drill, invented in 1701, was an important advance. It ensured even distribution of seeds and depth of planting and reduced losses to scavengers.

- Better plows, made from more durable iron and steel, also enhanced productivity. First was the Rotherham plow, introduced from Holland, that had a hard metallic plowshare that remained sharp with frequent use.

Rural Leaders

- A group of prominent rural leaders undertook systematic improvement of their estates, demonstrated the economic benefits that could ensue, and enjoyed the favorable notice of influential writers.

- Thomas William Coke of Holkham (1754–1842), a British politician, owned large and prosperous estates and ran a model farm, experimenting with best practices and encouraging information sharing. For about 40 consecutive years, he invited farmers from all over the country to his estates—in effect, introducing the world's first agricultural show. He also determined that differences in soil in selected areas would affect the usefulness of innovations.

- Arthur Young (1741–1820) was a farmer and regular writer on farming, producing 25 books on the topic during his life, beginning in late 1760s. His well-written works were widely translated and admired across Enlightenment Europe.
   - Young hated wastefulness and believed that far better use could be made out of land than was currently the case. He also voiced the Enlightenment notion that God or divine providence had created a universal abundance that just needed human energy to be realized.

   - Young understood the absolute centrality of security of tenure. One of his proposed reforms was to make farmers more confident that the land they rented would remain theirs or, ideally, that they'd be in a position to buy it.

- o He published *The Farmer's Kalendar* in 1770, a month-by-month account of jobs the diligent farmer needed to do to prosper. He founded the *Annals of Agriculture* in 1784, which eventually ran to 46 annual volumes.

- o The British government appointed Young secretary of the newly created Board of Agriculture in 1793. Young admired George Washington and the American Revolution. Washington corresponded with him about farming innovations at Mount Vernon.

- William Marshall (1745–1818) was Young's greatest critic. While Young toured the country and chatted with locals to get a sense of farm conditions, Marshall believed one had to farm an area for a few years before being able to discuss it with any authority. Marshall worked as a farm manager in several British regions and wrote a 12-volume account of British agriculture, published in 1798.

- Historians still find both Marshall and Young useful as they struggle to piece together the state of farming life in the late 1700s and early 1800s and to determine why farming became so much more productive at the time.

The Irish Experience

- The English experience diverged sharply from that of Ireland in the 18th and 19th centuries. England had developed a widely diversified agricultural sector. By the early 1800s, farmers were capitalists, eager to maximize profit from their lands, interacting with a large urban population, and able, in ordinary years, to meet demand even though population was rising.

- Ireland, by contrast, concentrated on one crop, potatoes, and thus, was caught in the catastrophe of the 1846 famine, which may have led to as many as a million deaths and resulted in the emigration of another million people.

- After some hard harvest years in the 1760s and a very bad year in 1816, England never again suffered from famine. In the long run, ironically, England did not continue to feed itself, coming in the late 19th century to rely increasingly on food imports. That strategy was acceptable most of the time, but it also had a perilous side, as the blockades of the two world wars made clear.

Suggested Reading

Kerridge, *The Agricultural Revolution*.

Mingay, *Arthur Young and His Times*.

Overton, *Agricultural Revolution in England*.

Pope, *Atlas of British Social and Economic History Since c. 1700*.

Questions to Consider

1. How did the development of scientific ideas contribute to improvements in British farming?

2. Which was more important to increases in British farm output: climate change, crop rotations, or new forms of land tenure?

The Agricultural Revolution
Lecture 3—Transcript

British agriculture became increasingly productive in the century after 1700, freeing up thousands of people to leave the land and move into manufacturing work. A combination of factors made these improvements possible, including new forms of land tenure and use, new crops, improvements in animal breeding, and new farm machinery. Some historians call these processes, collectively, the "agricultural revolution." Others deny that it was a revolution, but they're equally impressed at the overall achievement.

Population was growing rapidly after 1750 as we saw last time, but food production more than kept pace, so that the ancient spectre of famine receded ever further into the distance. The shift from the old open-field system to enclosure was the necessary first step for all other changes.

Traditionally in English farming, open fields had been broken into strips whose pattern can still very often be seen on English fields and meadows today: a line of swellings that show where the old strips were and the ditches between them. It's a very common pattern to see all over rural England. Different farmers had strips side by side on these open fields where a particular crop would be grown. It was inefficient, because each farmer's strips of land were scattered around the village, and he had to spend a lot of time moving from one to the next. Diligent farmers were at the mercy of lazy ones whose land sprouted weeds and, of course, the weeds would spread. After the harvest in the open field strip system, the farm animals were turned loose to graze on the stubble. The unfenced common land of the village, meanwhile, was open to everyone for wood gathering for firewood, and for the grazing of sheep, pigs, cows, and geese.

The process of enclosure, which is central to this story, was the consolidation of these strips into single fields that could then be fenced off so that just one farmer would be farming an enclosed field. This process of enclosure had begun in the Tudor era—that is, in the 1500s, particularly under Queen Elizabeth I—and it continued gradually through the 17th century, but then accelerated markedly in the 18th, the 1700s. The usual method was for the major local landowners to introduce a bill into Parliament for the enclosure of their village. Under these circumstances, the profession of "surveyor" developed. A group of trained men learned how to carry out surveys of the land efficiently and quickly so that the members of the community who are enclosing know exactly where the land lies. The land would be surveyed and then shared out in consolidated parcels to all those who had legal title to it, with the expectation, which was a justified one, that the farms would then become more efficient and more productive.

Wealthier farmers gained from this process, whereas landless men, denied their ancient commons rights, were the losers. The holders of traditional rights to graze or collect firewood on the common land or to live in cottages on the common often found that if they couldn't document these traditions, if they couldn't prove that they had an ancient right to live there, they would now be excluded. At that point, many of them had to either leave the land completely, becoming part of the first generation of industrial workers, or if they stayed in the countryside, they'd become landless farm laborers.

The enclosure and farming of previously common land increased the total volume of land under cultivation, and the average size of British farms began to increase. The average farm size of about 65 acres in 1700 increased to concentrated farm areas of about 150 acres in the counties south of the River Trent. The River Trent is a river that flows across the middle of England from west to east. South of the Trent—this is all the area around London—farms had come to be about 150 acres. North of the Trent—in the counties like Yorkshire, Lancashire, Durham, and Northumberland where industrialization was going to begin—they were of about 100 acres. But the total amount of land went up from about 21 million acres in 1700 to about 29 million in 1800. Waste land was cleared and seeded, often for the first time. Even more important, swamplands were drained—particularly in the East Anglia counties of Norfolk, Suffolk, Essex, and Lincolnshire—and because it's flat and fertile, it made some of the best and most productive new farmland starting in the 1700s.

The common pattern of English farming by the year 1800 was to have tenant farmers renting land from the big landowners while they themselves hired landless farm laborers. It was a three-tier system, a three-tier rural population, from the aristocracy at the top to the landless laborers at the bottom. Increasingly, also, the rural laborers tended to be men, as the number of women and children doing farm work went into decline. Farming also shifted in the 1700s from being principally a subsistence activity to principally a market-oriented business; that is, growing food that will be eaten by others rather than simply growing enough food to keep one's own family alive, the subsistence method.

As growing numbers of British people made their living from non-farm activities, farmers concentrated on looking for profitable ways to grow the food they needed. It's worth reminding yourself that every industrial society is an agricultural one, too. The food has to come from somewhere. You can have an agricultural society without industry, but you can't possibly have an industrial society without agriculture. Even today, here in the United States, where only about two percent of the population is farmers, still it's reasonable to say that the United States is an agricultural society. We think that food comes from the supermarket, but it doesn't; it comes from the land and it still has to be grown, even today.

But it was becoming more commercialized. In the 1720s, Daniel Defoe, whom we remember as the author of *Moll Flanders* and *Robinson Crusoe*, noted the beginning of what we'd call "sales" in farm produce futures by men called "corn factors." Defoe was very interested in this; he wrote: "These corn factors in the country ride about among the farmers and buy the corn, even in the barn before it is threshed, nay sometimes they buy it in the field standing, not only before it is reaped but before it is ripe." He suspected that the farmers were being defrauded in this way, but it might also suggest a maturing of a business model that offers farmers cash or credit at times other than once a year when the harvest goes to market. Think about this: From the farmer's point of view, if he sells his grain at harvest time in the autumn when everyone else is selling theirs, he's likely to get a low price. If he sells it the previous May or June, soon after it's been planted, he's speculating; he's taking a risk that he might have gotten more by waiting but he might also have gotten less. It's becoming commercialized, and it's becoming a speculative venture.

In the 18th century, new crops and new forms of crop rotation on the land led to increases in productivity. Ever since the discovery of America by Columbus, new food crops had become available to supplement the traditional wheat, oats, barley, and vegetables of the traditional English diet.

Potatoes, for example: Potatoes are a New World crop, and there were no spuds in Europe before Columbus. They offer a very high nutrition yield per acre. They were among the most important. They provide three or four times as much nutrition per acre as the cereal crops that were then common in Europe. They also provide Vitamin C, although in the 18th century nobody knew about vitamins. They were vital to the Irish food supply, where the population was growing very quickly, but less so in England, where potatoes were regarded as poor people's food. Obviously, they're central to the English staple fish and chips, but that only caught on in the late 19th and 20th centuries. In the 18th century, potatoes were looked down upon because they grow below the surface of the Earth and because they don't need the intensive cultivation of grain crops. They were regarded as poor people's food and were despised.

The introduction of root crops such as turnips, swedes, and mangel-wurzels, and the introduction of clover increased the food supply for people and for farm animals and they had a beneficial nitrogen-fixing effect. Clover and turnips would be grown instead of leaving fields fallow. The traditional method had been to grow a crop for a couple of years and then to leave the land unplanted, fallow, in order that it might recover its fertility. Now, instead, clover and turnips would be sown there. This was a system introduced from the Netherlands in the mid-1600s, and it caught on gradually throughout much of England. Clover in particular was highly effective in maintaining the nitrogen level in the soil.

One of the pioneers of this method was a man called "Turnip" Townshend; "Turnip" was his nickname. He lived from 1674–1738 and was a pioneer of what we'd call agricultural research. He was a politician, an aristocrat; very interested in agricultural improvements. At his estate called "Raynham" in Norfolk, he pioneered the four-year crop rotation in this sequence: wheat, turnips, barley, clover. The clover and the turnips were used as animal fodder, and that meant that more farm animals could be kept and they'd produce more manure, and the manure could be used on the fields to improve their fertility. It's kind of a benevolent cycle. Fallowing was excluded altogether because it was less effective than turnips and clover. Townshend himself, as his nickname implies, "Turnip Townshend," was a figure of fun in much of England. He was mocked as a great bore with a one-track mind. The poetry of Alexander Pope often takes him on and makes him look ridiculous. But nevertheless, from the point of view of the history of farming and the point of view of the increases of farm supplies, he's very, very important.

Farmers were also learning to set aside grains from the strongest and most disease-resistant plants as seeds to be planted in the following year. This was an early form of selective farming that led to yield increases. Replant the best grains, and the qualities they have will tend to replicate themselves. The crop itself was improving long before the era of scientific agronomy.

Fencing facilitated improvements in animal breeding. We take fences, walls, and hedges entirely for granted, but they had important effects by demarcating the land, by keeping animals off the crops, and by making selective breeding effective. Obviously, you can only breed your animals if you can decide exactly which ones are going to be introduced into the company of which other ones, and making sure that the animals that you don't want to breed are prevented from doing so. Breeders began to cultivate animals for specific characteristics, notably sheep for wool and meat, and cows for milk, leather, and meat. The best of the breeders was a man named Robert Bakewell, who lived from 1725–1795. He was a rigorously systematic cross-breeder who was extremely careful and methodical in working out which lines to develop and which to suppress. He created a new sheep breed called the New Leicester. It was a sheep that was made to grow rapidly, producing a very, very tasty form of mutton, which was then one of the standard parts of the English diet. Bakewell also joined up with Robert Fowler to produce a fast-growing cow ideal for beef production. Another sheep breeder named John Ellman bred a sheep called the Southdown, ideal for wool that was easy to card and spin into wool for weaving. As the textile industry begins to take off, it can be taken back all the way to the animal and more suitable wool can be created to make the process work better.

As with the crops, so with the animals: British cows and sheep by 1850 were completely different, stronger, and more useful than their predecessors had been in the year 1700. When Charles Darwin came to write his book *On the*

Origin of Species by Natural Selection, published in 1859, he began with chapters on domestic selection. In other words, he writes about how human decisions make it possible to modify the animals to make them bigger or faster, or more quick-growing, or yielding better wool or better milk, and so on. He says these are processes that have been going on for centuries. Darwin described how experts could select the best animals; and, of course, by best he means best from the point of view of the humans who are using them, who wanted more meat, or more wool, or quicker growth, or better meat-to-bone ratios. Darwin says these breeders actually create what are, in effect, new creatures and this is a very brilliant prelude to the rest of the book, because it enables him to argue convincingly that the same kind of process is going on in the natural world. When he talks about natural selection, he's using the word *selection* metaphorically by carrying it over from the artificial selection, which went on among animal breeders. Of course, in nature, it's the natural surroundings that decide which animals are best able to survive, rather than the farmer simply nurturing some and killing off others. But it certainly gave the theory added plausibility because his contemporaries, those of them who were interested in animal breeding, had actually witnessed the process in action and had witnessed the ways in which species could change.

One of the achievements of the farmers in these days was to replace oxen, which had been the standard draft animal for centuries, with bigger, stronger, and faster horses as their principal draft animal, and the horses are considerably more versatile.

The early mechanization of farming also increased productivity. Seed drills improved the regularity of plant distribution in fields. The traditional method of planting seeds was called "broadcasting." When we use the word *broadcast*, we're usually referring to television or radio signals being sent out into the world, but that's a metaphorical word as well; we've forgotten its metaphorical origins. Originally, *broadcasting* meant simply taking seeds from a pouch and sprinkling them, distributing them, as you walk along over the fields. The problem with broadcasting is that it's deficient in even distribution. Even a skilled planter can't get the seeds evenly distributed. They can't be buried to the right depth—in fact, they lie on the surface—and that, of course, means that a broadcasting farmer is usually followed by a great flock of birds who at once eat many of the seeds before they have the chance to germinate.

The first seed drill was invented by an eccentric farmer and farming theorist, a man named Jethro Tull, who lived from 1674–1741. He was a contemporary of Turnip Townshend. To anyone who, like me, lived through the popular music crazes of the 1960s and 1970s, Jethro Tull was a flute-playing rock musician. But the original, after whom he named himself, was this agricultural reformer. Presumably, the rocker originally heard about this man during his school classes. On some issues, Jethro Tull was completely wrong. He believed, for example, that air was the best fertilizer, and we know very well that that's simply not true. But his seed drill, invented in 1701, was an important advance. It made sure that distribution of the seeds was even, that the seeds were buried to the ideal depth, and that losses to scavengers would be slight. So a field planted by the seed drill is much more likely to yield a good harvest than one that's been broadcast. Seed drills caught on only slowly, like most new farming technologies, but in the long run they'd be one of many important technological improvements.

He also experimented with a hoe pulled by horses and wrote a book about it. The book's called *The New Horse Houghing Husbandry* from the year 1731. In a second edition of this book from the year 1762, by which time Tull himself had died, his editor made a familiar lament about farmers' chronic conservatism and their slowness to change. Here's what the editor says:

> How it has happened that a method of culture which proposes such advantages to those who will duly prosecute it, hath been so long neglected in this country, may be matter of surprise to such as are not acquainted with the character of the men on whom the practice thereof depends, but to those who know them thoroughly it can be none. For it is certain that very few of them can be prevailed on to alter their usual methods upon any consideration, though they are convinced that their continuing therein disables them from paying their rents and maintaining their families.

In other words, what he's simply saying there is farmers are very conservative and so change tends to be slow and uncertain. Even when a farmer has been shown the superiority of a new technology like the seed drill or the hoe, still he won't change his old ways.

Yet, from our point of view, the big story of 18th century is how much improvement was being achieved. Better plows, made from more durable iron and steel, increased attention to hoeing; these things enhanced productivity as well. One of the first of these better implements was the Rotherham plow, introduced from Holland and having a hard metallic plowshare that remained sharp with frequent use. Again, we're so familiar with good, hard steel implements, we forget how difficult they are to make and how rare they were until the last couple of centuries. Plowshares made of wood are much less good than ones made of metal, but even metallic ones had to be constantly sharpened until techniques of making hard steel developed, and this is a theme I'll get back to in later lectures in this course.

A group of prominent rural leaders undertook systematic improvement of their estates, demonstrating the economic benefits that could ensue, and they enjoyed the favorable notice of other influential writers at the same time. One of them was Thomas William Coke, whose estate was called "Holkham." He lived from 1754–1842; in other words, a generation later than Townshend and Tull. He, too, was a member of the elite, a Member of Parliament, and eventually he became the Earl of Leicester, one of the great aristocrats. He had a large and prosperous estate in Norfolk in East Anglia, and there he ran a model farm, experimenting with the best practices and encouraging the sharing of information among all the farmers whose notice he could attract.

Once each year, for about 40 consecutive years, at sheep-shearing time, he invited farmers from all over the country. Many of those who could afford it, including scientists and explorers like Joseph Banks, the friend of Captain James Cook, would go to visit. In effect, these were the world's very first agricultural shows, starting in the mid and late 18th century. He encouraged people to visit his Park Farm "because it is from them I gain the little knowledge I have and derive the satisfaction of communicating improvements among my tenantry." He recognized that differences of soil in different areas would affect the usefulness of innovations, which might not work everywhere. He also knew that many farmers were stubbornly traditional, and he once remarked that the rate of diffusion of his new methods was probably as low as one mile per year. This is a complaint that you see in the farming literature of Britain and, a little bit later, the farming literature of the United States as well. Why won't the farmers respond to the improved methods we've got, because they're so much better? It's usually the farmer's answer: "We've got methods that do work. Maybe they don't work as well as they possibly could, but at least we can be sure of them."

Another of these reformers was Arthur Young. He lived from 1741–1820. He was a farmer himself and a regular writer on farming, producing 25 books on the topic during his life, beginning in late 1760s. They're well-written books, too, and give a sense of the state of farming in the different parts of Britain. His books were widely translated, too, and admired across Enlightenment Europe. Ironically, Arthur Young was far more successful as a writer about farming than he was as a farmer in his own right, where he sometimes undertook risky experiments. If anything, he erred too much in the other direction. He hated wastefulness, and he believed that far better use could be made out of land than was currently the case. He also voiced the Enlightenment idea that God, or divine providence, had created a universal abundance that just needed human energy to be realized. It's this idea that comes up constantly in 18th-century literature from people like Voltaire also. God's reasonable. God created a perfect world. We've got to work out reasonably and rationally exactly how to put it to our best possible use.

Here's a little quotation from Arthur Young's book on farming in the north of England, published in 1771. He writes:

> It is acknowledged that nature does nothing in vain, and I cannot help thinking that every soil either contains within itself a remedy for its original barrenness, or at least that no large tract of country is destitute of some peculiar productions adapted to its fertilization, so as to render it fit for the production of vegetables and the support of animals. Thus has bounteous providence dispensed its blessings with an equal as well as liberal hand. The bleak mountain and barren rock contain the precious ore and sparkling gem, whilst the fertile plains and valleys are covered with wood, or produce corn and herbage. Every part of nature is conducive to the support, ease, and happiness of man. But as the exertion of the mental faculties, as

well as bodily labour, is requisite for the well-being of the human species, so the treasures of nature are not always obvious, nor her productions spontaneous.

Arthur Young also understood the absolute centrality of security of tenure. He said, "If people aren't certain that they can take advantage of the improvements to the land they make, they won't make the improvements." In other words, one of his proposed reforms was to make farmers more confident that land they rented would remain theirs, or ideally that they'd be in a position to be able to buy it. He wrote, "Give a man the secure possession of a bleak rock, and he will turn it into a garden. Give him a nine years' lease of a garden, and he will convert it into a desert." It's just not good enough to say "You can use this land for the moment"; it's got to be permanent.

He published *The Farmer's Kalendar* in 1770 (that's *Kalendar* with a "K"), a month-by-month account of jobs that the diligent farmer needed to do if he was going to prosper. It's a kind of farmer's almanac. He also founded the *Annals of Agriculture* in 1784, which eventually ran to 46 annual volumes. When the British government created a Board of Agriculture in 1793, it appointed Arthur Young as its Secretary.

He was an advocate of large-scale farming; he understood the benefits of doing it on a large scale. He wrote:

> The large farmer, with a greater proportional wealth than the small occupier, is able to work great improvements in his business. He also employs better cattle and uses better implements. He purchases more manures and adopts more improvements.

Among other people, he admired George Washington and the American Revolution. We tend to think that when the American Revolution took place, the British were all on the side of Lord North and King George III. They might've had to pay lip service to them, but, in fact, there was a great deal of admiration for what the Americans were doing and sympathy for their point of view. Washington himself modeled himself on Cincinnatus, the great old Roman hero who came from his farm at the hour of need but then went back to the plow when the emergency had passed. This resonated very,

very strongly with Arthur Young, who wrote admiring letters to Washington. Washington, knowing Young to be a great authority, corresponded with him about farming innovations at Mount Vernon. There was a strong transatlantic link there between the two men.

Another of these writers was William Marshall, who lived from 1745–1818. He was Young's leading critic. Young toured the country and chatted with locals to get a sense of farming conditions, but Marshall believed that you had to farm an area for a few years before you could discuss it with any authority. In other words, he was critical of what he thought of as Young's superficiality. He himself worked as farm manager in several different British regions and wrote a 12-volume account of British agriculture, published in 1798. He was a less talented writer than Young, lacking the gift of confident generalization and plausible inference from limited data. But historians still find both of them very useful as they struggle to piece together the actual state of farming life in the late 1700s and early 1800s and try to solve this question: Why was it becoming so much more productive?

We remember the 18th century as the era of the Enlightenment, and many of the era's philosophers showed an interest in agricultural improvements. It's impossible to overemphasize the era's faith that there's a relationship between theoretical and practical knowledge. Lord Kames, a Scottish scholar, wrote *The Gentleman Farmer: Being an Attempt to Improve Agriculture by Subjecting It to the Test of Rational Principles*. It came out in 1776, and it's exactly the kind of book which would've come out in that year.

Similarly, Humphrey Davy, a theoretical chemist but also a practical inventor—the inventor of the coal miner's safety lamp, as we'll see in a later lecture—in 1813, he wrote a pioneering work on *Elements of Agricultural Chemistry*. It was the best book of its kind until Liebig, the great German agricultural chemist, wrote his *Great Synthesis* about 40 years later.

English experience diverged sharply from Irish experience in the 18th and 19th centuries. England developed a widely diversified agricultural sector. By the early 1800s, farmers were capitalists, eager to maximize profit from their lands, interacting with a large urban population, and able, in ordinary years, to meet demand even though population was rising. Ireland, by contrast, concentrated on one crop, potatoes, with the short-term benefit of rapid population growth but the long-term catastrophe of the 1846 famine, which may have led to as many as a million deaths from famine and another million people emigrating. After some hard harvest years in the 1760s and a very bad year in 1816, England never again suffered from famine. In the long run, ironically, England didn't continue to feed itself, coming in the late 19th century to rely increasingly on food imports, particularly from the United States and Canada. That was fine most of the time, making the best use of Britain's own economic advantages to be more industrial, but it did have a dangerous side as the blockades of the two world wars made clear when German submarines threatened the approach of food convoys to Britain.

In the next lecture, we'll turn to people who'd already left the land and moved into cities in the very early stages of this great transformation. I'll also try to show what English urban life was like before the great age of factory manufacturing.

Cities and Manufacturing Traditions
Lecture 4

B y 1700, Britain already possessed a large urban population—not only in London, by far the single largest city, but also in several provincial towns. Britain was more urbanized than France and was rivaled only by the Netherlands and parts of urban northern Italy. Small-scale manufacturing of textiles, metal goods, and glassware; carpentry; and thriving brewing and distilling businesses had built up strong and distinctive trade traditions.

London

- It is no coincidence that nearly all major cities are coastal or on navigable rivers. At a time when water was the best means of transport, major cities historically were centered on route centers and ports.

- London, a city since the Roman era, was already a magnet to people from the English countryside. In the early 1700s, it was home to about 750,000 people—perhaps 15 percent of the entire population of Britain. Its sheer size made it an immense market, transforming the lands around it into farms to feed the townspeople and stimulating enterprise in the city to fulfill their needs.

- London was dangerous in many ways, however. With the city's many wooden structures, fire was a constant danger, especially given that heating, lighting, and cooking all depended on open flames. The Great Fire of London, in 1666, was one of the most notorious catastrophes in British history, destroying 13,200 houses and 87 churches.

- Rebuilding was itself an immense job and a tremendous economic stimulus. Christopher Wren's St. Paul's Cathedral is probably the best remembered post-fire structure. Following the fire, the London government began to regulate the width of streets, the use of brick

57

In the early 1700s, with a population of about 750,000, London surpassed Paris as the largest city in Europe.

or stone in construction rather than wood, and roofing with tiles instead of thatch.

- Other dangers included poor diet, adulterated food, and contaminated water. Indeed, in the late 17th and early 18th centuries, more people died in London than were born there. Although the city was economically attractive, it was the perfect breeding ground for epidemics. Plague was less common after the 1660s, but the city was still swept regularly by smallpox and typhus. In the early 19th century, cholera would add a new horror.

A Center of Trade

- Along with these drawbacks, London had many assets. The royal court was centered there, and around the court developed the *London season*. Wealthy gentry and aristocracy spent the winter and spring in London. Their presence stimulated luxury goods trades, such as watchmaking, jewelry making, stationers, coach making, cabinetry, and dressmaking. The aspiring middle classes, too, become urban consumers. London was a magnet to immigrants fleeing persecution abroad, such as the French Huguenots, many of whom brought their skills to the city, chiefly in the silk industry.

- Work in London was traditionally controlled by the old guilds, many dating back to the medieval era. But as the city grew rapidly outward and as new kinds of work arose, it became increasingly difficult for the guilds to keep a grip. They had grown out of an era of relative economic stability rather than sustained growth. New forms of work now arose. In a list from 1747, 215 different occupations were noted, but 50 years later, the list had expanded to 492, most of which were not regulated by guilds.

- London was also the center of colonial trade and colonial-related trades, such as tobacco processing and sugar refining. It was the headquarters of the monopoly companies that dominated Britain's empire: the Merchant-Adventurers, which held a monopoly on English textile trade in Europe; the Levant Company, with monopoly rights to the Ottoman Empire; the East India Company, the exclusive European trader in India; and Muscovy Company, trading with Russia.

- London dockyards thrived, with wharves on both banks of the Thames below London Bridge. Ships brought wares from around the country and around the world. The Navigation Acts specified that anything made in one of Britain's colonies had to be shipped to Britain first, then re-exported. These regulations were a source of grievance to the American colonies but a great stimulus to shipbuilding and ancillary trades in London.

Provincial Towns
- In early-18th-century Britain, no other provincial town or city had even 50,000 people. The next largest rank of towns included Bristol, Edinburgh, Norwich, York, Exeter, and Newcastle. All were either

ports or administrative centers with a smaller farming hinterland. Bristol, Liverpool, and Glasgow were port cities facing the Atlantic that grew prosperous through colonial trade in slaves, tea, tobacco, and sugar.

- Next in size were such towns as Birmingham in the Midlands. Birmingham produced metal goods, such as nails, buckles, buttons, knives, saddlers' ironmongery, and brassware. These goods were called "toys," and Birmingham was nicknamed "the toyshop of Europe." It was also the center of gun making.

- There was a distinctive attitude to business evident in the towns and cities. When young William Hutton first went to Birmingham in 1741, he was instantly aware of the difference between this thriving provincial manufacturing town (with a population of about 20,000) and the countryside where he had grown up. Hutton wrote: "I was surprised at the place, but more at the people. … They possessed a vivacity I had never beheld."

- Provincial towns were usually built around a central marketplace. On designated market days, farmers and craftspeople would gather in the town marketplace to sell their goods. The marketplace also served a labor exchange function.

- The 18th century also witnessed the growth of shops in provincial towns. Shops, which we take for granted, were once a novelty—places where particular goods were sold away from the places where they were made. Quaker shopkeepers pioneered the idea of having fixed shop prices instead of the tradition of haggling.

- Observers also noticed new towns springing up around one particular type of business. For example, Sheffield specialized in the cutlery trade, Burton-on-Trent specialized in beer, and St. Helens specialized in glass. Specialization was possible only when a town intended to supply a wider area—such as London—beyond the immediate market.

- Although the transport system was poor—and the Industrial Revolution would be greatly stimulated by its improvement—already in the early 1700s, goods were moving in large quantities not only by sea and river but also by wagon and packhorse.

The Guild System

- The guild system in many provincial towns regulated access to most of the important trades, many of which restricted membership to families that had been in a particular business for generations. The guilds also fixed prices and regulated quality control.

- Under the guild system, a young man would become an apprentice, often going to live in the household of a master craftsman. Often, the young apprentice's family would have to pay the master craftsman to take him on. Like female live-in servants, an apprentice was forbidden to marry. The system was subject to abuse, and apprentices could find themselves working as unpaid servants with no rights.

- When his apprenticeship was complete, the apprentice became a journeyman. The word is derived from the French *journée*, meaning "day." Journeymen were paid by the day.

- Journeymen could hope to accumulate enough experience and funds to become master craftsmen in their own right. This was a realistic expectation for blacksmiths, weavers, pin makers, wheelwrights, thatchers, glaziers, and coopers. However, there were other industries already growing too large in scale for that to be a common path, such as shipbuilders, breweries, and tanneries.

The 18th-Century Workplace

- A common pattern in the provincial towns was for businesses to be grouped together by type—for example, all the wheelwrights on the same street, all the butchers, all the candle makers, and so on. Work was regulated as much by daylight as by the clock, with craftsmen expecting to work longer hours in summer than in winter.

- In many workplaces, alcohol flowed freely, especially when safe drinking water was difficult or impossible to find. Beer making was already a big business, not least because it was actually less harmful to one's health in many areas to drink beer than to drink water. Urban water supplies were especially dangerous because wells were often contaminated by their proximity to cesspools. Rivers were also dumps for tanneries, dye works, and other polluting trades.

- Also common in the 18th century was the distilling of gin. However, gin contributed to poor health and premature death, and it was hard to regulate, often contaminated with turpentine. Generations of working people drank away their pay rather than struggle to get ahead.

- This was the fabric of social life that the first industrialists had to combat: trying to find ways to get people to work regular hours, by the clock and not the seasons, and to be sober throughout the working day. London businessmen were the first to push employees to work beyond daylight hours. A 1747 book called *London Tradesmen* describes workshops lit by lamps and candles, with work continuing after dark, especially in winter.

Combating Fatalism
- The first industrialists also had to overcome the workers' ancient sense of fatalism and instill the idea of progress and economic growth. They were materialists who needed others to share their sense that it was possible and desirable to gain wealth.

- Nevertheless, there was a constant drumbeat of criticism, not only from workers, who preferred the older, slower pace, but also from church leaders, who feared cities as centers of vice, luxury, and atheism. For example, in 1777, the bishop of Chester preached that a recent earthquake was God's warning to the cities of Manchester and Macclesfield.

- When we look back at the late 18th century, we're so impressed with the increased pace of economic activity that it's difficult to remember that it took place in the face of widespread skepticism that such improvement was possible. The changes required a radically new idea about the possibility of progress and of transforming the world as it was into something different and better.

- On the other hand, in those decades, fatalism, great though it was in Britain, was less prevalent there than almost anywhere else—a fact that helps explain the great transformation to the Industrial Revolution.

Suggested Reading

Borsay, *The English Urban Renaissance.*

Chalkin, *The Rise of the English Town, 1650–1850.*

Clark, ed., *The Cambridge Urban History of Britain*, vol. 2, *1540–1840.*

Corfield, *The Impact of English Towns, 1700–1800.*

Questions to Consider

1. How does the sheer proximity of large groups of people stimulate innovation and inventiveness?

2. Why were all of Britain's important preindustrial cities also ports?

Cities and Manufacturing Traditions
Lecture 4—Transcript

Britain already possessed a large urban population by the year 1700, above all in London, which was by far the single largest city, but also in several provincial towns. It was more urbanized than France and much more urbanized than Poland or Russia in Eastern Europe, its only rivals being the Netherlands and parts of urban northern Italy, the towns of the Renaissance. Small-scale manufacturing of textiles, metal goods, glassware, and carpentry, along with thriving brewing and distilling businesses, beer and spirits, had built up strong and distinctive trade traditions. Cities had grown up gradually over the centuries at route centers and ports when water transport provided the best communications. It's no coincidence that nearly all major cities are coastal or built on navigable rivers because water transport was by far the best method before industrialization.

London, a city since the Roman era, was already a magnet to people from all over the English provinces. In the early 1700s, it surpassed Paris to become the biggest city in Europe with about 750,000 people, about three-quarters of a million, perhaps as much as 15 percent of the whole population of Britain. Its sheer size made it an immense market, transforming the lands around it as places for growing food to feed the townsmen and stimulating enterprise in the city to fulfill its needs.

But London was a dangerous place; dangerous for many reasons. First of all, fire: Heating, lighting, and cooking all depended on open flames, and there was a constant danger of things burning down from all these open flames, especially because the city had so many old wooden structures. The Great Fire of London of 1666 is one of the most famous catastrophes in British history, much talked about in lore and legend but a real event. It destroyed 13,200 houses and 87 churches. The rebuilding of London in the 1660s, 1670s, and 1680s was itself an immense job and a great economic stimulus.

Christopher Wren's St. Paul's Cathedral is probably the best-remembered post-Great Fire structure. It's been greatly admired ever since, and rightly so. This is the domed cathedral in which the royal weddings take place. Perhaps its most famous moment came during a second terrible fire of London during the German air raids of 1940, the Blitz. There are some famous photographs of the dome of St. Paul's Cathedral rising above a landscape of smoke, fire, and catastrophe as many of the buildings around it in the city of London were being destroyed.

The London government, after the Great Fire of London, began to regulate the width of streets; the use of brick or stone rather than wood. They encouraged roofing with tiles instead of with thatch. But in practice, the government had little enforcement power and could rarely get its own way. There was no central London authority, no police force, until about 1830. Incidentally, don't sentimentalize thatched roofs. It's great to go to England on vacation on warm, dry summer's days and see thatched cottages in the countryside; they look lovely in midsummer in rural districts. But actually, thatch is a perfect haven for lice; it gets more and more infested the longer it stays there. It's not very waterproof; it's not very warm; its insulation properties are only fair; and it's not even always windproof. The passing of thatch isn't to be regretted. Fires remained common because flames were still needed for the basic activities of daily life.

Another of the dangers of living in London was the danger of premature death. More people died in London than were born there in the late 17th and early 18th centuries. Although it was economically attractive, it was the perfect breeding ground for epidemics. Bubonic plague was less common after the 1660s—in fact, there's a tradition that the Great Fire of 1666 ended the last great outbreak of the plague of 1665—but even so, the city was still swept regularly by smallpox and typhus; I mentioned in a previous lecture the development of smallpox inoculations 140 years later in the 1790s. In the early 19th century, 1829 and 1830, cholera would add a new horror: an urban epidemic disease that could spread extremely rapidly. Most people in London had a poor diet. They were forced to eat adulterated food. They were forced to drink contaminated water because there was no alternative. There was no food and drug regulation, and poor stuff was being sold to credulous consumers. All these things made urban life hazardous.

But along with these drawbacks, London had many assets. The Royal Court was centered there. Around the Court developed the London season, according to which the gentry and the aristocracy—that is to say, the wealthiest people in the kingdom—spent the winter and the spring in London in their town houses before going out into the provinces for the rest of the year. If you read the novels of Jane Austen or Anthony Trollope, you get a very good feeling for the London season; the way, just before Christmas, the aristocracy comes into town, and that's where social life takes place until early in the following summer.

The presence of all the wealthiest people in the kingdom, or many of them, stimulated the luxury goods trades such as watchmaking, jewelery, stationery, coach making, and cabinetry. It's also in the late 1600s and early 1700s that the idea of annual fashions begins to catch on, particularly in women's dress. So the clothing historians can now look at a picture of a dress and know, sometimes to the year or certainly to the two or three closest years, exactly when the picture was done and when the dresses were being worn; this idea that you'll use something and dispose of it and pick up a new one because it's fashionable. This was also an environment—London was big enough—where there was a lot of emulation of the rich by the aspiring middle classes; the commercial classes themselves that are supplying this need are also hoping to be able to imitate the fashions that they make. They, too, are becoming a big urban consumer group.

The famous furniture maker, Thomas Chippendale, maker of what's now an extremely valuable form of furniture, thrived in early- and mid-1700s in London in exactly this environment as a maker of furniture for the upper and middle classes.

London was also a magnet to immigrants fleeing from persecution abroad, particularly the French Protestants, the Huguenots, all of whom were expelled from France in 1685 by King Louis XIV. Many of them brought to England valuable skills, particularly the silk industry, centered in the Spitalfields district of London. London's long had a reputation as being a haven for refugees; it still has that reputation right up to the present. Many of the refugee communities brought in with them valuable new skills and crafts.

Work in London was traditionally controlled by the old guild system, and many of the guilds dated right back to the Middle Ages. But as the city grew rapidly outwards and as new kinds of work arose, it became increasingly difficult for the guilds to keep a grip. They were the creations of an era of relative economic stability rather than what was now becoming normal, an era of sustained economic growth. The innovations of the 18th century meant that new types of work kept arising. In a list from 1747, 215 different occupations were listed. But another list from 50 years later, near the end of the century, gives 492 separate occupations as part of the Division of Labor, which Adam Smith was going to talk about. Many of these new jobs weren't guild-regulated.

London was also the center of the colonial trade, and it was headquarters of the monopoly companies that dominated the British Empire before the 1800s. The Merchant-Adventurers Company, for example, held a monopoly of the English textile trade in Europe. The Levant Company had monopoly rights to trade with the Ottoman Empire at the eastern end of the Mediterranean in the days when the Turkish Empire was still a massive concern. The East India Company, founded in 1600, grew steadily in power and wealth as Britain became first the dominant and then, after the 1750s, the exclusive European trader in India. In fact, the East India Company became a government in its own right, and from the late 1700s to the mid-1800s, the East India Company, this private trading company, ran India itself. The Muscovy Company had monopoly rights to trade with Russia. London was also the center of the Colonial-related trades like tobacco processing, an enormous business with the Maryland and Virginia trades, and sugar refining as sugar came in from the West Indies, then also very, very valuable colonies.

The dockyards of London thrived. Wharves on both banks of the River Thames below London Bridge were swarming with people—just a narrow passage up the center of the river—and ships were bringing wares from around the country and, indeed, from around the world into the port of London itself.

The Navigation Acts specified re-export from Britain: Anything made in one of Britain's colonies had first to come to Britain and then would be re-exported. As I mentioned previously, that was a source of grievance to the American colonies and one of the sources of the American Revolutionary War. But it was a source of prosperity to London; a terrific stimulus to shipbuilding and ancillary trades like the rope makers, the navigational instrument makers, the sail makers, all of whom we'll visit in the next lecture.

Now let's move out of London and shift to the provincial towns and cities. No other city in England had even 50,000 people. In other words, none was even 1/10th the size of London in the early 18th century. The next rank of towns was Bristol, Edinburgh, Norwich, York, Exeter, and Newcastle on Tyne. Many of these were either ports or else administrative centers. For example, Edinburgh is the capital of Scotland in addition to being a port. Some of them were the seat of bishops, which would have a great cathedral, and some were county towns, the local administrative center with the administrative functions employing townsmen. Each one of these towns had a smaller farming hinterland; so whereas a lot of the area around London fed London, each of these also had a farm supply area. Bristol, Liverpool, and Glasgow were all ports. They all faced the Atlantic Ocean, and they all grew prosperous by the colonial trade in slaves, tea, tobacco, and sugar.

The single biggest source of work for English men after farming was as sailors, and the port towns were rough places. Not only were there taverns and brothels along the waterfront; these were also the places where the press-gang prowled. The press-gang was the Royal Navy's method of recruiting sailors when it suddenly needed more, usually when a war broke out, and they were legally entitled. There were gangs of sailors who'd kidnap men—ideally men who already had seafaring skills—and carry them off into the men of war, into the warships, to serve at the king's pleasure, sometimes for years at a time. You could suddenly be seized by the press-gang and carried off, and this was a source of terrible anxiety to generations of people who lived near the coast.

Next in size were towns like Birmingham in the Midlands. Today, Birmingham is Britain's second-biggest city. It's always been a manufacturer of metal goods. In Birmingham, things like nails, buckles, buttons, knives, saddlers' ironmongery, bits and bridles for horses, and brassware were made. Metal goods in those days were called "toys" and Birmingham was nicknamed "the toyshop of Europe," but these aren't the kind of toys that children would appreciate. In other words, the meaning of *toys* itself changed emphatically in meaning. Birmingham was also a center of gun-making; anything made of metal in the days before the industrialization of metal manufacture.

There was a very distinctive attitude to business evident in the towns and cities. They were altogether more thriving, more energetic, more lively places. When a young man called William Hutton first went to Birmingham in 1741, he was instantly aware of the difference between this thriving provincial manufacturing town, then of a population of about 20,000, and the countryside where he'd grown up: "I was surprised at the place, but more at the people. They were a species I had never seen. They possessed a vivacity I had never beheld. I had been among dreamers, but now I saw men awake." This is something we get often from travelers; this idea that the towns are places where the possibilities of a commercial life are far more evident, and people respond to it. The French philosopher Voltaire came to England and admired it very much. He wrote: "Commerce, which has enriched the citizens of England, has helped to make them free, and that liberty in turn has expanded commerce. This is the foundation of the greatness of the state." Voltaire was a great admirer of Britain.

The provincial towns were usually built around a central marketplace, often an open space with a market cross at the center. On designated market days, farmers and craftsmen from the neighborhood would gather in town market to sell their goods. It also operated as a labor exchange. If you were seeking work, you'd go to the marketplace on market day in the hope of being hired. Even in the late 1800s, that was still going on. In Thomas Hardy's novel *Far From the Madding Crowd*, farmer Gabriel Oak needs a job as a shepherd and goes to the market until one of the farmers comes along looking for a shepherd and hires him.

The 18th century also witnessed growth of shops in provincial towns. Shops are things that we take absolutely for granted, but once they were a novelty. These were places where particular goods were sold away from, different from, the places where they'd been made. One writer in 1720 was surprised to see elaborate decoration in the shops, and he wrote, "Never was such painting and gilding, such sashings and looking glasses among the shopkeepers as there is now." Quaker shopkeepers pioneered the idea of having fixed shop prices instead of the older tradition of haggling over the price. You'd go to the shop, the price of the object would be clearly stated, and you'd either accept it or reject it like that. Now we're so familiar with it, we need to be reminded that even that method and the shops themselves had to be invented.

Daniel Defoe, whom I mentioned previously in the lecture on farming, the man who's best remembered as the author of *Robinson Crusoe* but also a very shrewd observer of life in England, wrote this in 1728:

> Let the curious examine the great towns of Manchester, Warrington, Macclesfield, Halifax, and many others. Some of these are mere villages. The highest magistrate in them is a constable, and few or no families of gentry among them. Yet they are full of wealth and full of people, and daily increasing in both; all of which is occasioned by the mere strength of trade and the growing manufactures established in them.

When Defoe says that they're "mere villages," he doesn't mean that they're little clusters of huts; obviously not, because he said how big they are. What he means is that they don't yet have the administrative structure of the older towns; they've grown up very rapidly and very recently. Often these new places lacked members of Parliament. They weren't adequately represented, and that was going to be a bone of contention politically in the politics of later industrialization.

Observers also noticed new towns springing up where one particular type of business was specialized. The town of Sheffield specialized in knives, forks, and spoons; the cutlery trade. Burton on Trent specialized in brewing beer. St. Helen's specialized in glass. These are traditions that persisted well into the 20th century. Of course, specialization of this kind is only possible when a town intends to supply a much wider area than the immediate market. Again, especially this is true of supplying London. Here's Daniel Defoe again: "This whole kingdom, as well the people as the land and even the sea, in every part of it, are employed to furnish something, and I may add, the best of everything, to supply the city of London."

The transport system in England was wretchedly bad before the Industrial Revolution. In fact, the Industrial Revolution itself would be greatly stimulated by the improvement of internal communications, as we'll see in subsequent lectures. But already in early 1700s, goods were moving in large quantities, especially by sea—the coastal trade—and by river, but also, where it was the only possible alternative, by wagon and by packhorse.

The guild system in many provincial towns regulated access to most of the important trades, many of which restricted membership to members of families who'd been traditionally in that business through the generations. The guilds also fixed prices and regulated quality control. Each of these various jobs was regulated by the guild. Here's how it worked: A young man would become an apprentice, usually at the age of about 10 or 12, often going to live in the household of a master craftsman. Often the young apprentice's family would have to pay the master craftsman to take him on. Like female live-in servants, an apprentice was forbidden to marry, even when he reached the end of his apprenticeship and was 17, 18, or 19. Ideally, the master would teach him the mysteries of the trade. The word *mystery*, like the word *toy*, is a word whose meaning has changed extensively. Now we think of a *mystery* meaning a detective story where you're trying to work out who did the killing or sometimes mystery relating to the supernatural. But a mystery used to be a body of knowledge that some people had gotten, but that most other people hadn't gotten. So you talk about the mysteries of the carpenters' trade, or the mystery of the coopers' trade (a cooper is a barrel maker). The apprenticeship system was subject to abuse. Apprentices could find themselves working for years as unpaid servants with no rights. But at its best, it was a good way of enabling members of new generations to learn the mysteries of the craft and pass it on to the next generation.

When his apprenticeship was complete, usually after seven years, the apprentice became a journeyman. This, again, doesn't mean that he went traveling. It comes from the French word *journee*, which just means "day," and it meant that he'd be paid by the day. He's learned the mystery, he's good at the craft, and he can be paid by the day by other masters who need extra help. A journeyman could hope to accumulate enough experience and enough capital to become a master craftsman in his own right. That was the expectation: Your career would start in apprenticeship, move on to the journeyman, and end up as a master craftsman. It was a realistic expectation for blacksmiths, weavers, pin makers, wheelwrights, thatchers, glaziers, and coopers. But there were other industries already growing too large in scale for that to be a common pattern; for example, shipbuilding, as we'll see in the next lecture. Already the capital required to break into shipbuilding was far too great for most journeymen ever to be able to aspire to do so. It was already true also of the brewing business, the beer industry, and the tanneries, where leather goods were made.

There was a common pattern in the provincial towns for businesses to be grouped together by type. All the wheelwrights would be on the same street, all the butchers on another street, all the candle makers on a third, and so on. We need to remember that this is a world where work was regulated as much by the daylight hours as by the clock, with craftsmen expecting to work longer hours in summer, when it was lighter, than in the winter.

Many trades observed the tradition of Saint Monday. Saint Monday means carrying the weekend's revelry over into the new week, but then making up for it later in the week with long hours of hard work. At the time of the Protestant Reformation, when England was still a Catholic country before the 1530s, lots and lots of saint's days would be days off from work. But because the Protestant churches rejected the cult of the saints, suddenly there was the prospect of having far more days at work. So English workers created this ironically-titled day, Saint Monday, saying "Oh, we're going to make a three-day weekend of it and not go to work this day." Maybe the fact that we still celebrate public holidays often on Mondays is a little vestige of the Saint Monday tradition. Benjamin Franklin worked at a London printer's shop in the 1720s, and he impressed the owner because he never celebrated Saint Monday.

Let me quote to you now from a Sheffield song, "The Jovial Cutler." This is about a man who makes knives and forks, and about how he always sits around the smithy fire on Mondays drinking with his friends, and how he won't get down to work. It goes like this: "Brother workmen, cease thy labor. Lay your files and hammers by. Listen while a brother neighbor sings a cutler's destiny. How upon a good Saint Monday sitting by the smithy fire we tell what's been done at Sunday, and in cheerful mirth conspire." So he's drinking and enjoying himself with his friends. But in one of the later verses of the poem, his wife comes in and berates him. She says, "I slave for you, but you won't even work hard enough to buy clothes or even basic food for the house." It ends with her making threats to her husband, the cutler: "Thou knows I hate to broil and quarrel, but I've neither soap nor tea. God burn thee, Jack. Forsake thy barrel, or nevermore thou'st lie with me." She makes a wife's threat to try to get him back to work.

Alcohol in many workplaces flowed freely, especially when safe drinking water was difficult or impossible to find. As I've said, beer making was already a big business, not least because sometimes it was actually less harmful to your health in some areas to drink beer than it was to drink water, which was contaminated. Urban water supplies especially were dangerous because the wells were so often contaminated by their proximity to cesspools, and the bigger cities got and the more problems they had with lack of main drainage, the more serious this problem became. Rivers also, from which clean water might've been drawn, were in effect dumps for tanneries, dye-works, and other dirty trades. Clean water was itself a very, very hard thing to come by in the middle of the towns.

Also very common in 18th century was the distilling of gin, and a lot of British people were very heavy gin drinkers. It contributed to poor health and premature death. It was very hard to regulate, and the gin itself was often contaminated with turpentine and other additives. William Hogarth, the English artist, made a famous pair of prints in 1751. The first one is of a street called Beer Street, where the citizens are drinking good old English beer and they're happy, round, and prosperous. But the second picture is of Gin Lane, where they're emaciated, thieving, letting their children die from neglect. Even some of the houses are toppling into the street. It's the most vivid pictorial rendering you can imagine of the difference between good beer and bad gin. The only prosperous business in Gin Lane is the pawnbroker, and in the beer picture, his shop was falling into disrepair. These pictures were part of a campaign to suppress the epidemic of gin drinking that had developed among poor people.

But, of course, even the beer wasn't necessarily that great, despite Hogarth's depiction of it. Generations of working men drank away their pay rather than struggling to get ahead. Again, it's very useful here to turn to the autobiography of Benjamin Franklin, because he spent a few years in London in the 1720s just before the Industrial Revolution started to get underway. Franklin, who was only about 19 or 20 at the time, explains how he tried to persuade the men in the London printing shop where he worked to eat better and pay less, because they're wasting all their money on beer. But he says most of them were determined to stick with beer, and he'd then front them the money because they'd run out of credit at the ale house. Here's a direct quote from the book:

> From my example, a great part of them left their muddling breakfast of beer and bread and cheese, finding they could with me be supplied from a neighboring house with a large porringer of hot water-gruel sprinkled with pepper, crumbled with bread, and a bit of butter in it, for the price of a pint of beer, viz, three hay-pence [in other words, three half-pennies]. This was a more comfortable as well as a cheaper breakfast, and kept their heads clearer. Those who continued sotting with beer all day were often, by not paying, out of credit at the ale house, and used to make interest of me to get beer; their light, as they phrased it, being out.

So they'd say "Mr. Franklin, my light's out. Can you lend me some money?" meaning "I can't get credit at the pub anymore."

This was the fabric of social life that the first industrialists had to combat: trying to find ways to get men to work regular hours by the clock and not the seasons, and to be sober throughout the working day. London businesses were the first to push men to work longer hours than just daylight. For example, a book from 1747 called *London Tradesmen* describes workshops lit by lamps and candles, with work continuing after dark, especially in the winter. The days are very short in the English winter because England is so far north. It's on the same latitude as Labrador in northern Canada. But on the other hand, the days are very, very long in summer and workers were used to the idea that you'd work when it was light, and that you'd stop working when it was dark. This is one of the things the industrial magnates tried to change.

The first industrialists also had to overcome an ancient sense of fatalism and instill the idea of progress and economic growth. They were materialists who needed others to share their sense that it was possible and desirable to gain wealth. But a constant drumbeat of criticism against this idea came not only from the workers who preferred the older, slower pace, but also from churchmen who feared the cities as centers of vice, luxury, and atheism. For example, here's a little quote from the Bishop of Chester in 1777, preaching after an earthquake, which he explained as God's warning to the cities of Manchester and Macclesfield. He said that cities encouraged:

> … intemperance and licentiousness of manners, a wanton and foolish extravagance in dress, in equipage, in houses, in furniture, in entertainment; a passion for luxurious indulgences and frivolous amusements, a gay, thoughtless indifference about a future life, a neglect of divine worship, a profanation of the day peculiarly set apart for it, and perhaps to crown all, a disbelief and contempt of the gospel.

When we look back at the late 18th century, we're so impressed with the increased pace of economic activity, it's difficult to remember that it took place in the face of widespread skepticism that such improvement was possible and required a radically new idea about the possibility of progress; of transforming the world as it was into something different and better. On the other hand, fatalism, great though it was in Britain, was less so there than almost anywhere else in those decades, and must contribute to explaining the great transformation.

This lecture has shown, I hope, that it was in the towns and cities that ideas about economic development took root. In the next lecture, we'll look at one business that had already by 1700 shifted to a far larger scale than the domestic workshop: the shipbuilding business.

The Royal Shipyards
Lecture 5

Shipbuilding was one of the first industries to bring together large numbers of men to undertake complicated precision work. When we look at ships from the 1600s—such as the *Mayflower*—and those from the early 1700s, we're astonished that something so small could cross the Atlantic Ocean. But for their time, these ships were amazingly large and complex; in essence, they were floating towns that could keep several hundred people alive for months at a time away from land. Making, maintaining, and running them stimulated many new manufacturing methods. Historians point out that ships at sea anticipated what factories would be later and that many of the techniques of industrial discipline can be found first in nautical discipline.

Anticipating Industrialization

- Many of the methods of organizing work and many of the logistical principles that would become common in the factories of the 1700s were pioneered in shipbuilding, especially for the Royal Navy, starting in the late 1600s.

- The shipyards of the Royal Navy created the large-scale organization of work, materials, logistics, and complex construction that would be characteristic of later factory-era industrialization and pioneered many of these methods in a nation still using techniques that were slow, labor intensive, tradition bound, and based on organic materials.

- What is so striking to us now is that the shipyards were successful in an era of poor internal communications and preindustrial work traditions. By later standards, the Royal Navy shipyards were nightmarishly inefficient, but by the standards of their own time, they made crucial organizational advances.

- Already before 1700, the Chatham naval shipyards near London employed more than 800 people, at a time when most manufacturing was done in the workshop system or by a master craftsman with one or two journeymen and apprentices.

- Shipyards pioneered the bulk ordering of raw materials (wood, rope, barrel hoops and staves, and cannons) and refined logistics and materials flow. The industry also gave rise to ancillary businesses, an arrangement that would later be common in industrial towns.

- The only group with sufficient capital to maintain operations on this scale was the government, which ran the yards and was reluctant to contract out to private companies. Historians know much about the shipbuilding industry because the Royal Navy kept good records and because we have such valuable documents as Samuel Pepys's diary from the 1660s and 1670s.
  - Pepys became chief clerk of the Navy Board after the Restoration of 1660 and rose to be chief secretary to the Admiralty in the 1670s.

  - Pepys doubted that the Royal Navy dockyards were being run as efficiently as they could be. He was discouraged by indifference over quality control, was eager to create systematic methods, and deplored slavish reliance on tradition.

The Process of Shipbuilding

- The Company of Shipwrights, one of the guilds that restricted entry into the shipyards, was founded in 1605. Its apprenticeship system limited who got jobs, often a privilege that descended through families. These jobs were highly coveted because they were secure and paid well. The guild listed 26 distinct jobs—many of them eccentric—including rat killer, keeper of the clock, keeper of the plugs, scavelmen, and treenail mooters.

- The only power source available in the shipyards was provided by draft animals, mainly horses, but most of the work was simply done by men using muscle power. Jobs that are easy today with power tools were painfully slow. Sawing through pieces of oak, for example, required a two-man saw and the use of a saw pit.

- Ships of the line required enormous quantities of materials and were tremendously expensive. They had to be strong enough to bear the weight of their cannons and to endure the recoil of a broadside but also streamlined enough to make good progress in pursuit of other ships or in fleet movements. They had to be stable enough so that a quantity of guns could be placed well above the waterline for more versatility and to obviate flooding danger.

- When a ship was being made, paper plans were first drawn up at the scale of 1 to 48. Once the plans were agreed upon, full-size templates of the various components were made out of thin and relatively light fir wood. They would then be copied in oak by the ship's carpenters. A first-rate ship of the line would use the timber from 100 acres of land, about 4,000 mature trees.
  - English oaks grow very slowly, reaching full maturity only after more than 100 years. Previous deforestation of Britain meant that much of the timber for ships had to come from abroad, especially from the Baltic lands.

  - One of the many benefits of developing colonies in America was that wood for masts could come from New Hampshire and Maine instead. Builders were delighted by the high quality of American wood.

- Certain parts of a ship's frame had to be made from oak trees whose trunk had divided into massive limbs along certain angles. These were the angled pieces that attached keel to sternpost and ribs to deck beams. The grain of the wood had to flow properly to ensure the strength of the frame.

- Careful forestry over the centuries had taught people how to make trees split at certain angles and certain heights or how not to. Even so, those who cut trees for the Royal Navy were aware of 65 possible defects that could make wood unsuitable.

- Oak cut in winter had a reputation of being less liable to rot than that cut in summer, but all wood had to be seasoned for a few years before actually being used in construction. Seasoning prevented warping and helped make ships strong enough to absorb enemy broadsides and to be able to stay at sea for months.

- The Royal Navy sent out surveyors to identify ideal trees and reserve them with distinctive marks: the broad arrow. By the late 1600s, this was a slow, tedious business, and master builders had to scrounge wood from all over the country. There were severe penalties for cutting a tree with the broad arrow marked on it.

- A first-rate ship of the line could take 10 years to complete. The danger was that it would begin to rot even before completion.

A Complex Operation

- The head of the shipbuilding operation was a master shipwright, who relied on drawings, models, tradition, and rule of thumb. The shipwright chose the essential pieces of wood for the keel and ribs of the ship.

- Also important were the block makers, who created the blocks through which ropes were drawn to raise and lower sails. Caulkers, pitch heaters, oakum boys, smiths, joiners, carpenters, wheelwrights, plumbers, bricklayers, sail makers, and even gilders, who decorated the stern and the cabin, all worked in the same place.

© Library of Congress Prints and Photographs Division, LC-DIG-ppmsc-08801.

There was relatively little change in ship design from the early 1600s through the early 1800s, although sizes increased, as did the number of ships.

79

- Shipyards would have a mast house, often more than 100 feet long, where the masts, made of several pieces of fir wood, could be assembled before fitting to ships. The logs were kept in mast ponds, underwater, until assembled, to prevent them from drying and splitting.

- Sail makers also required a great deal of space where the canvas could be laid out, cut to size, and stitched. Canvas was used for sails, boat covers, tarpaulins, and even sailors' clothes.

- Even larger were the rope houses, which were up to 1,000 feet long so that rope could be made indoors, protected from the rain.
    - To make rope, hemp was imported in bulk, mainly from the Baltic. Hemp fibers were dragged across spiked boards to disentangle the fibers. Spinners would then attach the ends to a turning wheel and walk along the rope house, carrying bundles of the fibers and twisting them into yarn. Then, a bundle of 400 yarns would be tarred for weatherproofing. Tar was imported at first from the Baltic and, later, from the Carolinas.

    - After drying, the yarns would then be woven together into thick rope. Depending on its intended use, rope could be up to 24 inches thick. Making an anchor cable of 24-inch diameter rope would require the labor of 200 people.

    - A first-rate ship of the line required huge quantities of rope for many uses—often more than 100,000 feet in all. Rope needed to be replaced frequently, as did the sails.

    - The smithery, or dockyard blacksmith's shop, made anchors, the single biggest preindustrial metal objects, often weighing two tons or more. Smitheries also made links of anchor chain, bolts for main timbers of the ship, and iron bands to hold mast sections together. Guns were made from bronze, an alloy of copper and tin, or from iron.

Preindustrial Methods and Materials

- One of the clearest ways we can describe this process of shipbuilding is preindustrial. The materials used were primarily organic—wood for the timbers of the ship and flax for the rope and canvas sails. These materials were produced by slow rural processes, with long periods of growing and seasoning.

  - Not only was wood hard to find by the 1700s, but it was also difficult to transport over long distances, when roads were poor and there were no canals or railways.

  - Further, everything was susceptible to rot and decay, and there was the chronic problem of boring creatures damaging hulls and seaweed and crustaceans attaching to hulls and slowing the ships down.

  - Historians have shown that even with good maintenance and major refits, a fighting ship could rarely be kept going longer than 20 years; replacement was required not because the design was obsolete but because the ship was made of organic materials that were decaying.

  - In 1761 came the first experiment with copper sheathing of hulls. This method was successful and became universal in the Royal Navy fleet in the early 1780s. Use of copper sheathing meant that ships could stay at sea for two years instead of the previous four months before coming in to dry dock for hull repairs.

- Although there were constant laments from Pepys about corruption, waste, pilfering, and incompetence, in fact, Royal Navy ships usually held their own in long blockade service and in battle. In the great sea battles of the 1700s and early 1800s, English ships, though they burned or were dismasted by enemy fire, hardly ever sank. French ships had the edge in grace of design and were slightly more innovative, but British ships had superior solidity and durability under fire.

- The Royal Navy shipyards created the large-scale organization of work, materials, logistics, and complex construction that would be characteristic of later factory-era industrialization. Even more impressive, the shipyards pioneered many of these methods in a nation still using techniques that were slow, labor-intensive, tradition-bound, and dependent on organic materials.

Suggested Reading

Coad, *Historic Architecture of the Royal Navy*.

———, *The Royal Dockyards, 1690–1850*.

Coote, *Samuel Pepys*.

Dodds and Moore, *Building the Wooden Fighting Ship*.

Questions to Consider

1. In what ways were the Royal Navy shipyards like an industrial enterprise and in what ways were they still preindustrial?

2. How successfully did the navy balance the various requirements of making effective fighting ships?

The Royal Shipyards
Lecture 5—Transcript

Shipbuilding was one of the first businesses that brought together large numbers of men to undertake complicated precision work. Many of the methods of organizing work, and many of the logistical principles that would become common in the factories of the 1700s, were pioneered in shipbuilding, especially for the Royal Navy, starting in the late 1600s.

What's so striking to us now is that they did it in an era of wretched internal communications and preindustrial work traditions. By later standards, the royal shipyards were nightmarishly inefficient, but by the standards of their own time they were making crucial organizational advances. Already, before 1700, the Chatham naval shipyards near London employed over 800 men at a time when most manufacturing was done in the putting-out system, done in cottages where the work would be distributed by a master to people working each in their individual houses rather than collectively in one place, or was being done by a master craftsman with one or two journeymen and apprentices. The historian Jonathan Coad, who studied the pre-industrial Navy, writes this:

> The construction, fitting out, and the subsequent maintenance and repair of a warship then, as now, is one of the most complex of all tasks. The concentration of skills and the variety of materials used meant that in pre-industrial England the dockyard towns could lay claim to being probably the most versatile industrial communities in the country.

When we look at ships from the 1600s—ships like the *Mayflower*—and from the early 1700s, we're astonished that something so small could cross the Atlantic. But for their time, they were amazingly big and complex; floating towns that could keep several hundred people alive for months at a time away from land. Making and maintaining devices like this stimulated many new methods, and so did running them. The historians Marcus Rediker and Peter Linebaugh point out that ships at sea were a kind of premonition of what life in factories was going to be like later, and that many of the techniques of industrial discipline can be found first of all in nautical discipline. They write: "The ship provided a setting in which large numbers of workers cooperated on complex and synchronized tasks under slavish, hierarchical discipline in which human will was subordinated to mechanical equipment. The work, cooperation and discipline of the ship made it a prototype of the factory." I think that's a wonderful insight: that the first glimpse we get of industrial-scale work is in the making and the running of these big sailing ships.

The shipyards themselves, mainly around London at Chatham, Woolwich, Sheerness, and Deptford and others on the south coast of England in Portsmouth and Plymouth, pioneered the bulk ordering of raw materials, things like the wood, the rope, the barrel hoops and staves, and the cannons. They also organized the first complicated logistical problems: how to make sure that the right materials arrive at the shipyards at the right time and can be put through the necessary sequence in order. They also gave rise to ancillary businesses—ship-related work that clusters around the shipyards— that would also become common later in the industrial towns.

The only group with sufficient capital to run operations on this scale before the year 1700 was the government, which ran the yards. It was reluctant to contract out to private companies although sometimes, if a war started unexpectedly or if war was imminent, they'd relax that principle and contract out to get more work done quickly. We know a lot about all this because the Navy kept good records and because we have such valuable documents as Samuel Pepys's diary from the 1660s and 1670s. Samuel Pepys became the Chief Clerk of the Navy Board after the Restoration of King Charles II in 1660, and he rose to the position of Chief Secretary to the Admiralty in the 1670s. His diaries are fascinating documents. He wrote it all in code, partly because some of the things would've been embarrassing if they'd been discovered at the time; he was chronically unfaithful to his wife and wrote down his erotic adventures. But he's high-spirited, naughty, talented, loyal to the king, and eager to achieve British naval supremacy; a great patriot and a great bureaucrat for his time.

In the Chatham dockyards in 1662, soon after starting the job, he found "a great disorder by a multitude of servants and old decrepit men." What he meant by that simply was that there seemed to be more men in the shipyards, more men present being paid, than there were actually at work, and lots of old men who'd once perhaps been effective shipbuilders but were still there then, still somehow on the payroll. He believed that Peter Pett, who was the king's chief ship designer, was crooked, and this is quite possibly true because it was an age of very, very widespread dishonesty and petty corruption. Pepys doubted that the shipyards were being run as efficiently as they could be, and he was sometimes discouraged by men's apparent indifference to questions of quality control: "I was weary and vexed that I did not find other people so willing to do business as myself when I have taken pains to find out what in the yards is wanting and fitting to be done." Pepys was eager to create systematic methods and he deplored the men's slavish reliance on tradition. "Their ignorance and unwillingness to do anything of pains and what is out of their old dull road."

One of Pepys biographers, Stephen Coote, writes this:

> The dockyards themselves were the sites of England's greatest industrial enterprise and covered many acres. Here, Pepys met the clerical and executive officers, supervised their work, and monitored the discipline they tried to impose on their often turbulent workmen—that army of sawyers and sail makers, coopers and caulkers, joiners and jacks of all trades, who toiled—or were supposed to toil—through an 11-hour day, and who, at harvest time, were apt to abscond in pursuit of extra work.

So he couldn't even be certain that they'd stay at work when there was money to be made gathering the harvest.

There was restricted entry into the shipyards. The Company of Shipwrights, one of the guilds, had been founded in 1605. Their apprenticeship system limited who got the jobs in the yards, and often these jobs descended from father to son through a certain set of privileged families. Work in the shipyards was coveted because it was so secure. You had a government contract. It was well-paid, and even had paid sick days, something that was almost unheard of in other professions in the 1600s.

There were 26 distinct jobs listed in the shipyards, some of them eccentric, all the way down to the rat killer, a man whose job was called "the keeper of the clock," and another man called "the keeper of the plugs." The keeper of the plugs, his job was to remove all the plugs at low tide from the scuppers of the ships so that all the water could drain out, and replace them as the tide rose, saving an enormous amount of hand pumping work. Another of the jobs listed is that of the paviours, whose job was to keep the stone slabs flat and even; the scavelmen, whose job was to keep yards free from rubbish and debris; and, perhaps most exotic of all, a job called "treenail mooters." All this actually means is that these are the people who made the long nails that were used to bind together some of the great timbers.

The only power source available in these shipyards was provided by draft animals, mainly horses, but most of the work was simply done by men using muscle power. Jobs that are easy today with power tools were painfully slow. Sawing through pieces of oak, for example, required the use of a saw-pit. One man would stand above the pit with his foot on the log, the other would be down in the pit, and they'd have a two-man saw, cutting by hand through these timbers. Drilling through the main solid timbers of a ship's keel, which was made of solid oak, to insert bolts holding different members together had to be done with an auger, a big hand drill an inch and a half diameter. The drilling of one of these holes through several timbers could itself take nearly a week. Another vital job was caulking, filling the gaps between the planks of the ship with a mixture of oakum; that is to say, old rope fragments, tallow, tar, and goat hair. This had to be done while building the ship, and it had to be constantly redone to keep ships leak-proof and seaworthy.

Ships of the line, the big fighting ships, required enormous quantities of materials. They had to be strong enough to bear the weight of their cannons. A ship of the line was essentially a floating gun platform, and the way in which the fighting took place was that the ships would come alongside one another and fire broadsides into each other. The idea was to fire simultaneous, annihilating broadsides to shatter the opposing ship, kill as many of its crew as possible, break their morale, and prevent the ship from continuing to fight. The ships had to be built strong enough to endure the recoil, which is caused when you fire a broadside, but also strong enough to make the ships capable of pursuing an enemy ship if it was fleeing or if the fleet itself was in movement. They had to be versatile, they had to be maneuverable, and they had to be strong.

Ideally, also, these ships of the line needed to be stable enough that a lot of guns could be placed well above the water line for more versatility. Obviously, the closer the guns are to the water line, the more stable it's going to be because its center of gravity will be lower. But if they're too close to the water line, in rough weather when you open the gun ports, there's the liability of flooding. It's good to have higher gun decks, but the higher they are the higher the center of gravity of the ship itself will be, and the more unstable it's going to be, and it's going to be more liable to severe rolling in rough weather. The designs had to be a series of compromises to accomplish both these ends: stability and good vantage point for the guns. The ships were immensely expensive. Parts of them were nearly two feet thick, made of first-class oak.

When a ship was being made, paper plans were first drawn up at the scale of 1 to 48. Once the plans were agreed upon, then full-size templates of the various components would be made in the place called the "mould loft" out of thin and relatively light fir wood. They'd then be copied in oak by the ship's carpenters. A first-rate ship of the line would use the timber from 100 acres of land, about 4,000 mature trees. English oaks grow very slowly, reaching full maturity only after about 100 years. The previous extensive deforestation of Britain meant that much of this wood had to come from abroad. In particular, it had to come from the Baltic lands, from Sweden and Denmark. That meant that the British government had to stay on good diplomatic terms with the governments of Sweden and Denmark so that its naval convoys could be able to enter the Baltic Sea through the Narrows, through the Skagerrak and the Kattegat. This had the effect of making the town of Hull in northeast England the chief importing center for Baltic wood. The Baltic trade was a primary consideration of British foreign policy through all the years of wooden sailing ships.

One of the many benefits of England developing colonies in America was that wood for the masts, for example, could now for the first time come from New Hampshire or Maine instead of from the Baltic lands. Starting in the year 1705, there was a Surveyor General of Her Majesty's Woods in North

America, whose job was to mark broad arrows on the trees. The broad arrow designated that the royal government had claimed this tree for its own. The ship builders in the English yards were delighted by the high quality of the American wood that they found. In fact, one of the reasons that America seemed like such a rich place to its early settlers was because of the amount of woodland because wood was scarce in England and therefore it was a form of wealth, whereas in America it was incredibly plentiful.

Certain parts of the ships' frame, such as the "knees" and the "futtocks," had to be made from oak trees whose trunk had divided into massive limbs along certain particular angles. These angled pieces were crucial to the design of the whole ship. They were the pieces that attached the keel to the stern post or the ribs to the deck beams, the places where a lot of stress is placed on a join. The grain of the wood had to flow right for them to be strong enough. Careful forestry over the centuries had taught men how to make the trees split at certain angles, to make them split at certain heights, or how not to. Foresters learned how to make the spaces between the trees just right to get the angles appropriate, and they knew which compass bearing on which side of the slope to plant the tree, and so on. All these things had to be taken into consideration in growing the trees and then eventually in harvesting them.

Even so, the men who cut the trees for the Navy, the "fellmongers," were aware of 65 possible defects that could make the wood unsuitable. Cutting down these great oak trees was done with axes, and cutting down one tree could take several days because this is in the time before they had good quality metal blades. The blades of an axe would blunt far more quickly than they do today because they didn't have steel alloys, so that the fellmongers were constantly re-sharpening their blades. Oak trees cut in wintertime had a reputation of being less liable to rot than oaks cut in the summer. But even so, whenever it was cut, all the wood then had to be seasoned for a few more years before actually being used in construction. This process of seasoning prevented warping and helped make the ships strong enough to absorb enemy broadsides and strong enough to be able to stay at sea for months at a time. To make "green" ships—in other words, to make ships from wood that wasn't seasoned long enough, as the Navy sometimes did in emergencies such as during the French and Indian Wars of the 1750s and 1760s—was to jeopardize their seaworthiness and also to reduce their life expectancy.

Occasionally, ships could be built quickly, but their durability was then in doubt.

The Navy sent out surveyors to identify ideal trees and to reserve them with distinctive marks; the broad arrow, which I mentioned previously. Already by the late 1600s, it was a slow and tedious business, and master builders like Phineas Pett had to scrounge from all over the country. There was a great deal of complaining in the Navy literature about the lack of suitable oak trees. There were also very severe penalties for cutting a tree once the broad arrow had been marked on it, as this meant that it was reserved to the government.

For a first-rate ship of the line, not only did it take 100 acres of woodland, it could also take 10 years to complete. There was the very real danger that it would begin to rot even before its completion, hence the anxiety about the seasoning of the wood. The first stage of the project was to build the hull on a slipway, and when the hull had been built to launch it backwards into the river. Most of these yards were on the river Thames itself or on its tributary, the Medway River. Once the hull was floating, it would be fitted out with masts, with blocks, with ropes, with cannons, and so on, and it would be fitted out and completed while it was already floating. Old ships, old hulks, fitted with cranes were used to raise the masts into position.

The head of the whole operation was the master shipwright. He relied on drawings, he relied on models, but above all, he relied on tradition, the way in which the job had long been done, and rule of thumb. There was relatively little change in design from the early 1600s right through to the early 1800s, though the size of the ships did gradually increase, as did the number of ships in the fighting Navy. One of the shipwright's crucial jobs was to choose the essential pieces of wood for the keel, the very bottom of the ship, and for the ribs, the frame of the ship itself, all of which had to be just right. Also important were the blockmakers; the blocks through which the ropes were drawn to raise and lower the sails. The making of the blocks was done out of elm wood, and about 1,000 of them were needed for a big ship. The pulley inside the block, which rotates as the rope is pulled through it, was made of a foreign wood called lignum vitae. Also hard at work on the ship during the construction phase were the caulkers, whom I've mentioned, the pitch heaters who warm up the tar, the oakum boys who are fragmenting pieces of old rope, the smiths, the joiners, the carpenters, the wheelwrights, the plumbers, the bricklayers, the sail makers, and even the gilders, the people who decorated the stern and the cabin, all at work in the same place at the same time.

One of the distinctive buildings at the shipyard would be the mast house. This was a building, often more than 100 feet long, where the masts, made of several pieces of fir wood, could be assembled before being fitted to the ships. The logs for the masts were kept in mast ponds; that is to say, they were kept underwater until they were assembled to prevent them from drying and splitting, in which case they'd be far less useful.

Another group at work was the sail makers. They required a lot of space as well where the canvas for the sails could be laid out, cut to size, and stitched, often on the top floor of one of the buildings where no floor supports were needed. Hence, the place where the sails are made is called the "sail loft," even if it's on the ground floor. Canvas was used for sails, for boat covers, for tarpaulins, and even for the sailors' clothes. The Royal Navy had no uniforms for ordinary sailors until 1857. Until then, they simply wore whatever they owned when they went on board until it wore out, after which they wore rough canvas shirts and trousers made essentially of sailcloth.

Even bigger were the ropehouses, up to 1,000 feet long so that rope could be made indoors, protected from the rain that would impede the work. "Ropewalks" was the name of these places. The Woolwich ropehouse was built in 1612, and the other dockyard towns followed suit later in the 1600s. The principle material for rope was hemp, and hemp was imported in bulk, also mainly from the Baltic countries, by the Eastland Company, which held a monopoly there. Hatchelling was the process of dragging hemp fibers across metal spiked boards to disentangle all the fibers. Next, spinners would attach the ends of the fibers to a turning wheel and would walk along the ropehouse carrying bundles of these fibers and gradually twisting them into a yarn. Next, a bundle of 400 of these yarns would be tarred for weatherproofing. The yarn had to be dragged through the tar at just the right speed. If it went too slowly, the tar would sink in too much and weaken the fibers. But if it went through too fast, it would only protect the outer layer. So even the tarring of the layers of rope was a skilled craft. The tar itself came at first from the Baltic, but a bit later on from the Carolinas, where pine forests were plentiful and where men learned how to make slow-burning pine fires that would be covered in turf so they're built slowly, and then pine tar would gradually flow out down a sloping channel into buckets ready to catch it.

After they were dry, the yarns of a rope would then be woven together into the thick finished rope itself. Depending on the use to which the rope was going to be put, it could be as much as 24 inches in diameter. Making an anchor cable of 24-inch diameter rope would require the labor of 200 men, with all the sailors available in the shipyard called in to provide the extra manpower during most laborious phases. Again, even something like rope, which we tend not to think about, was extremely labor-intensive and very, very slow and difficult to make. A first-rate ship of the line required huge quantities of rope for many uses, particularly for the sails. Often more than 100,000 feet, several miles of rope, would be carried on a first-class ship.

Everything needed to be replaced frequently; the sails, for example, the ropes, the planking itself. "To the sailing navy, roperies, mast houses and sail lofts were what machine and boiler shops were to be to the steam-driven navy of the late nineteenth century." This is a remark from the historian Jonathan Coad, talking about the labor intensiveness of it.

The smitheries, a special name for a dockyard blacksmith, made anchors. An anchor was the single biggest metal objects made before the Industrial Revolution, at a time when metal was hard to get and difficult to make. An anchor could weigh two tons or more. Links of anchor chain also were made there at the smithery, and bolts for the main timbers of the ship and iron bands to hold mast sections together.

The guns on these great ships were made from bronze, which is an alloy of copper and tin, or from iron. They were muzzleloaders; that is, you loaded them from the same point where they'd eventually fire their projectile. A solid piece of metal would be drilled out with a touch hole at breach end, the back end, where a fuse could be introduced to light the charge.

Iron cannons in the early 18th century were feared; they were regarded as inferior because they were more likely to explode, killing their users. For several generations, old bronze cannons would be melted down and reused and iron ones, too, because the metals themselves were being produced in such small quantities. By 1780, as we'll see in one of the later lectures, the quality of iron was improving along with the iron industry itself.

One of the clearest ways that we can describe all this is pre-industrial. It was so dependent on things growing: the wood for the timbers of the ship and the flax for the rope and for the canvas sails. All these materials were produced by slow rural processes: long rhythms of growing, and then of seasoning. Not only was the wood hard to find by 1700, it was also very, very difficult to move long distances, when British roads were awful and there weren't yet any canals or railways. You can imagine that the size of some of these timbers is very big, and the sheer act of moving them from one place to another was difficult. Everything was liable to rot and decay, especially when the ships were laid up "in ordinary." Being "in ordinary" means between wars. Obviously, when war is on, the ships are all in service. Between wars, most of them are simply waiting and rotting in the yards. There was a chronic problem of boring creatures damaging the hull, boring into it and damaging its seaworthiness. There was also the chronic problem of seaweed and crustaceans attaching themselves to the hull and slowing the ship down.

Historians of the Navy have shown that even with good maintenance and major refits, a fighting ship could rarely be kept going longer than 20 years before it had to be replaced, not because the design was obsolete, which might be an issue these days, but because it was made of organic materials that were decaying. More likely, a ship would last for 12–16 years. In other words, it could take nearly as long to build the first decade as it would then enjoy in service. Nelson's flagship at the Battle of Trafalgar in 1805, the *Victory,* a famous warship, was built in 1759, so it was unusually old at the time of its great battle in 1805. But it had had several "great repairs," as they were called, which is to say rebuilds, to keep it going.

In 1761, for the first time, the Royal Navy experimented with copper sheathing for the hulls of its ships below the waterline. It worked out very well and became universal in the fleet by the 1780s. It meant that ships could stay at sea for two years instead of the previous four months before coming back in to dry dock for hull repairs. Copper sheeting would be attached to the hull with copper nails, and this proved very, very effective. It meant that during the Napoleonic Wars, the Royal Navy could patrol just outside the French ports to prevent Napoleon's navy from coming out into the waters. Sometimes these ships would stay on station for two years at a time.

Through most of the 1700s, the yards were overstaffed because when there was a wartime crisis, many skilled men were needed all at once. So, as you can expect, the men took it easy between times. Traditionally, the men who worked in the shipyards were entitled to what was called "chips." In other words, they could carry away for their own use any piece of wood that he could carry under one arm; that was the tradition. You weren't allowed to carry away the great oak pieces, the heavy members of the ships, which were the most important of all, but the privilege of chips was itself subject to abuse.

This constant lamentation from Samuel Pepys went on in the 1660s right through to the end of the 1700s about corruption, waste, pilfering, and incompetence, but the ships usually held their own in long blockade service and in battle. In fact, in the many, many great sea battles of the 1700s and early 1800s, the English ships, though they sometimes caught fire and burned and were often dismasted by enemy fire, hardly ever sank. It was almost impossible to sink a wooden fighting ship. The French navy probably had the edge with grace of design and the French were slightly more innovative, but the British had superior solidity and durability under fire, which in these naval battles was usually the crucial issue.

Another constant problem that they had to worry about was the fire hazard in the shipyards themselves. Shipyards were the perfect medium for conflagrations, with vats of boiling tar, blacksmiths' fires in the smithery, rope, sails, wooden ships, gunpowder in barrels, wooden buildings all cheek-by-jowl together at the yards. There were several catastrophic fires, particularly in the 1760s and 1770s. Finally, the Navy Board ordered the comprehensive rebuilding of the yards in brick and stone, simply to cut down on the fire hazard. Many of those buildings survive right up to the present, including the Portsmouth block mills where one of the very first industrialized processes was introduced in the early1800s when Samuel Bentham and Marc Brunel set up block-making machines, a point I'll come back to in a later lecture.

To summarize, the royal shipyards created the large-scale organization of work, materials, logistics, and complex construction that would be characteristic of later factory-era industrialization and pioneered many of these methods in a nation still using techniques that were slow, labor-intensive, tradition-bound, and using organic materials.

In these first five lectures of the course, I've outlined the conditions that made industrialization possible. In the next lecture, I'll turn to the way in which the actual process of industrialization got underway, first of all in the textile business.

The Textile Industry
Lecture 6

For centuries, Britain had a thriving domestic and export trade in woolen cloth. In the late 18th century, a group of entrepreneurs invented machines to spin thread and weave cotton cloth, then built some of the world's first factories to house them. The invention of the cotton gin in 1793 enabled American planters to grow cotton in bulk, most of which was shipped to Liverpool. Key advancements realized by the textile industry included the gathering of workers into the same place to work under close supervision; the invention of machines that could work faster and more consistently than hand workers; the application of power sources to those machines; and the development of huge domestic and foreign markets.

The Early Textile Trade

- For centuries, the clothing trade in wool in Britain had been a small-scale domestic industry, often practiced by farming families. Clothiers took raw wool to families and collected their finished cloth at the end of each week. Women usually carded the raw wool and spun thread, while men wove cloth on hand looms.

- Surplus broadcloth, the kind of woolen cloth that was being made, was exported to Antwerp in the Netherlands by the Merchant Adventurers' Company. This was a steadily expanding trade, and it was open to competition after 1690.

- The county of Lancashire in the northwest and the regions around Liverpool and Manchester became cotton-producing areas, using imported cotton from India and the West Indies. The clothiers were small-scale capitalists long before the first textile machines arrived, and the area had a fund of workers who were familiar with carding, spinning, and weaving.

- Cotton cloth being imported from India was called *calico*. Women liked the cloth because it was light, it could be printed in bright colors, and it enabled them to adopt new fashions, but domestic textile manufacturers persuaded Parliament to ban calico in 1700, fearing that the competition would undermine their livelihoods. The ban on cotton imports wasn't repealed until 1774.

- In the early 1700s, certain experiments raised the possibility that textile manufacturing might be centralized and mechanized. The Lombe brothers' silk mill in Derby is often regarded as the world's first water-powered factory. It profitably employed 300 workers, making silk thread for weavers.

- Silk was a luxury item, however; mass production would take off in cotton and wool manufacturing, where demand was potentially much greater.

Weaving and Spinning Machines
- An early attempt to make a weaving machine was John Kay's *flying shuttle*, developed in 1733. It worked at twice the speed of a conventional loom.

- Weaving became far faster than spinning, which remained the bottleneck in the production process. The first practical spinning machine was James Hargreaves's *spinning jenny*. Hargreaves saw a way to increase the output of the spinning wheel from one spindle at a time to six or eight. His device was patented in 1764.

- Richard Arkwright improved on the spinning jenny and created the *water frame*, which could spin strong cotton yarn. Arkwright built a factory at Cromford, in Derbyshire, where the fast-flowing Derwent River could turn waterwheels linked to the spinning machines. He installed overshot waterwheels, which were far more efficient than the traditional undershot wheel.

- Although hand spinners could make about 20 hanks to the pound, Arkwright's factory could produce 60 hanks to the pound— much finer yarn to make smoother and thinner fabric. Arkwright also mechanized other stages of the process—cleaning, carding, drawing, and roving—that preceded spinning.

- Inventor Samuel Crompton created a hybrid machine called the *mule* in the late 1770s that could produce 300 hanks to the pound—incomparably finer than any yarn seen before and strong, as well. One mule could contain 1,000 spindles; watched by just two or three people, this device could do the same work that previously required dozens or even hundreds of people at spinning wheels. Mules remained the basic spinning machines into the 20th century.

Growing Demand for Textiles

- The overpowering superiority of machine spinning rapidly drove hand spinners out of business. Early manufacturers encountered severe resistance from local people, who were afraid that machines would destroy traditional ways of life and work. Modern economists are familiar with the concept of economic growth and rising productivity, but at this time, workers believed that a machine five times as efficient would put four out of every five workers out of a job.

- A rash of machine-breaking riots took place in 1779. Parliament investigated machine-breakers' complaints but concluded that a lucrative new industry was springing up with far more benefits than harm and that traditional ways would have to yield. Former cottage workers must now move to factory jobs. The nation was beginning to adapt to the concept of government support for economic growth.

- As it turned out, the demand would continue to grow, absorbing labor that had been threatened by mechanization. From the late 18th century to the late 19th century, Britain exported a huge percentage of its cotton textiles to Europe, the United States, and more often, to captive colonial markets in Africa, India, and the West Indies. In this era, productivity rose rapidly, quality improved equally rapidly, and prices continued to decrease. By the 1820s, half of all Britain's exports, by value, were cotton goods.

- New technologies were complemented by American Eli Whitney's invention of the cotton gin in 1793, which facilitated the massive growth of plantation cotton. The American cotton crop increased from 2 million pounds in 1791 to 182 million in 1821.

The Fortunes of Hand-Loom Weavers

- Between 1770 and 1810, as spinning technology improved, there was a heightened demand for hand-loom weavers. They were often gathered together in workshops but continued to work individually—a halfway stage to the integrated factory.

- In the 1790s, William Radcliffe employed about 1,000 hand-loom weavers and was always on the lookout for more. These years would be remembered later as the golden age of the hand-loom weavers.

- Once weaving technology caught up in the 1810s, however, the hand-loom weavers' trade went into a long decline. A famous example is the family of Andrew Carnegie, who left Scotland, penniless, to try their luck in America. Hand-loom weavers lacked the capital to shift over to the far more expensive power looms.

Employment Conditions

- The cotton spinners were pioneers of factories as social systems, as well as production centers. They struggled to assemble and keep a workforce, a problem that persisted for the first half-century of cotton factory production.

- Arkwright found that to lure people to Cromford, he had to hire entire families, offer them houses, and create a cohesive community, complete with a pub. Even when paying higher wages than those available to farm laborers or domestic manufacturers, these early entrepreneurs struggled to keep a steady workforce.

- The textiles industry was vulnerable to shifts in fashion and to intermittent booms and busts, making employment unpredictable. When Friedrich Engels wrote about the condition of the English working class in 1844, he said that the mental stress and uncertainty about work from day to day was even worse than the slum conditions, poor housing, and bad food the workers were forced to endure.

• Engels also made a point noted by other observers at the time: As steam power displaced waterwheels after about 1825, manufacturers showed a preference for women and children as workers. The machines did the hard work, and "operatives" or "hands" were needed mainly to watch or to repair broken threads. Children's small hands and ability to get into tight spaces and women's dexterity were assets. Owners also knew that women and children could be paid less and were less likely to strike.

The possibility of using women and children as textile workers coincided with the Napoleonic Wars (1790s–1815), when large numbers of men were in the armed services.

Rapid Advancements in Methods

• Historians have long debated whether the Industrial Revolution, beginning in cotton, actually impoverished the workers or whether—despite the undeniable miseries—they were better off than their rural predecessors, who could also experience severe poverty. Certainly, the textile revolution created far more affordable, popular clothing than British people had ever had access to before.

- Methods developed for cotton manufacture were later adapted for linen, wool, and worsted. Other textile processes advanced rapidly, as well. For example, in 1750, bleaching a piece of fabric using sour milk (lactic acid) could take several months. Experiments with the manufacture of sulfuric acid brought the time down to about one month, and by 1800, the perfection of bleaching powder (lime chloride) reduced the time scale to one or two days.

- Similar advances were made in the printing of fabric. The old method, still in use in the late 1700s, was to have a master printer carefully ink wooden blocks and apply them to the fabric. Inventor Joseph Bell's printing rollers created far greater regularity in pattern on large pieces of cloth and worked 100 times as quickly.

- The industry continued to grow. In 1813, there were 2,400 power looms in Britain; in 1829, 55,000; and in 1850, 224,000. The British textile industry never rose to near-monopoly status, however. Even by the mid-19th century, most companies were medium sized and specialized in a particular fabric or process.

Factories as Model Communities

- Conditions in many of the factories were regimented, and the work was unpredictable. Manchester manufacturers championed the idea of laissez-faire; they resisted government regulation and wanted to be free to run their factories in their own way. In contrast, some employers tried to create model communities in which the residents would be happier, healthier, and organically unified.

- Robert Owen was among the first of such employers. He was Welsh by birth but ran textile mills in Scotland. On first entering the business, he was horrified by the squalor of workers' homes, widespread drunkenness, mass illiteracy, and appalling work conditions.

- Owen strove to create a humane working environment, with shorter hours, rudimentary education for children in the mill, and improved housing. Utilitarian philosopher Jeremy Bentham invested in the mill and accepted a lower rate of return than if profit had been the only consideration.

- In the 1850s, Titus Salt created a community called Saltaire for the manufacture of alpaca worsted. It was a state-of-the-art factory designed to carry out all phases of manufacture. Salt built a workers' village next door, with a chapel, almshouse, bathhouse, a hospital, and a library. The sign over the entrance arch read: "Abandon beer, all ye who enter here."

Suggested Reading

Chapman, *The Cotton Industry in the Industrial Revolution*.

Fitton, *The Strutts and the Arkwrights, 1758-1830*.

Lemire, *Cotton*.

Mathias, *The First Industrial Nation*.

Questions to Consider

1. Why did the textile industry start out in remote rural districts but later move to such cities as Manchester?

2. What were the most important technical and social challenges faced by early textile entrepreneurs, such as Arkwright?

The Textile Industry
Lecture 6—Transcript

The first British industry to be transformed by mechanization was textiles. For centuries, Britain had had a thriving domestic and export trade in woolen cloth. In the late 18th century, a group of entrepreneurs invented machines to spin thread and weave cotton cloth, then built some of the world's first factories to house them.

The invention of the cotton gin in 1793 enabled American planters to grow short-staple cotton in bulk, most of which they shipped across the Atlantic to Liverpool. It became America's most important export in the years between the Revolution and the Civil War, and also the most important raw material of Britain's industrial revolution in textiles. In a burst of phenomenal growth, Britain's textile factory output rose between 1780 and 1820 by 2,200 percent.

For centuries, the clothing trade in wool had been a small-scale domestic industry, often practiced by farming families. In Yorkshire, in the West Country, the counties of Somerset and Dorset, and East Anglia, Norfolk and Suffolk and Lincolnshire, clothiers would take raw wool to families each week and collect their finished cloth at the end of the week ; this was part of the "putting out" system that I mentioned last time. Inside the family, the labor was divided like this: The women usually carded the raw wool and spun the thread on spinning wheels while the men wove cloth on hand looms. Carding is running the wool taken from the sheep between two boards with short metal spikes, drawing out the fibers. By drawing the boards across each other, the fibers are straightened and loosened, and then it's ready to be spun into yarn on a spinning wheel. Handloom weaving works like this: The weaver sets up parallel threads, the "warp," and then weaves a shuttle among them to create the "weft" or the "woof." Surplus broadcloth, the kind of woolen cloth that was being made, was exported to Antwerp in the Netherlands by the Merchant Adventurers' Company. This was a steadily expanding trade, and it was open to competition after 1690.

The county of Lancashire in the northwest, the area around Liverpool and Manchester, became cotton-producing area, using imported cotton from India and from the West Indies. The clothiers, the people who organized this business, were already small-scale capitalists long before the first textile machines arrived, and the area had a fund of workers who were familiar with carding, spinning, and weaving.

Cotton cloth being imported from India was called calico. Women liked calico because it was light, it could be printed in bright colors, and it enabled them to adopt new fashions, but domestic textile manufacturers persuaded Parliament to ban calico in 1700. They feared that the competition would undermine their business and their livelihood. It still found its way into England by smuggling, but during a business slump in 1719–1720, the wool makers in Norwich and in London rioted, ripping calico clothes off women who were wearing them in the streets and even throwing acid at people wearing calico clothes. To make matters worse from the victims' point of view, the juries often refused to convict. They sympathized with the wool workers who thought that their jobs were threatened rather than sympathizing with the victims of the violence. Parliament responded with another act in 1721, strengthening the ban on cotton imports, so something seemingly as innocent as pieces of cotton cloth could become highly controversial.

It wasn't until the 1770s, much later, that Parliament finally bowed to the reality that cotton importation had continued in increasing volume. It bowed to this reality and repealed the ban on cotton imports in 1774. In those same years, however, experiments raised the possibility that textile manufacture might be centralized and mechanized.

The Lombe Brothers's silk mill in Derby, built in 1721, is often regarded as the world's first water-powered factory. It employed 300 workers, profitably, making silk thread for weavers. I mentioned earlier that Derby is my hometown, and according to a local story that I grew up with in that town, John Lombe had sent his brother Thomas to Italy where silk was being spun by simple machines. He got a job there, learned how to operate the machine, sneaked back in to the factory during the night to draw the machine accurately, and then hurried back to England with the design. The Lombe Brothers then established a patent for machine silk making, giving them a 14-year monopoly inside the British Isles. This is perhaps the earliest known case of industrial espionage in British history. The Lombe Brothers's mill is still there; until very recently it was a museum of science and technology.

But silk, which they were making, was a luxury item. Mass production was going to take off not in silk, but in cotton and wool manufacture, where the demand was potentially much greater because the cost was so much lower.

John Kay's "flying shuttle" was an early attempt to make a weaving machine. This was an invention of 1733. It worked at twice the speed of a conventional loom, speeding up the weaver's ability to make cloth. You can still see a John Kay "flying shuttle" at a place called Quarry Bank Mill. It's a working textile museum in Cheshire, just south of Manchester. Quarry Bank Mill also contains working examples of nearly all the other machines I'm going to mention in this lecture. If you're English, go there really soon. Quarry Bank Mill is the perfect accompaniment to this part of the history of industrialization. If you're elsewhere, put it on your itinerary for your next visit to Britain. It's one of many sites that enable visitors to get a lively sense of what these early industrial devices actually looked like, and perhaps even more important, what they sounded like, because they were deafening.

With the flying shuttle, weaving was now a far faster process than spinning. Spinning had become the bottleneck in the production process. The first practical spinning machine was James Hargreaves's "spinning jenny." Hargreaves was a tinkerer from Lancashire, good at woodwork and familiar with the fact that weavers could use yarn faster than spinners could spin it. He saw a way to increase the output of a spinning wheel from one spindle at a time, which was the traditional way, to six or eight spindles all attached to the same wheel. A very simple machine, named after his wife, Jenny, but it worked. He patented it in 1764.

A second spinning machine was patented by Richard Arkwright. He was a wig maker and a barber from Preston in Lancashire. He improved on the spinning jenny and created a device called the "water frame" that could spin strong cotton yarn. Arkwright, who's one of the biggest names in the history of the revolution in cotton textiles, saw the need for a centralized production, a factory, next to a reliable power source, a fast-flowing river, to turn the water wheels, which would be connected to the machinery. He built his factory at Cromford in Derbyshire, where the fast-flowing River Derwent could turn water wheels linked to the spinning machines. It, too, is still there today, now a museum of early industrialization, as are the nearby factories of the Strutt family in Belper, his contemporaries and rivals. Arkwright installed overshot waterwheels. An overshot waterwheel is one where the water flows onto the wheel from the top and then carries the wheel down, as opposed to an undershot waterwheel where the river simply flows past the bottom of the wheel and turns it.

A famous mid-century engineer named John Smeaton had shown in 1751 that overshot wheels were far more efficient than the traditional undershot. It also meant that if you could build a little reservoir and have a canal carrying water, called the mill race, you'd always be able to have a water supply flowing over the wheel, whereas variations in river level, if it got low enough, could leave an undershot wheel high and dry. Hand spinners couldn't make more than about 20 hanks to the pound—a hank is 840 yards of thread—but Arkwright, with his water frame, could produce 60 hanks to the pound; in other words, much finer yarn to make smoother and thinner fabric. Arkwright's factory at Cromford also mechanized other stages of the process: the cleaning of the cotton, carding, drawing, and roving; the various techniques that precede the actual spinning.

Another inventor named Samuel Crompton created a hybrid machine in the late 1770s, adopting the best features of Hargreaves and Arkwright, hence its name, the "mule." A mule is an animal that's a cross between a horse and a donkey, and this also was a crossbreed, the bringing together of two different types. It could produce 300 hanks to the pound, incomparably finer than any yarn seen before, but still strong enough to be woven. One mule could contain 1,000 spindles. It's fascinating to watch one at work, minded by just two or three people doing the same work that previously had required dozens or even hundreds of people at individual spinning wheels. The mule remained the basic spinning machine right into the 20th century, often improved and updated in small ways, but remaining essentially the same device.

The overpowering superiority of machine spinning very rapidly drove the hand spinners out of business. Early manufacturers encountered severe resistance from local people who were afraid that machines would destroy traditional ways of life and work. Today, we're familiar with the concept of economic growth and rising productivity, but back then they assumed that a machine five times as efficient would put four out of every five workers out of a job, and they protested against it very vigorously indeed. There was a rash of machine-breaking riots in 1779, and a petition to Parliament 1780 complained of "the introduction of patent machines and engines of various descriptions, which have superseded manual labor to such a fatal and alarming degree that many thousands, with their families, are pining for want of employment." Parliament investigated in response to the machine-breakers' complaints, but the parliamentary committee concluded that a lucrative new industry was springing up with far more benefits than harm, and that traditional ways would have to yield. Former cottage workers must now move to factory jobs if they wanted to stay in the textile trades. This wasn't a foregone conclusion, but it shows that times were changing and that the nation was beginning to adapt to the concept of government support for economic growth. So towards the end of the 18th century they sided with the manufacturers, whereas at the beginning of the century they'd sided with the workers who were protesting against calico imports. That's a fairly major switch in policy.

As it turned out, the demand would continue to grow, absorbing labor that had been threatened by mechanization. A huge percentage of British cotton textiles were exported from the late 18th right through to the late 19th centuries, sometimes to Europe and to the United States but more often to captive colonial markets in Africa, India, and the West Indies. This was an era in which productivity rose very rapidly, quality improved equally rapidly, and the price kept going down. Better and better goods at lower and lower prices, one of the very distinctive characteristics of industrial capitalism.

By the 1820s, half of all Britain's exports by value were cotton goods. These technologies were complemented by Eli Whitney's invention of the cotton gin in 1793. It facilitated the massive growth of plantation cotton growing in the American Deep South, all the more so with the Louisiana Purchase of 1803, which opened up a vast suitable area to cotton planting and hence also to the continued spread of slavery. The American cotton crop rose from 2 million pounds in 1791 to 182 million in 1821, a gigantic rise facilitated by the cotton gin.

The spinning technology improved first, and it created a heightened demand for hand-loom weavers. This was in the period from about 1770 to about 1810. Hand-loom weavers began to gather together in workshops rather than continuing to work each in his own home, but they continued to work individually. This is a kind of halfway stage to the integrated factory that came a bit later. In the 1790s, a man named William Radcliffe employed about 1,000 hand-loom weavers, and he was always on the lookout for more as demand kept rising and the supply of cotton thread came in. He wrote, "Their dwellings and small gardens are clean and neat—all the family well clad—the men with each a watch in his pocket, and the women dressed to their own fancy." In other words, they're prospering; as working men, they could afford to buy a watch, then a sign of modest wealth. These years would later be remembered as the Golden Age of the hand-loom weavers.

The first modern weaving machine was invented by a clergyman named Edmund Cartwright and patented 1785, but it didn't prove economically viable and a factory run by his brother failed. Once the weaving technology caught up, however, in the 1810s, the hand-loom weavers' trade went into a long decline. Men who were earning five pounds a week in 1800 could scarcely make a tenth as much 30 years later, despite working for grim, long hours. Mechanized weaving had driven them out of the business. A famous example of the poor hand-loom weaver includes the family of Andrew Carnegie, who left Dunfermline in Scotland, penniless, to try their luck in America instead. The hand-loom weavers lacked the capital to shift over to the far more expensive power looms. It wasn't that they were unaware of what was happening; they knew exactly what the problem was, but they couldn't afford to capitalize the shift to power production.

The cotton spinners were pioneers of factories as social systems as well as production centers. They struggled to assemble and keep a workforce, a problem that persisted for the first half-century of cotton factory production. Perhaps their biggest difficulty was to find sufficiently skilled workmen to assemble the machinery to put together the water frames themselves to build the waterwheels to link everything up. These were skills that were new. During post-1780 boom in cotton manufacture, such men were in very high demand.

But unskilled workers to actually manage the factory were also hard to find and even harder to keep. They disliked the constant labor, as opposed to the more intermittent style of working in domestic work. There was no more Saint Monday. These are people who are required to come to work six days a week and work 12 or 15 hours continuously. They disliked the close supervision; it reminded some of them of the workhouse, where the very poorest people were forced to go. They disliked the switch from seasonal and daylight time to clock time, and we have stories of workers who, in the summer would appear as soon as it got light at five in the morning but during the winter couldn't be persuaded to show up until eight o'clock, much later, because they were used to the idea that they worked by the daylight. These early workers very much disliked the noise of the machines. Their hours had always been long and their pay poor, but previously it had been possible to pause, to chat with each other, and to reflect. Now the noise itself was very alienating, as was the regimented, continuous work.

Early manufacturers like Arkwright himself tended to be martinets, as they struggled to impose a sense of order, punctuality, sobriety, and cleanliness on people who were unfamiliar with all these concepts. Arkwright discovered that to lure people to Cromford, his factory, he had to hire entire families. He had to offer them housing; that is, he had to create an entire community, complete with its own pub, in order to get people and keep them. Even when paying higher wages than were available to farm laborers or domestic manufacturers, the first generation of employers struggled to keep the same steady workforce.

The textile industry was vulnerable to shifts in fashion, and also to intermittent booms and busts, which made employment unpredictable. At one point, there'd be a sudden surge in demand and everyone would be working the maximum number of hours to get to fulfill the demand; but then suddenly there'd be a glut on the market. No more was needed, they'd be laid off, and they never knew from week to week whether work was going to be available. When Friedrich Engels wrote his famous book about the condition of the English working class in 1844, he said that the mental stress, the uncertainty about work from day to day, was even worse than the slum conditions, the horrible housing, and the bad food that the workers had to endure.

Engels also noticed a point that was often made at the time by other observers: that as cotton manufacture moved out of the river valleys and into the Lancashire cities, and as steam power gradually displaced waterwheels after about 1825, the manufacturers showed a preference for women and children as workers. 1825 was the year of Richard Roberts's "power mule"; this is a very significant improvement over earlier types of the mule. From then on, the machine did the hard work, and the operatives—people who were often called the "hands"—were needed mainly just to watch, or to repair broken threads; to keep an eye on the machine as it did all the actual labor. Children's small hands and their ability to get into tight spaces and women's dexterity were now assets. In a series of 12 engravings by J. R. Barfoot called "The Progress of Cotton" from 1840, children can be glimpsed inside the machinery, small enough to mend the threads in inaccessible places and to pick up the cotton waste. It was dangerous, but children were required to go into the machinery itself while it was in operation.

The possibility of using women and children in the factories also coincided with the Napoleonic Wars. In the 1790s and early 1800s, up to the Battle of Waterloo in 1815, which finally ended Napoleon's reign, this was a period in which the factory system was developing rapidly. Large numbers of men were in the armed services, and this was a further incentive for the employers to adapt to other workers: women and children. Some London parishes began to send poor children, orphans, north to Lancashire to the textile towns so that they could get work there and save a local burden of poor relief. But the employment of women and children could lead to very painful gender reversals inside families, where now suddenly the man was humbled by being left at home while his wife became the breadwinner. The factory owners also knew that women and children could be paid less and were less likely to go on strike.

Historians have long debated whether the Industrial Revolution, beginning in cotton, actually impoverished the workers, or whether, despite the undeniable misery of the work, they were slightly better off than their rural predecessors, where poverty could also be very severe. Were they, in fact, on the road to eventual improvement? Certainly, the textile revolution created far more affordable popular, low-priced clothing than British people had ever had access to before. It was very common before 1800 for poor working people to only have one set of clothes, which they'd wear until they literally fell to pieces. Now, in the 1800s, even the poorest could start expecting to own more than one set of clothes.

This was an industry that was innovating constantly. The cotton textile industry was the first to build iron-framed factory buildings; the first to experiment with gas lighting to make a brighter-lit environment for night work. The methods that they developed for cotton manufacture, which takes very, very nicely to machines, were then adapted to other fabrics: for linen, for wool, and for worsted, which is a blend of cotton and wool with some of the good qualities of each. Other textile processes advanced rapidly as well. For example, in 1750, bleaching a piece of fabric could take several months. The main ingredient was sour milk, whose active ingredient is lactic acid. Experiments with the manufacture of sulphuric acid brought the time of bleaching down to about one month, but by 1800 the perfection of bleaching powder, whose principle component is lime chloride, made the time scale of that one or two days; again, an enormous increase in the pace at which the process can be done.

Similarly, in the printing of fabric, the traditional method, still in use in the late 1700s, was to have a master printer very carefully inking wooden blocks and then applying them by pressing them onto the fabric. An inventor named Joseph Bell came up with printing rollers instead. Fabric would now be fed through these rollers, which were constantly being inked as they rotated. These created a far greater regularity in the pattern on large pieces of cloth and worked 100 times as quickly. On the other hand, once the bleached or printed fabric was sold, making it up into clothes was still done mostly by hand until the invention of effective sewing machines around 1860 in a later stage of the industrialization of textiles.

The industry continued to grow. There were 2,400 power looms in Britain in 1813, but there were 55,000 of them by 1829 and 224,000 of them by 1850. Later in this course, we'll see how in some industries, such as Rockefeller's Standard Oil in America, one or a few owners rose to near-monopoly power. British textiles were never like that. By the mid-19th century, most companies were medium-sized and specialized in a particular fabric or a particular job, spinning, weaving, dyeing, or bleaching.

Conditions in many of the factories were regimented and the work unpredictable. The Manchester manufacturers championed the idea of laissez-faire, the opposite of the old patriarchalism of the countryside. They wanted to resist government regulation and be left free to run the factories in their own way. On the other hand, a few employers tried to create model communities that would be happier, healthier, and organically unified.

Among the most famous and among the pioneers was Robert Owen. He was a Welshman by birth, but he ran the textile mills at New Lanark in Scotland, powered by the water of the River Clyde. On first entering the textile business, Robert Owen was horrified by the squalor of the workers' homes, the widespread drunkenness among the workers' families, the mass illiteracy, and the appalling work conditions to which they were subjected. He tried to create a humane working environment, shorter hours, a rudimentary education for children in the mill at the school he provided, and improved housing. The utilitarian philosopher Jeremy Bentham, who believed in the greatest good for the greatest number, invested in this mill and accepted a lower rate of return than if profit had been the only consideration. Owen eventually developed into an early socialist, attracted the attention of idealists throughout Europe, and later ran an experimental model community called New Harmony in Indiana in the United States.

In the 1850s, another of these social experimenters, a man named Titus Salt, created a community called Saltaire outside the town of Bradford. This was for the manufacture of alpaca worsted. It's a blend of cotton and the wool that comes from the alpaca, the South American mammal. It was a state of the art factory designed to carry out all the phases of the manufacture. Titus Salt also built a workers' village right next door to the factory, with better-than-average workers' houses, and the corner houses at the end of each block were superior. They were for the foremen and the skilled workers, a reward for being a valued workman. Saltaire included a chapel, an almshouse for old workers, a bath house, a hospital, and a library. But it also had a requirement for all workers that they must not drink alcohol. Titus Salt was no socialist, but he was a well-intentioned paternalist, and what we call a prohibitionist. Hence sign on entrance arch: "Abandon beer all ye who enter here." That's a lovely parody of Dante's *Inferno*, where over Hell says the message "Abandon hope all ye who enter here." Titus Salt understood perfectly well that drinking could lead to loss of work and housing, and so he insisted that he have a sober workforce. Saltaire is also still there to be visited today. It's now a world heritage site.

To sum up, the key transitions in the textile industry were: gathering the workers together in the same place to work under close supervision; the invention and proliferation of machines that could do the work faster and more evenly than hand workers; and the application of power sources to these machines, first water power, then steam. The development of immense domestic and foreign markets as the price of the finished goods continued to go down and the quality to go up was one of the central characteristics of industrial manufacturing.

In the next few lectures, we'll go on to investigate the key technological breakthroughs that made mechanization possible in coal mining, in iron manufacture, and in transportation. We'll turn first to coal mining.

Coal Mining—Powering the Revolution
Lecture 7

The Industrial Revolution ran on coal. Immense coalfields underlie parts of Britain, and coal had been mined and quarried to a small extent ever since pre-Roman times. Improvements in mining technology in the 18th century, however, along with rising demand, transformed coal mining into a large-scale capitalist enterprise. Coal fueled the steam engines that turned the textile machines, and it powered the furnaces that created large-scale iron and steel manufacturing.

Dangerous and Dirty Work

- Since ancient times, inhabitants of Britain burned coal from geological outcrops, but weathering made it poor fuel. Already by the time of the Romans, the British understood the need to dig into the ground to recover coal that would burn better.

- Coal is fossilized carbon—the compressed remnant of plants that grew millions of years ago. Mining it has always been, and still is, among the most dangerous jobs in the world. Mines are subject to subsidence, with tunnels suddenly caving in to crush miners or to trap and suffocate them behind a rockfall.

- The activity of coal mining releases poisonous gases, such as carbon monoxide, trapped in the coal seams. Other gases, especially methane, can explode. Miners breathe in coal dust and are susceptible to lung diseases, including silicosis and pneumoconiosis "black lung." In addition to all this, the work is backbreaking and carried on in near-total darkness.

- The traditional coal mine had a shaft about eight feet in diameter. This shaft was dug straight down into the earth until it met the coal seams, and the lateral tunnels were dug out from the bottom of the shaft to dig up the coal itself.

- Coal was hauled up in baskets made of woven sticks by a team of horses turning a windlass. Underground, the miners at first used a system in which they cut out part of the coal but left large pillars of it standing to hold up the roof. An alternative method was the longwall system, which shored up the area already dug out, leaving just a narrow passage.

The Expansion of Mines

- By 1700, coal mines were becoming larger and deeper. These large mines were susceptible to flooding, which could be severe, especially near the coast, such as the huge mining area around Newcastle. If a mine was on high ground, it was sometimes possible to build a tunnel from which floodwater would drain away. But better methods were urgently needed by 1700.

- A second problem was that of transport. Coal is high in bulk and relatively low in value. In fact, Newcastle developed partly because of its proximity to the river Tyne and the North Sea, which allowed

Because of the inherent dangers in mining, conflict between miners and mine owners has been acute in Britain from before 1700 up to the 1980s.

transport by water to London. If a mine was further inland, the cost of getting the coal to the coast for shipment was simply too high.

- Ventilation was also a serious problem; it was difficult to get circulating air into the mines. There was a constant hazard of "choke damp" and "firedamp," poisonous gases. In the Tyne area, shallow mines had a flooding problem; although this problem lessened with greater depth, the flammable gas problem worsened. As mines went deeper, owners' investment increased, making accidents and cave-ins financial as well as human disasters.

- Lesser but also significant problems included lack of illumination, difficulty of access, underground transportation, and subsidence. When coal faces were no longer in production, often the weight of the rock strata above an area would gradually press down on pillars of coal, leading to subsidence above.

An Early Steam Engine

- Responses to all these problems began to increase in the 1700s. One of the first was Thomas Savery's *atmospheric engine*, patented in 1698. It was the first steam engine in history, and it was designed to pump flooded mines. But it could raise water only about 80 feet and had to be sited inside the mine itself. Miners believed it increased the likelihood of fires or explosions.

- Thomas Newcomen, an ironmonger from Devonshire, greatly improved Savery's design. The new engine could operate at only two or three strokes per minute at first and depended on the creation of a vacuum in a steam-filled cylinder. The first one was used at a Staffordshire colliery in 1712 and caught on quickly; some engines stayed in use throughout the 18th and 19th centuries.

- Newcomen installed 78 engines during the 20 years of his patent. When the patent expired, others got into the business, installing 300 more in the next 40 years—nearly always as mine-pumping engines but occasionally to lift water into high ponds that fed waterwheels for rotary motion.

Improved Transport

- Tramways—the world's first railways—were a response to the coal transport problem. Tramways were wooden, low-friction tracks, easing the way for horses to draw coal wagons down to wharves at the river. The world's first railway bridge, Causey Arch, built in 1726, carried a mine tramway down to Tyneside from a mine seven or eight miles from Newcastle. At the time, it was the highest and longest single-span bridge in England.

- In Northumberland, the normal pattern was for railways to run mainly downhill to the riverside. Wagons rolled under own weight, with a brakeman riding them and a horse hitched behind. After the wagon was emptied, the horse would drag it back up the hill to the mine.

- At the river, coal was dumped in covered sheds to keep it dry until boats arrived to take it to London. Coal was tipped from overhanging spouts into keelboats rowed by four men. They transported the coal downstream (working with the tide) to ships in the Tyne River estuary and loaded it by hand into ships, which carried it to London.

- After 1800, mine owners tested stationary steam engines on the railways in winding houses, using them to lower coal wagons down to the waterside and haul them up. A stationary steam engine at that point was more suitable than a locomotive and, in fact, remained so on steep gradients, because a direct pull is better than a locomotive-powered railway on steep ground.

- As mines went deeper, owners experimented with sending tunnels out farther and equipping them with underground tramways. After about 1750, horses were taken underground to pull baskets of coal. That meant making the tunnels higher and wider, but it added much-needed power.

- To draw coal out of the mine, innovations with waterwheels turning windlasses demonstrated a great increase in speed and reliability over the horse-drawn method.

Safety Lamps

- The next issue to address was the need for improved lighting. Following a terrible accident in 1812, when 92 men and boys were killed in a gas explosion during a shift change, philanthropists became interested in the idea of finding ways to improve safety.

- The challenge was to find a way to carry a light into the mine that would not cause fires and explosions when it encountered gas. Two similar designs were proposed, one by a practical mine engineer, George Stephenson (later, the great pioneering railway builder), and the other by an upper-class scientist, Sir Humphrey Davy. Both were effective in preventing explosions of firedamp.

- Safety lamps had both economic and safety consequences; they enabled many "fiery" mines to be reopened and the most dangerous areas of working pits to be fully exploited. However, miners were slow to adapt to safety lamps or exposed themselves to danger by taking their covers off in the mine. Late in the 19th century, candles were still being used in many mines.

Improved Ventilation

- Increased ventilation was another important mining improvement. Miners realized that it was better to have two mine shafts than one; especially if a draft could be drawn through to keep air circulating. Miners learned how to set a fire at the top of one shaft to draw air through from the other, a process called "coursing the air." They also learned that it was essential to guide air through all the workings— even those not currently in use—to prevent the concentration of flammable or poisonous gases.

- Mine owners installed doors to guide airflow while keeping underground communications as direct as possible. One shocking example of child labor was to have children serve as *trappers*, sitting alone and in total darkness next to trapdoors to open and close them when coal was being dragged to the pithead. The trappers made sure that fresh air got to the areas where miners were currently at work.

- Even when hazards had been known for centuries and remedies had been available for decades, not all mine owners showed a concern for safety. In 1862, at Hartley Colliery, 204 men and boys were killed in an accident that blended bad management with bad design and bad luck. The accident led to such a public outcry that Parliament passed design regulations in response.

Women and Children in the Mines

- As mining developed, owners sought a more efficient method of sorting out coal at the surface.

- From about 1760, mine owners utilized inclined planes with screens of metal bars, so that the *small coal* (less valuable) would fall through the screens, while larger pieces of *round coal* were preserved. Another typical children's job was as a coal picker, sorting rock from coal on conveyor belts below the screens.

- By the Victorian era, a literary protest against women and children in the mines was gaining momentum, however. Such labor would soon be prohibited by law.

The Importance of Coal in Industrialization

- Coal was involved in every aspect of the British Industrial Revolution:
  - Coal fueled steam engines, which made mine drainage possible and then made manufacturing independent of wind or water mills.

  - Coal fueled railways.

  - Coal released the iron industry from dependence on charcoal.

  - Coal provided a cheap, reliable fuel for domestic heating and for nearly all industries that required some form of heating: brewing, salt making, glassmaking, papermaking, and so on.

- The statistics demonstrate that coal, industrialization, and economic growth are inextricably linked. In 1700, 3 million tons of coal were produced; in 1750, 5 million tons; in 1830, 30 million tons; and in 1870, 128 million tons.

- Economic historian Michael Flinn estimated that the rate of increase of coal use accelerated about one percent per year in the early 18th century; two percent per year in the late 18th century; and three percent per year after 1830.

- By the 1850s, many economists were anxious that Britain's coal reserves would be exhausted, bringing the economy to a grinding halt. There are, in fact, still hundreds of years' worth of coal reserves, but the fear bears witness to the centrality of coal in the Industrial Revolution.

Suggested Reading

Atkinson, *The Great Northern Coalfield, 1700–1900.*

Galloway, *A History of Coal Mining in Great Britain.*

Griffin, *Mining in the East Midlands, 1550–1947.*

Lewis, *Coal Mining in the 18th and 19th Centuries.*

Questions to Consider

1. Were most of the dangers associated with coal mining unavoidable in the early stage of the Industrial Revolution?

2. Why did the problem of mine drainage have such far-reaching consequences for other areas of British industrial development?

Coal Mining—Powering the Revolution
Lecture 7—Transcript

The Industrial Revolution ran on coal. Immense coalfields underlie parts of Britain, and it's been mined and quarried in small ways ever since pre-Roman times. Improvements in mining technology in the 18th century, along with rising demand, transformed coal mining into a large-scale capitalist enterprise. It fueled the steam engines that turned the textile machines and it powered the furnaces that created a large-scale iron and steel industry. Coal also ensured that for two centuries industrial Britain would be coated in soot and that its people would have to breathe smoky air and cope with dense urban fog.

When I was a child in England in the 1950s and '60s, we still kept warm at home with coal fires. I've made hundreds of them. We had a coal shed behind the house, and brawny men with blackened faces delivered sacks of coal every month. Coal itself is shiny, black, and angular. You can't just hold a match to coal; you have to create a fire from paper and sticks to generate enough heat, and then gradually the coal catches fire from the glowing embers of the burning sticks. To get it started properly, you also have to help the coal "draw"; that is, you have to force air through the flames to make the fire self-sustaining. The simplest way is to blow on it. As it burns down, a coal fire creates heaps of glowing red and yellow embers that are very warm, beautiful, and home-like; much loved. But it's also dirty and polluting. If you start the fire poorly, the house will fill with smoke. This was an early morning job for generations of English people—cleaning ashes out of the grate—and it's a dirty job. No wonder every family that could possibly afford it hired servants to do the work instead.

Since ancient times, inhabitants of Britain had burned coal from geological outcrops, but weathering made it poor fuel. By the time of the Romans, they understood the need to dig into the ground to recover it to find fuel that was going to burn better. Coal is the compressed remnant of plants that grew millions of years ago. Mining it has always been, and still is, among the most dangerous jobs in the world. Mines are subject to subsidence, with tunnels suddenly caving in to crush the miners or to trap and suffocate them behind a rock fall. Poisonous gases like carbon monoxide trapped in the coal seams are released by mine workers and can kill them. Other gases, especially methane, explode. Miners breathe in coal dust all the time and are liable to lung diseases like silicosis and pneumoconiosis, "black lung." In addition to all this, the work is back-breakingly hard and exhausting and, until the invention of electric lights, was carried on in near total darkness.

In view of all these things, it's not surprising that this is an industry where conflict between miners and mine owners has been so acute. Every miner every day knows that he's in mortal danger, and he has every reason to detest the people who profit from his work without taking the same risks. In the history of British workers, there's a long tradition of miners' militancy, from before 1700 right up to the days of Margaret Thatcher when she was Prime Minister in the 1980s.

The major British coalfields are in the northeast of the country in Newcastle on Tyne and County Durham, Northumberland; also in the Scottish lowlands, the area around Glasgow and Edinburgh; in Yorkshire around Sheffield; in Nottinghamshire and Derbyshire; in South Wales; and in the coastal Lake District. Each of these areas has its own distinctive type of coal, with its characteristic difficulties. Each area has special names for the equipment that's used and for the different types of workers, and each has a colorful history of legends, songs, folklore, and memories. Still, we can disentangle much of this and make some useful generalizations about the history of the development of coal mining nationwide.

The traditional coal mine had a shaft about eight feet in diameter. This dug straight down into the earth until it meets the coal seams, and then lateral tunnels are dug out from the bottom of the shaft, the pit head, to dig up the coal itself. It's hauled up the shaft in woven baskets, made of sticks originally, called "corves," by a team of horses or turning a windlass at the top to drag the corves up the shaft. Underground, the miners at first used the bord and pillar system. This means that with pick axes, they'd cut out part of the coal but leave big pillars of it standing to hold up the roof. That wasted about half the coal, which had to be left in place to keep the roof up. The coal hewers at the face itself, with picks and shovels, often worked in near darkness. Sometimes they'd also blast with black powder to loosen coal, another hazard among the many they faced. An alternative to the bord and pillar system was the long wall system: Shoring up the area that's already been dug out with spoil—that is, waste material from the diggings that you're currently working on—and leaving just a narrow passage to squeeze through.

The coal seams sometimes obliged the miners by being level so they could work on a relatively flat surface, but at other times the seams themselves are angled because of the geological folding of the Earth itself. There are parts of the Earth's crust that have been buckled by millennia of geological activity. Sometimes the coal seams are narrow, so much so that worthless rock has to be removed along with the valuable coal. Of course, the thinner the seam, the less valuable the seam itself is to work.

By 1700, much of the easily-accessible coal had been dug out, and the mines were getting bigger and deeper. As they got deeper, the problems proliferated. One of the worst problems was flooding. Flooding was severe, especially in mines near the coast, such as the huge mining area around Newcastle upon Tyne, which developed early on. Primitive pumps were unsatisfactory. Chains of buckets drawing water out of the mines simply weren't efficient enough. If the mine was set on high ground, it was sometimes possible to build an adit or a drain lower down; that is to say, a sloping tunnel from which the flood water could be diverted and drain away. But better methods were urgently needed by 1700.

A second problem was that of transport. The problem with coal is that it's high in bulk and relatively low in value. In fact, Newcastle developed partly because of its proximity to the River Tyne and to the North Sea. The coasting trade—meaning ships sailing from Newcastle down to London, which is the principle market—coasting ships could take the coal. If the mine was much further inland, the cost of getting the coal to the coast for shipment was simply going to be too high. Packhorses and wagons were both too inefficient and too expensive.

A third problem was with ventilation. It's very difficult to get circulating air into the mines, and meanwhile, the gases in the mines are often lethal. There was a constant hazard of "choke damp." This is a mixture of carbon dioxide, nitrogen, and water vapor; it's unbreathable and it could asphyxiate a miner.

A related problem was "fire damp"; this is methane, which can explode. Newcastle on Tyne had a reputation for "fiery pits"—in other words, pits that were full of firedamp—and there were frequent lethal explosions. For example, 30 men were killed in Gateshead near Newcastle in an explosion of 1705; 69 more were killed at Chester-Le-Street in a 1708 explosion. In the Tyne area, the shallow mines had a flooding problem. The flooding got less bad as the mines got deeper, but the flammable gas problem got worse. Safety problems were paramount. As the mines got deeper, the owners' investment increased. It costs more and more to dig further down into the Earth, making accidents and cave-ins financial as well as human disasters.

Lesser but also significant problems included the illumination problem. Taking down tallow candles increased the risk of explosions, and tallow candles don't have a very bright flame. All sorts of expedients were tried to get light into the mine, even phosphorescent rotting fish. A flint wheel was tried; this is known as the "steel mill." It was thought to be less dangerous than candles, but actually it often caused fires. The mill works like this: A child wears a frame; it has a series of metal gears. The boy cranks a handle that holds a piece of flint next to a fast-turning metal wheel, which has the effect of creating a shower of sparks. But as you can see, all these are fairly primitive methods of illumination.

There was the problem of access. If the mine is shallow, it's possible to simply go down a series of ladders. But once the mine's 100 feet deep or more, the sheer act of getting to the bottom of the mine is itself becoming problematic. Underground transport was another major issue; an appalling hardship for men and women to drag baskets of coal from the coal face to the bottom of shaft. You need to imagine that once the shaft has been established, then tunnels are sent out in every direction following the seams, sometimes a long way, a half a mile or a mile further away, making it very difficult to drag the baskets of coal back to the shaft.

Subsidence was a continuous problem. When coal faces were no longer in production, very often the weight of the rock strata above the area would gradually press down on the pillars of coal, leading to subsidence from above. It wasn't as bad as sudden cave-in, but still it could lead to shifting of the buildings on the surface; so coal mining areas often had buildings that would subside, doorframes that would become jammed, and windows that wouldn't open.

Responses to all these problems began to increase in the 1700s. One of the first was Thomas Savery's "atmospheric engine," patented in 1698. It was the first steam engine in the history of the world, and it was designed to pump flooded mines. The problem with Thomas Savery's engine was that it could only raise the water about 80 feet and it had to be sited inside the mine itself, which terrified the miners because they thought it was going to make fires or explosions more likely; the fire-damp danger. The author of a book called *The Compleat Collier*—collier is the name for a coal miner—from 1708 wrote that miners feared the Savery engine:

> ...because nature doth generally afford us too much sulfurous matter, to bring more fire within these our deep bowels of the earth, so that we judge cool inventions of suction or force would be safest and best for this our concern, if any such could be found that would do so much better and with much more expedition than what is done generally here.

In other words, we don't like the Thomas Savery engine. It strikes us as solving one problem but creating another.

Thomas Newcomen, an ironmonger from Devonshire—this is in the extreme southwest of England; tin mining country—greatly improved the design that Thomas Savery had made. The Newcomen steam engine could only make two or three strokes per minute. It's a great beam engine with a reciprocating beam, and at first they moved very, very slowly. The Newcomen engine depended on creation of a vacuum inside the steam-filled cylinder that would then draw the piston to fill the cylinder. It used a lot of coal, but at a coalmine that doesn't matter. The coal costs less than the feeding of teams of horses, which until then had to turn a windlass.

The first Newcomen engine was installed at a Staffordshire colliery in the English midlands in 1712, and it worked well and the technology caught on quickly. Some Newcomen engines stayed in use right through the 18th and 19th centuries; they had life expectancies of more than 100 years. Newcomen himself installed 78 of them during the 20 years of his patent. When the patent expired, other manufacturers got into the business, installing about 300 more of them in the next 40 years, nearly always as mine-pumping engines; that's where steam technology started out. Occasionally, though, Newcomen engines could also be used to lift water into high ponds that could then be used to feed water to the top of the millrace for an overshot waterwheel. In other words, the steam engine would put the water in the pond and the rotary motion would actually come from the waterwheel itself.

Steam engines were gradually improved over the 18th century, particularly by James Watt, who's the big name in steam engine technology, as we'll see in a later lecture.

In response to the transport problem that the coalmines faced, tramways were developed, and these were the world's very first railways. The rails were made of wood, but the great thing about a railway is that it's a low-friction environment. A smooth wooden wheel on a smooth wooden rail is much better than a horse dragging a wagon along a muddy road. It eased the way for horses to draw coal wagons down to the wharves at the riverbank.

The world's very first railway bridge was built 1726, a place called Causey Arch. It's fascinating to us now because this is about 100 years before steam-driven trains of the sort we've become familiar with. It carried a mine wagonway down to Tyneside from a mine that was seven or eight miles from Newcastle itself, and it was used to cross a deep valley through which a stream flowed. It's 90 feet high, and at the time was the highest and longest single-span bridge in England. Causey Arch fell into disuse after the mine closed, but it's been restored and is still there today. You can still go and visit it.

In Northumberland in the northeast of England, the normal pattern was for the railway to go mainly downhill to the riverside with full coal wagons. The wagons were called "chaldrons," and they rolled under their own weight down the sloping track, with a brakeman riding them and with his horses hitched behind. The brakeman's job was to make sure it didn't go too fast. Then, after they'd been emptied out, the horse would drag the empty wagons back up the hill to the mine where the process could be repeated. At the river itself, the coal was dumped at "staithes." These are big covered sheds to keep the coal dry until boats could arrive to take it off to London. The coal was tipped from overhanging spouts into keelboats rowed by four men. They rowed it downstream, working with the tide, to ships in the Tyne River estuary below the Tyne bridges, loaded it by hand into the ships, after which it would be carried off to London. This was a business that was going on for centuries.

After 1800, mine owners experimented with stationary steam engines on these railways in winding houses, lowering the coal wagons down to the waterside and hauling them back up. A stationary steam engine at that point was more suitable than a locomotive and, in fact, remained so on steep gradients because a direct pull is better than a locomotive-powered railway on steep ground.

As the mines went deeper, the owners experimented with sending out tunnels further and equipping them with underground wagon ways, too. After 1750, horses were taken underground to pull the corves instead of people. But, of course, that meant making that the tunnels had to be made higher and wider to accommodate the horses. On the other hand, having a little underground tramway added a component of much-needed power there to cover the big distances and the greater weights.

There's a wonderful mine that you can visit today. It's called "The Big Pit" in South Wales. It was a mine that closed down in 1980 and is now a fascinating underground museum of mining. You can be taken around by some of the retired miners. It's still possible to see down there the stables. Horses were used there right into the second half of the 20th century. They were good in terms of being a power source, but it meant that the horse feed had to be taken down there and rats often went down with it. They smelled terrible because they had to be mucked out all the time. It's a gruesome environment; fascinating to visit briefly, but not at all the sort of appetizing place where you'd want to spend your entire working life.

To draw the coal out of the mine from the bottom of the shaft, experiments were made with waterwheels turning windlasses, and these showed a great increase in speed and reliability over using horses on the windlass.

The next big issue was to find an improved type of lighting. In 1812, there was a terrible mining disaster at Gateshead near Newcastle when 92 men and boys were killed in a gas explosion during a shift change. Both shifts of miners were in the mine, and all but 30 of them were killed. Many of the survivors were badly wounded and burned. An immense explosion showered the whole area with coal dust, which fell like snow. The mine owners had tried to suppress publication of news about disasters because it was such bad publicity, but this one was so bad that a local clergyman called John Hodgson created the Sunderland Society, dedicated to publicizing the disaster and looking for ways of preventing a recurrence. He stood up to the bullying of the local mine owners and insisted that the news of the disaster and the search for safer techniques in the mine must be found.

The news of the accident spread through the kingdom, and philanthropists became interested in the idea of finding ways to improve mine safety. Was there a way to carry a light into the mine that wouldn't cause fires and explosions when it encountered methane gas? Two very similar designs were proposed, one by a practical mine engineer called George Stephenson, who later on was going to be one of the great pioneers of railway building, the other by an upper-class scientist, Sir Humphrey Davy. I mentioned Davy in the lecture on agriculture; he was very interested in the chemistry of farming. Both of these safety lamps were effective in preventing explosions of fire damp. Also, the changing character of the lamp flame gave the miners a warning that they were in dangerous areas. They still use a flame, but now it's shrouded in such a way that contact won't instantly lead to an explosion. John Buddle, who was a safety-conscious entrepreneur of northeastern mining, urged Humphrey Davy to patent his lamp, which would've given him between 5,000 and 10,000 pounds per year. Buddle wrote, "The reply of this great and noble minded man was 'No my good friend. I never thought of such a thing. My sole object was to serve the cause of humanity, and if I have succeeded, I am amply rewarded in the gratifying reflection of having done so.'"

Safety lamps had economic as well as safety consequences. They enabled many "fiery" mines to be reopened, and the most dangerous areas of the working pits to be fully exploited for the first time. Now it would be possible to extract the coal without explosions. Groups of grateful miners made collections to give to Davy, and wrote him letters of tribute. Robert Galloway, who wrote a superb early history of English coal mining in the 1880s, wrote of the lamp: "Difficulties there are even with its aid, but in the case of deep mining, what vastly greater, what insuperable difficulties would have existed, had science not armed the miners with the wonderful insulated lamp, which warns them of the presence of their invisible enemy, and protects them from its power." But the miners themselves were often slow to adapt to safety lamps, or they exposed themselves to danger by taking the safety cover off inside the mine, things they weren't supposed to do. Late in 19th century, candles were still being used in many mines, 70 or 80 years after the safety lamp had been developed.

Another improvement came with better ventilation. Miners realized that to have two shafts is much better than to have one, especially if you could draw a draught of air down one shaft, through the tunnels, and up the other side; that is, to keep the air circulating inside the mine. They learned how to set a fire at the top of one shaft, such that it would draw air through from the other and keep the circulation going. That was called "coursing the air." They quickly understood that it was important to guide the air through all the workings, even those that weren't currently in use, to prevent the concentration of flammable or poisonous gases. That meant the installation of doors so that the air would be guided to flow through all the workings underground, often which became labyrinthine after they'd been worked for a few decades, while keeping underground communications as direct as possible. How do we get the air to circulate everywhere while still keeping the shortest possible distance from the face to the bottom of the pit?

One horrible example of child labor was to have children as "trappers," sitting alone and in total darkness by these trap doors to open and close them when coal was being dragged to the pithead. The trappers made sure that fresh air was getting to the areas where the miners were currently at work. It was a necessary job, but a terribly boring, lonely, and frightening one, especially for little children.

Even when all these hazards had been known for centuries and remedies for many decades, not all mine owners showed a concern with safety, and there was very little political regulation of the mines themselves. In 1862, at

Hartley Colliery, 204 men and boys were killed in an accident that blended bad management with bad design and bad luck; a perfect storm, everything came together. This was a mine where there was still only one shaft rather than the two, which were known to be best for ventilation. The one shaft was therefore used for sending people up and down, for pulling up coal, for ventilation, and for the flood pumping of the Newcomen engine. These various uses were partially separated by "brattices," which is to say a mass of wooden framing to keep the various sections separate.

Here's the historian Frank Atkinson describing what actually happened there at Hartley:

> The beam of the pumping engine, the largest and most powerful in the north and weighing more than 40 tons, suddenly and without warning broke. About half of it plunged down the shaft, tearing away the brattices, ripping off the stone and timber that protected the walls, carrying piles, gearing, and hundreds of tons of debris in its descent. The accident happened just after the back shift men had gone down to relieve the fore-shift. Six days elapsed before a way could be made through the debris, and by that time all had died, suffocated by poisonous gases and lack of fresh air.

This disaster finally led to such a public outcry about safety that Parliament passed a law specifying two shafts in every coal mine from then on.

As coal mining developed, the owners sought a more efficient method of sorting out the coal once it was brought to the surface. From about 1760, they started to use inclined planes with screens of metal bars so that coal tipped onto them at the top, would run down into containers but permit the smallest pieces, which is called "small coal," to fall through (it's less valuable) while the larger pieces of "round coal" were preserved. Another children's job at the mines was as coal pickers, sorting rock from the coal on conveyor belts below these screens.

By the Victorian era—Victorian era: Queen Victoria became queen in 1837—a literary protest against women and children working in the coal mines was gaining momentum. One of the writers who showed an interest in it was Benjamin Disraeli, who later on was going to be the great conservative Prime Minister. In his novel *Sybil,* published in 1845, he describes boys and girls coming out of a coal mine at the end of a hard shift. He writes:

> Troops of youth, alas, of both sexes, though neither their raiment nor their language indicates the difference; all are clad in male attire, and oaths that men might shudder at issue from lips born to breathe words of sweetness. Yet, these are to be, some are, the mothers of England. But can we wonder at the hideous coarseness of their language when we remember the savage rudeness of their lives? Naked to the waist, an iron chain fastened to a belt of leather runs between their legs clad in canvas trousers, while on hands and feet an English girl for 12, sometimes for 16 hours a day, hauls and hurries tubs of coal up subterranean roads . . . circumstances that seem to have escaped the notice of the Society for the Abolition of Negro Slavery.

In other words, he's making the claim: It's all very well for philanthropists here in England to worry about people far away who are enslaved; that's bad enough. But dreadful things are happening right here in England, too. Soon the work of women and children would be prohibited by law.

Coal was involved in every aspect of the British Industrial Revolution. Its importance would be difficult to exaggerate. It fueled steam engines, which made mine drainage possible; then it made the manufacturing of all other things independent of wind or watermills. It fueled the railways. It released the iron industry from dependence on charcoal, as we'll see in the next lecture. It provided a cheap, reliable fuel for domestic heating, and for nearly all the industries that required some form of heating: brewing, salt making, glass making, paper making, and so on.

The statistics bear out the idea that coal, industrialization, and economic growth are linked in the most intimate way possible. In 1700, about 3 million tons a year of coal were mined in Britain. By 1750, it had risen to 5 million; by 1830, to 30 million; and by 1870, to 128 million tons. The historian Michael Flinn has estimated that the rate of increase of use was about one percent per year in the early 18th century, two percent per year in late 18th, and three percent per year after 1830; in other words, an accelerating rate of increase.

By the 1850s, many economists were anxious that Britain's coal reserves would be exhausted, bringing the economy to a grinding halt. We know that was a false fear; there are, in fact, still hundreds of years' worth of coal reserves. But it bears witness to the centrality of coal in the industrial revolution.

One of the principal uses of coal was for smelting iron. In the next lecture, I'll turn to the rising iron industry of the 18th century to show how a succession of technical breakthroughs enabled ironmasters to produce ever greater quantities of high-quality iron. Coal and iron advanced together as the raw materials of the Industrial Revolution.

Iron—Coking and Puddling
Lecture 8

Throughout most of world history, metals were very scarce and expensive. Until the late 18th century, use of iron was confined mainly to horseshoes, nails, knives, weapons, and cooking pots. The availability of inexpensive ferrous metals (iron and steel) was one of the necessary conditions for the Industrial Revolution. Iron is much more durable than wood; a wooden industrial machine would be vibrated or pounded to pieces after a year's work, but one made of iron would last for decades. Like coal mining, the iron industry has origins stretching back well before 1750, and its transformation took place in gradual stages.

Ironworking

- Initial evidence of ironworking from around 1500 B.C. has been found in the Middle East. To have metal objects of any kind in the ancient world was a sign of wealth and status. Bronze and gold were valued because of their appearance; iron, because of its hardness. The first evidence of ironworking in Britain appeared around 500 B.C.

- Making iron requires crushed iron ore, limestone (a catalyst of the reaction), and a fuel that burns hot enough to melt the iron out of the rock. A temperature of about 2,550° F is needed. To make iron, the fuel, ore, and limestone were fed in at the top of a blast furnace, and the fire was made hotter by high-pressure air blown in from below.

- Early blast furnaces in England were usually sited near iron ore mines and beside fast-flowing streams so that a waterwheel could power the bellows and supply the vital air stream. Once a furnace was in operation, it would be kept going in a continuous *campaign*, sometimes for a year or more.

- At the bottom of the blast furnace, liquid iron flows out and into a long trough (the *sow*); it then flows into molds, which are placed at right angles to the sow (*pigs*).

- The standard fuel for blast furnaces was charcoal. A great deal of woodland—about 10 acres of forest—was required to produce one ton of iron in the 1500s and 1600s.
  - The heavy population of Britain over the centuries meant that wood was being used far more quickly than it could regrow. Wood was the main material for building houses, barns, and fences and the main source of fuel in areas away from coal mining districts. As we saw in Lecture 5, shipbuilders also needed it in large quantities.

  - Britain was so severely deforested by the early 1700s that ironmasters feared their business would soon come to a stop—an irony given that it was poised to take off. But for the moment, the lack of charcoal seemed like an insuperable obstacle.

- Many manufacturers of iron goods imported iron from Russia or Sweden rather than make it from scratch. Import of the metal meant that the price of metal goods was high. Imports remained high throughout most of the 1700s; thus, Britain had both a strategic and a commercial interest in generating more home production.

- The major types of iron were cast iron, which is hard but brittle, and the more costly wrought iron, which is more flexible and malleable. The first stage of the process, drawing the metal out of the ore, produced pig iron. The second stage was forging, or remelting the pigs and beating them to drive out the impurities, especially sulfur and carbon compounds.
  - That made the iron workable for wire drawing, pin and nail making, locks, horseshoes, and much later, for railway tracks and machine tools. Making wrought iron was more labor intensive and required specially trained workers; hence, the end product was more costly.

  - Some iron was also used for the still more difficult steel-making process. Steel contains more carbon than wrought iron but less than cast iron. Steel was used only in fine goods in the 18th century, such as watch and clock springs. Working it was an intricate and small-scale craft, again, ironically, in light of what would happen later.

Abraham Darby I

- An important breakthrough was made in the early 18th century by Abraham Darby I (1678–1717), a Quaker ironmaster and the first in a great dynasty of ironmasters. In 1709, he worked out how to smelt iron by burning coke.

- Coke is coal that has been heated to drive off sulfur and silicon impurities, leaving it nearly pure carbon. In the 1640s, English brewers had experimented with it for beer making because ordinary coal gave an off-taste to the beer. Glassmakers, ceramics makers, and manufacturers of copper and brass all experimented with different types of coal to determine the uses for which they were best suited. Because Britain was well stocked with coalfields, this advance improved the industry's prospects.

- Abraham Darby made cast iron pots and pans, kettles, water pipes, boilers, and metal ovens. He also pioneered making molds out of sand. Darby's cast iron wares sold widely; they were cheaper than wrought iron wares because there was no need for skilled workers to make them. Darby also made a deal to supply parts to John Newcomen, the pioneer of early steam engines, to supply cast iron parts for the engines.

- Darby was already making iron as a capitalist—that is, as a master with a large wage-earning workforce. Like mining and shipbuilding, the iron industry was becoming too capital intensive for an ordinary person to break into.

Use of Coke to Smelt Iron

- The coke method of smelting caught on slowly at first, but it gradually became standard after the 1750s, as charcoal became scarcer and British manufacturers looked for ways to make good-quality iron at home rather than import it.

Coalbrookdale, near the site of the world's first iron bridge, is in a beautiful rural valley that has now been converted into a museum of industrial archaeology.

- There were even discussions in the 1730s and 1740s about exporting the first stage of the process to the American colonies, where the wood and charcoal supply was thought to be endless, then concentrating on forge work in Britain. The success of the coke process made that unnecessary, however.

- Britain's constant wars against France throughout the 18th century created a steady demand for metal weapons. In fact, most improvements in ironworking technology were in response to military demand.

- In 1779, Abraham Darby III, grandson of the coke innovator, built the world's first bridge of iron, a high single span over the Severn River. Coalbrookdale, where Darby worked, was also the scene of a famous painting, *Coalbrookdale by Night*, by Philip James de Loutherbourg. It shows a blast furnace at work, with great leaping flames of red and yellow lighting up the district and casting lurid shadows over the people and horses toiling in the foreground. It is a dramatic image of the power and vitality of industrialization.

- Once the coke process became standard in the late 18th century, the iron industry migrated away from remote country valleys, where it had sought out woods and water power, onto the coalfields. An area near Birmingham became known as the "Black Country" because it was home to so many dirty, smoky metal workshops.

Cort's Puddling Process

- The industry was still bedeviled by the problem of impurities that made much of the coke-produced iron unsuitable for wrought iron work. Henry Cort's *puddling* process, patented in 1783, helped solve that problem.

- Puddling was the process of stirring and agitating molten iron, releasing more of the sulfur and carbon impurities. Puddling was done in what was called a *reverberatory furnace*, in which the iron did not come into contact with the fuel of the fire but was melted by extremely hot air passing over and around it.

- In Cort's process, the iron was brought out of the furnace, hammered, and then shaped into bars or rods by passing it through rollers, which also removed more of the impurities. It enabled forges to increase weekly output by several hundred percent in comparison to traditional methods.

- Cort was a contractor to the Royal Navy, looking for a way to displace reliance on Swedish iron imports by making high-quality iron locally at competitive prices. Unfortunately, he profited little from his vital discovery because his partner had embezzled money from the Royal Navy. Cort's patents were seized, forcing Cort into bankruptcy.

- Even so, the importance of the method was recognized at the time. In fact, Lord Sheffield said that Cort's method, along with James Watt's steam engine, were two technologies that more than compensated for Britain's loss of America in the Revolutionary War.

- Cort's puddling method caught on quickly. The Royal Navy used the less-brittle wrought iron for anchors, metal fittings for decks and rigging, and barrel hoops. After 1791, it would offer contracts only to iron makers who used Cort's puddling process.

"Iron-Mad" Wilkinson

- Another central figure in the ironworking industry was John "Iron-Mad" Wilkinson, who regarded iron as a miracle product. He made the first metal boat, understanding Archimedes's principle that it would float so long as the volume of water displaced weighed more than the combined weight of the boat's metal hull and the air it contained. Skeptics believed it would sink; Wilkinson proved otherwise.

- Wilkinson patented a method of boring extremely accurate cannons for the army. James Watt hired him to make cylinders of the same accuracy for his greatly improved steam engines. Watt's steam engines were a huge stimulus to the industry after 1775. They replaced water power as a source for blowing high-pressure air into blast furnaces.

- Wilkinson made and was, in the end, buried in an iron coffin. As he and others learned how to make iron in volume, it became available for even more uses—for example, as a substitute for wood in industrial machines, for precision instruments and machine tools, and later, for bridges and railroad tracks.

Rapid Increases in Production

- Iron manufacturing caught on rapidly in the late 18th century, supplying a growing number of other industries. The quality kept rising and the price kept falling—one of the recurrent features of industrial capitalism. By the 19th century, iron was the obvious material for such vital innovations as railway locomotives and metal ships (which could be made far larger than traditional wooden ones).

- Again, statistics tell the story. In 1700, Britain produced 12,000 tons of iron; in 1750, 18,000 tons (a modest gain despite early innovations); in 1790, 90,000 tons; and in 1820, 400,000 tons.

- The iron industry continued to expand throughout the 19th century and was given an immense boost by the invention of railways. It also came to be the standard structural material for a wide variety of machines and tools.

Suggested Reading

Ashton, *Iron and Steel in the Industrial Revolution.*

Evans and Ryden, eds., *The Industrial Revolution in Iron.*

Harris, *The British Iron Industry, 1700–1850.*

Hyde, *Technological Change in the British Iron Industry, 1700–1870.*

Questions to Consider

1. Why was the switch from charcoal to coke so vital to the development of British iron making in the 18th century?

2. What characteristics of iron made it the basic raw material of so many other industries?

Iron—Coking and Puddling
Lecture 8—Transcript

We are surrounded by metal objects today, and we use them all the time. It's difficult to remember that throughout most of world history, metals were very scarce and expensive. Until the late 18th century, iron was confined mainly to horseshoes, nails, knives, weapons, and a few cooking pots. The availability of cheap ferrous metals, iron and steel, was one of the necessary conditions for the Industrial Revolution. It's much more durable than wood. Industrial machines that would've been vibrated or pounded to pieces after a year's work if made of wood could be made of iron and last for decades. Like mining, the iron industry is one that has origins stretching far back before 1750, and its transformation took place in gradual stages.

The first signs we have of iron making come from around 1500 B.C.E. in the Middle East. To have metal objects of any kind in the ancient world was a sign of wealth and status; bronze and gold because of their appearance, iron because of its hardness. In the Biblical book of Judges, describing events from around the year 1000 B.C.E., God gives the Promised Land to the Children of Israel, Canaan, but they have to fight the peoples who already live there. Here's a fascinating quotation from the book of Judges: "The Lord was with Judah, and he took possession of the hill country, but he could not drive out the inhabitants of the plain, because they had chariots of iron." That implies that iron weapons are too much, even for God and his chosen people.

Similarly, in the first book of Samuel, there's a passage about the fact that there were no blacksmiths in Israel, because the Philistines kept a monopoly on ironwork. The most famous of the Philistines was Goliath, and here's the long biblical description of Goliath was like immediately before he encountered David with the sling: "He had a helmet of bronze on his head, and he was armed with a coat of mail, and the weight of the coat was 5,000 shekels of bronze. The shaft of his spear was like a weaver's beam, and his spear's head weighed 600 shekels of iron."

The first evidence we have of ironworking in Britain comes from about 500 B.C.E. Making iron requires crushed iron ore, limestone, which acts as a catalyst of the reaction, and a fuel that burns hot enough to melt the iron out of the rock at about 1,400 degrees Celsius, which is 2,550 degrees Fahrenheit. A blast furnace is the place where this process happens. Early ones in England consisted of tower about 20 feet high. Fuel, iron ore, and limestone were fed in at the top, and the fire was made hotter by high-pressure air being blown in from below. Early blast furnaces in England, not surprisingly, were usually sited near to ironstone mines, what we call iron ore, beside fast-flowing streams so that a waterwheel could power the bellows to supply the vital air stream that increases the temperature of the fire. Often there would be a dam built upstream to ensure a continuous flow of water down to the wheel itself. The earliest ones we know about are in the Weald of Sussex in southeastern England, casting shot and cannon balls for the king.

Once a blast furnace was in operation, it would be kept going in a continuous "campaign"—that was the word for it, the same as a military campaign—sometimes for a year or more. What happens at the bottom of a blast furnace is that liquid iron flows out and to a long trough that's called the sow, and then it flows into molds that are placed at right angles to it that are called "pigs," because it looks like baby pigs feeding from their mother, hence our use of the word "pig iron"; that's where it comes from.

The standard fuel for the blast furnaces was charcoal. It required a lot of woodland—about 10 acres of forest, in fact—to produce one ton of iron in the 1500s and 1600s. The heavy population of Britain over the centuries meant that the wood was being used more far more quickly than it could regrow. Wood was the main material for building houses, for barns, for fences, and the main source of fuel in areas away from coalmining districts. As we saw in Lecture 5, the shipbuilders also needed it in very large quantities. Britain was so severely deforested by the early 1700s that ironmasters feared that their business was going to have to come to a stop, ironic in light of what happened next; it was just about to take off. But for the moment, the lack of charcoal seemed like an insuperable obstacle.

Many manufacturers of iron goods imported iron from Russia or Sweden rather than make it from scratch. The import of the metal meant that the price of metal goods was high. The Royal Navy insisted on high-quality

Swedish bar iron for its anchors; as I mentioned before, the biggest metal objects that were then being made. Imports from the Baltic remained high through most of 1700s, so Britain had a strategic as well as a commercial interest in generating more home production. Charcoal is friable; it breaks up. It couldn't be transported far without breaking up into useless fragments or powder. Its brittleness also restricted the size of blast furnaces, because the sheer weight of the ore, which was also being introduced, would crush it and prevent the burning from taking place properly.

The major types of iron were cast iron, which is hard but brittle, and the more costly wrought iron, which is more flexible and malleable; it can be beaten into shapes and it can be drawn out. The first stage of the process, taking the metal out of the ore, produces pig iron. The second stage was forging: re-melting the pigs and then beating them to drive out the impurities, particularly of sulfur and carbon compounds. That made it workable for wire drawing—it becomes very, very ductile—pin and nail making, locksmithing, horseshoes, and much later for railway track and machine tools. But wrought iron is more labor intensive, and it needs specially trained workmen— blacksmiths and others—hence, it's more costly. Some iron was also used for the still-more-difficult steel making process. Steel contains more carbon than wrought iron, but less than cast. Steel was confined to fine goods in the 18th century like watch and clock springs. It was an intricate and small-scale craft, again, ironically, in light of what was going to happen later.

A very important breakthrough was made in the early 18th century by a man named Abraham Darby I. He lived from 1678–1717. He was a Quaker iron-founder, the first in a great dynasty of ironmasters. He worked out how to smelt iron by burning coke in Coalbrookdale in Shropshire in the year 1709. This is the valley of the River Severn, which flows south near the Welsh border and reaches the sea at Bristol.

Coke is coal that's been heated to drive off the sulfur and silicon impurities, leaving it more nearly as pure carbon. In the 1640s, English beer makers, the brewers, had experimented with it because ordinary coal gave a horrible taste to the beer. Abraham Darby probably learned about its possibilities from the brewers or from copper makers because he began his life as a metalworker in the copper wire industry. Glassmakers, ceramics makers, and non-ferrous metal manufacturers, copper and brass, were all experimenting with coal and getting to know the many different types that could be found from the mines around Britain and the uses to which they were best suited. Britain was very well-stocked with coalfields, as we saw last time, so this advance suddenly improved the industry's prospects. Users were getting to know the many varieties, and Darby was lucky that Coalbrookdale coal—that is, the coal from the place where he worked—was suitable for coking.

In 1741, an account of the variety of types of coal and their usefulness in the iron business was written, and here's part of the author's remarks:

> Our sea coals, or Newcastle coals, or in general all the fossil coals which cake in burning and run into cinders, abound with sulfur and therefore are improper to be used about iron, always making it brittle; but pit coals, Kennel coals, and Scotch coals, which burn to a white ash like wood, and abound in bitumen, may be used in the first fluxing of the iron from the ore, and if the iron prove not so malleable as is required, this property may be given to it by melting the metal a second time with wood.

Abraham Darby made cast iron pots and pans, kettles, water pipes, boilers, and metal ovens. He also pioneered in making molds out of sand. His cast iron wares sold widely, being cheaper than wrought iron wares because there was less need for skilled forgemen to work on them. He also made a deal to supply parts to John Newcomen, the pioneer of the early steam engines. That is, he would supply the cast iron parts for the engines themselves; so there's a link between the iron and coal industries. Abraham Darby was already making iron as a capitalist; that is, as a master with a large wage-earning workforce. Like mining and shipbuilding, iron was becoming too capital intensive for an ordinary workman to break into. Instead, there was a paid workforce of laborers who didn't face the prospect of being able to become ironmasters themselves.

The coke method of smelting caught on very slowly at first, but it gradually became standard after the 1750s, as charcoal continued to become more scarce and as British manufacturers looked for ways to make good-quality iron at home rather than import it from Sweden. There were even discussions in the 1730s and '40s about exporting the first stage of the process to the American colonies, where the wood and charcoal supply was thought to be endless, and then concentrating on the forge work, the more skillful part, back in Britain. But the success of the coke process eventually made that scheme unnecessary. I've mentioned this already, but it bears repeating, because it's something that's so hard for us to grasp: One of the things that had amazed the first generations of British settlers in the New World was the abundance of wood. To them, it looked like wealth growing right out of the ground. In fact, they boasted that in America even a poor man could have a roaring fire. That's a reminder to us of just how scarce wood was becoming.

Britain's constant wars against France through the 18th century created a steady stimulus for metal weapons. Most improvements in this technology were in response to military demand, and then later on they were diverted into more peaceful uses, like the making of plowshares.

In 1779, Abraham Darby III—that is, the grandson of the man who worked out how to use coke in smelting iron—built the world's first bridge of iron, a high single span over the River Severn. It's still there today, and it's still in use for pedestrians. The local people were so proud of it that they renamed the town Ironbridge, and that's how it is still today.

Coalbrookdale, where the Darby ironmasters worked, is a beautiful rural valley, and it's now been converted into a museum of industrial archaeology. It's one of many places that ought to be on the itinerary of every visitor to Britain; just as important in its way as the battlefields and the great medieval castles. I urged you during my lecture on textiles to visit Quarry Bank Mill, and I'm equally enthusiastic about encouraging as many people as possible to visit Coalbrookdale. Coalbrookdale is also the scene of a famous painting, *Coalbrookdale by Night*, painted by Philip James de Loutherburg. This was an artist who was born in Strasbourg on the French and German border, but who settled in England. It shows a blast furnace at work in the valley at night, with great leaping flames of red and yellow lighting up the district and casting lurid shadows over the men and horses that are toiling in the foreground. It's so eloquent about the power and vitality of industrialization that it's been used countless times in textbooks to illustrate the Industrial Revolution. Probably far more people will recognize it than can recognize the artist's name. If I had to single out one image that personified industrialization that would be the one: *Coalbrookdale at Night*.

Once the coke process became standard in the late 18th century, the iron industry migrated away from the remote country valleys like Coalbrookdale, where it had sought out woods and water power, and it moved onto the coal fields. An area of southern Staffordshire near Birmingham became known as the "Black Country" because there were so many dirty, smoky metal workshops there. Here's a description of the district, the Black Country, by a traveler in the early 1800s, Samuel Sidney. He writes:

> In this Black Country, a perpetual twilight reigns during the day, and during the night fires on all sides light up the dark landscape with a fiery glow. The pleasant green of pastures is almost unknown. The streams, in which no fishes swim, are black and unwholesome. The natural dead flat ground is often broken by high hills of cinders and spoil from the mines. The few trees are stunted and blasted. No birds are to be seen, except a few smoky sparrows. And for miles on miles, a black waste spreads around, where furnaces continually smoke, steam engines thud and hiss, and long chains clank, while blind gin horses walk their doleful round. From time to time, you pass a cluster of deserted, roofless cottages of dingiest brick, half swallowed up in sinking pits or inclining to every point of the compass, while the timbers point up like the ribs of a half-decayed corpse. The majority of the natives of this Tartarian region are in full keeping with the scenery—savages, without the grace of savages, coarsely clad in filthy garments, with no change on weekends or Sundays. They converse in a language belarded with fearful and disgusting oaths, which can scarcely be recognized as the same as that of civilized England.

This is the part of England from which my family originates on my father's side.

The iron industry was still bedeviled by the problem of impurities that made much of the coke-produced iron unsuitable for wrought iron work. Henry Cort's puddling process, patented in 1783, helped to solve that problem.

Puddling is the process of stirring and agitating molten iron, releasing more of the sulfur and carbon impurities. Puddling was done in what was called a "reverberatory furnace," in which the iron didn't come into contact with the fuel of the fire but was melted by extremely hot air passing over and around it. Here's a contemporary description of puddling:

> Iron, when melted, spits out in blue sparks the sulphur which is mixed with it. The workman keeps constantly stirring it about, which helps to disengage the sulphurous particles and, when thus disengaged, they burn away in blue sparks. In about an hour after melting, the spitting of these blue sparks begins to abate and the melted metal begins to curdle, and to lose its fusibility just like solder when it begins to set.

Puddling was an exhausting job requiring immense strength from the workmen and stamina, working in burning-hot conditions with rods that eventually became too hot to hold. As the metal becomes purer, it begins to solidify, making the work even harder. This is kind of the strong man's version of churning butter, a job which gradually gets harder as the butter congeals.

In Cort's process, the iron was then brought out of the furnace, hammered, and shaped into bars or rods by passing it through rollers, which also had the effect of removing more of the impurities. It enabled forges to increase their weekly output by several hundred percent by comparison with traditional smithing methods. The rollers are much more effective than simply a blacksmith hammering away at an anvil. Henry Cort himself was a contractor to the Royal Navy, looking for a way to displace Britain's reliance on Swedish iron imports by making high-quality iron locally at competitive prices. His business was at Fontley, near Portsmouth, the big south coast naval dockyard.

But unfortunately for Cort, he profited very little from this vital discovery because his partner had embezzled money from the Navy (not to his knowledge). His patents were seized as the Navy tried to recover its money, forcing Cort himself into bankruptcy. Even so, the importance of the method of puddling was recognized at the time. Lord Sheffield said that

Cort's method, along with James Watt's improved steam engines, were two technologies that more than compensated for Britain's loss of its American colonies in the American Revolutionary War. Lord Sheffield wrote, "It is not too much to say that the result will be more advantageous to Great Britain than the possession of the thirteen colonies, for it will give the complete command of the iron trade to this country, with its vast advantages to navigation."

Sure enough, the method caught on very quickly. The Royal Navy used the less-brittle wrought iron for anchors, for metal fittings of deck and rigging, and for barrel hoops. After 1791, it would offer contracts only to iron makers who used Cort's puddling process. Cort was given the compensation of a modest pension in 1794, but he lived to enjoy it for only six more years.

Another central figure in the business was John Wilkinson, nicknamed "Iron-Mad Wilkinson", who regarded iron as a miracle product and wanted to build many more things from it. There are stories that he'd go home to his wife and say "Great news, darling. I've made some knives and forks and plates from iron." I'm not sure that everyone was so keen as he. One historian of the industry describes him like this:

> His was a dominating, assertive nature, almost titanic in the force of its elemental passions, in its ambitions, its inflated egotism, and its capacity for hatred and revenge. When differences arose, whether with rivals, with customers, or with employees, he was relentless in his bitterness and bland to all consequences.

Wilkinson made the first metal boat. He understood Archimedes's principle that it would float so long as the volume of water displaced weighed more than the combination of the boat's metal hull and the air it contained. Skeptics believed it would sink. Everybody was familiar with the fact that if you take a piece of iron and throw it into the water, it'll sink. But he understood that it's a combination of the air, which is much lighter than the water, and the metal. As long as that, combined, is less than the water, it'll float, and so it proved.

146

Wilkinson is important also because he patented a method of boring extremely accurate cannons for the army. Cannons had been subject to explosion, becoming lethal to the people who were wielding them, and vulnerable also to an imperfect fit. Ideally, you want the cannonball to fit as snugly as possible into the bore of the cannon so that the energy of the exploding charge is maximized in pushing the projectile much further. Wilkinson worked out a very, very good way of doing exactly that.

James Watt hired him to make cylinders of the same kind of accuracy for his greatly improved steam engines, as we're going to see in Lecture 12. Watt's steam engines were themselves a huge stimulus to the iron industry after 1775. They could replace water power as a source for blowing high-pressure air into the blast furnaces. Again, there's an obvious symbiosis between these two developing industries.

Wilkinson made, and was at last buried in, an iron coffin. As he and others learned how to make iron in volume, it became available for ever more uses; for example, as a substitute for wood in industrial machines, for precision instruments, machine tools (the subject of Lecture 13 in this course), and later on for bridges and for railroad track. It was much better than wood because it was so much more durable.

The ironmasters themselves were tough, humorless individuals. Thomas Ashton, the historian of the industry, writes this:

> The austerity of the ironmasters affected every side of their lives. Successful themselves, they were intolerant of what might appear weakness or inefficiency in others. And though their charities were numerous, there was little of the milk of human kindness in their constitutions. At that time, more than any other, industrial leadership demanded men of an autocratic mould; and, individualists as they were both by nature and circumstance, they resented any attempt on the part of the workers to determine, in any measure, the conditions of their working life.

So to work for one of these ironmasters was to subject yourself to an autocratic boss.

Iron manufacturing caught on rapidly in the late 18th century, supplying a growing variety of other industries. The quality kept rising and the price kept falling, one of the recurrent features of industrial capitalism. By the 19th century, it was the obvious material for such vital innovations as railway locomotives and metal ships, which, as we'll see, could be made far larger than the traditional wooden ones. Here are some statistics on British iron production: 12,000 tons in 1700; 18,000 tons in 1750, a modest gain despite early on innovations like coking; but then, 90,000 tons in 1790; and 400,000 tons in 1820. The industry continued to expand throughout the 19th century, given an immense boost, as we'll see later, by the invention of railways. Iron came to be the standard structural material for a wide variety of machines and tools, too.

From iron, we're going to move on in the next lecture to pottery. Pottery making, like iron founding, was an ancient art, but in the late 18th century, a group of pioneers, led by Josiah Wedgwood, abandoned the traditional English method of making pottery, put it on a scientific footing, and greatly expanded the accuracy, variety, and scale of manufacture. Wedgwood, whose products are still available today and still highly valued, also exploited many new avenues of marketing, which was sometimes as important to the spread of industrialization as changes in manufacturing technique.

Wedgwood and the Pottery Business
Lecture 9

I n the late 18th century, a group of pioneers, led by Josiah Wedgwood, abandoned the traditional English method of making pottery, put it on a scientific footing, and greatly expanded the accuracy, variety, and scale of manufacture. Wedgwood, whose products are still available and highly valued today, also exploited many new avenues of marketing, which was sometimes as important to the spread of industrialization as improvements in manufacturing techniques.

Josiah Wedgwood

- Wedgwood pottery is among the most famous in the world. Josiah Wedgwood (1730–1795), the man who turned his family's traditional cottage industry into an immense, lucrative, and up-to-date manufacturing concern, was a contemporary of Arkwright and Abraham Darby III.

- Wedgwood accomplished for pottery what Arkwright did for textiles and Darby did for iron making: He expanded the scale of manufacture, perfected techniques, rationalized the business, and found innovative ways to improve quality while cutting costs.

- He also befriended many of the leading business innovators, intellectuals, and scientists of his era, including Matthew Boulton, business partner of James Watt, and Joseph Priestley, the man who first isolated oxygen. He was the grandfather of Charles Darwin.

- Wedgwood was the son, grandson, and great-grandson of potters and was born in an area still called "The Potteries."
  - The area was close to a coalfield for fuel, was close to Derbyshire for lead glazes, and was well supplied with clay. Around 1700, it was discovered that ground-up flint made the area's reddish clay whiter.

- - However, the area was plagued by poor communications because it was not on any of the navigable rivers. It was very difficult to bring in supplies or ship out finished goods. The roads were poor, and transport depended on heavy wagons and packhorses.

- Wedgwood received a basic education and was then apprenticed to his brother. An attack of smallpox in 1747 nearly killed him. Because of his illness, he suffered for years in his right knee and ultimately had his leg amputated in 1768. He became an expert workman, especially in delicate branches, such as spouts and jug handles, because he could not use the treadle of the potter's wheel. He went into business on his own in 1759.

- A profitable element of the business was repairing high-quality china that was chipped, cracked, or smashed. Wedgwood studied Chinese designs, as well as Meissen from Germany and Sèvres from France. Grateful customers spread word of his skill, including local gentry, whose patronage he sought. An early patron was Sir William Meredith, Member of Parliament from Liverpool.

- Wedgwood's company had a great breakthrough in 1765, when it received an order from King George III's wife, Queen Charlotte, for a creamware set. Creamware is a cream-colored pottery, stronger than Chinese porcelain but still pale and delicate. Wedgwood appealed to the queen successfully for permission to rename the style "queensware," and it became a key part of his marketing efforts.

- Wedgwood's letterhead and bills now carried the header "Josiah Wedgwood, Potter to Her Majesty." This is what is known in Britain as a "royal warrant"—a superb marketing point in a monarchy.

Systems and Innovation
- Potters in Wedgwood's era found it difficult to make two batches of pottery quite the same. Color or glaze quality varied, and many pots were still lost in kiln firing.

- Wedgwood carried out systematic experiments with clay, glazes, colors, and kiln temperatures, keeping meticulous notebooks that were written in code to discourage industrial espionage. He was more interested in the science of his materials than most of his contemporaries, trying to discover relevant principles in application of glazes, behavior of clay, and firing techniques.

Wedgwood was the most innovative and enterprising of the pottery entrepreneurs; his rivals included John Turner and Josiah Spode.

- He invented a high-temperature thermometer for kilns to eliminate as much guesswork as possible. In addition, he created a stronger and more consistent creamware, duplicating color and thickness in repeated batches. Willing to innovate, Wedgwood adapted a lathe originally designed for woodworking to the process of finishing and decorating pottery.

Wedgwood Factories

- The Wedgwood factory was characterized by a strict division of labor, with different people doing mixing, firing, painting, and glazing. Wedgwood abandoned the traditional system consisting of the apprentice, journeyman, and master and substituted intense specialization.

- Wedgwood studied bottlenecks in production and tried to establish rates of work in each operation so that materials flowed evenly through the factory from start to finish. He battled constantly against traditional laborers, who were not used to factory hours and systems. Wedgwood also recognized the advantage of taking on children to learn his new methods, as opposed to converting older workers already set in their ways.

- In 1769, Wedgwood founded a factory and workers' model village at Etruria. Etruria was named after Etruscan ware, one of the styles of pottery that made Wedgwood famous. This was the era of the excavation of Herculaneum; Wedgwood had the early books translated and sought images of the excavated pottery to copy.

- A distinguished-looking factory, with a cupola and Georgian façade, Etruria became the standard model of pottery factories for more than a century. Every room had a different function. Each room even had a separate entrance in order to segregate workers at each stage of the process, so that no one would learn all the processes and carry the secret off to a rival. This was an early example of what historians call the "deskilling" of labor.

- Wedgwood was the first pottery master to buy a James Watt steam engine; he used it to turn potters' wheels at uniform speeds and to grind colors and flint.

- On opening day at Etruria, Wedgwood and his business partner, Thomas Bentley, made six vases in the Etruscan style. On them were painted classical figures and the legend: "One of the first day's productions at Etruria in Staffordshire by Wedgwood and Bentley." Also on the vases was the Latin phrase *Artes Etruriae Renascunter* ("the Etruscan arts are reborn").

- Wedgwood biographer Robin Reilly noted: "It was not only the products of the Etruria factory that were innovative; the layout of the factory and the management techniques employed there were exceptionally advanced … From 1772, it was Wedgwood's policy to mark everything made at Etruria. He was the first earthenware potter consistently to mark his goods and the first ever to use his own name, which was impressed in the clay."

- Wedgwood's only patent was in 1769, for a method of imitating Greek vases. These were made of red clay covered in a black glaze and then carved through the black. Knowing that patents were hard to enforce and could often enrich lawyers more than patent holders, when Wedgwood invented *jasperware* (the characteristic blue and green matte-finish pottery with white decoration), he relied on secrecy rather than patenting.

A Marketing Pioneer

- A marketing pioneer, Wedgwood opened a London showroom in Soho, designed to draw in wealthy customers. He offered a wide inventory, frequent novelties, and free delivery. He issued his first catalog in 1773 to enable customers to see and order the full range of his offerings.

- Winning a large order from Catherine the Great of Russia was another coup. In 1773, she ordered a 952-piece tea set of creamware, all with the same frog motif but each with a different landscape painted on it.

- Filling the order required an immense effort for more than a year, including hiring first-class landscape painters. The price was £3000 (more than £1 million today), and Wedgwood was terrified that Catherine might die before it was delivered and he wouldn't be paid. She did pay, however, and he put the whole thing on display in London before sending it off to Russia—a marketing sensation.

Investment in Better Transport

- As the Wedgwood pottery business expanded, effective communications with Liverpool and London became essential. Getting clay for queensware was quite difficult; the clay was quarried in Cornwall, brought by ship to Liverpool, carried by boat up the Mersey and Weaver rivers, and put on a wagon. Wedgwood joined schemes for building an improved turnpike road.

- Understanding the importance of canals for bulk transport, Wedgwood also became an investor in the Trent and Mersey

Canal, which linked Liverpool and Manchester with the Midlands. He supported it, bought shares, urged family members and other pottery owners to invest, and became its unpaid treasurer.

- The canal, which opened in 1771, went right past the front of the Etruria factory—resulting in vastly improved communications and a reduction in transport costs.

A Distinguished Intellectual and Scientist

- Wedgwood was a member of the Lunar Society, a group of distinguished businessmen and intellectuals who met regularly to exchange ideas. They sometimes called themselves "the lunarticks" but were, in fact, the opposite: enlightened, empirical, sensible, and dedicated to the idea of human improvement in every way.

- Members of the Lunar Society were strongly sympathetic to the American cause in the Revolution, and many were antislavery advocates, as well. Wedgwood had deplored British tax policy for many years and anticipated a political rift. But he was discreet, knowing that he could not afford to offend his customers, and would share his real views only with close friends and Lunar Society associates.

- In 1783, Wedgwood presented papers to the Royal Society on his "pyrometer" and on the scientific analysis of different clay samples. The scientific exactitude he practiced soon caught on when it became clear that it enabled the manufacture of a more dependable, durable product and one that could be turned out reliably on a large scale.

Suggested Reading

Burton, *Josiah Wedgwood: A Biography*.

Dolan, *Wedgwood: The First Tycoon*.

McKendrick, Brewer, and Plumb, *The Birth of a Consumer Society*.

Mokyr, *The Enlightened Economy*.

1. Why was marketing as important as production for Wedgwood?

2. What challenges did Wedgwood face in his factories, and how well did he address them?

Wedgwood and the Pottery Business
Lecture 9—Transcript

Wedgwood pottery is among the most famous in the world. Josiah Wedgwood, the man who turned his family's traditional cottage industry into an immense, lucrative, and up-to-date manufacturing concern, was a contemporary of Arkwright and Abraham Darby III. He was born in 1730 and died in 1795. He did for pottery what they did for textiles and iron making, expanding the scale of manufacture, perfecting techniques, rationalizing the business, and finding ways to improve quality while cutting costs. He also befriended many of the leading business innovators, intellectuals, and scientists of his era, including Matthew Boulton, the business partner of James Watt, and Joseph Priestley, the man who first isolated oxygen. One of his daughters was the mother of Charles Darwin.

Josiah Wedgwood was born in Burslem in Staffordshire 1730. He was the son, grandson, and great grandson of potters, a network of intermarried families in the business, mainly on a very small scale. This area of the country is still today called "the potteries." It's close to a coal field for fuel. It's close to Derbyshire, which provides lead mining for the glazes, and it's well supplied with clay. But it's plagued, or was plagued, by poor communications, not being on any of the navigable rivers. Heavy, slow wagons on miry tracks brought goods in and carried them out. There were no good roads. Or else, they were forced to depend simply on packhorses. It was difficult to bring things in, difficult to ship out finished goods.

We've known about pottery from the very first human sites that we've encountered. It's developed extremely gradually in many, many parts of the world, including in England, where it had a kind of glacially low advance over the centuries. Around 1700, shortly before the birth of Wedgwood, there was the discovery that ground up flint, powdered flint, would make the area's reddish clay whiter. Early in the 18th century, the introduction from Holland of the salt glazing process transformed the glazing techniques used in Staffordshire, creating a harder and a more even glaze. The way it works is that when the pots have been made on wheels and then have been finished by specialists, they're placed inside "saggars," which are fireproof containers. Then they're placed in the kiln, usually a great bottle-shaped kiln, and then with this new technique from Holland, salt would be poured into the top of the kiln and because its temperature was so great, the salt would vaporize. Here's a traveler's description of what it looked like when they were doing salt glazing. He wrote:

> The vast volume of smoke and vapor from the ovens, entering the atmosphere, produced that dense white cloud, which from about eight o'clock till twelve on the Saturday morning so completely enveloped the whole of the interior of the town as to cause persons often to run against each other; travelers, to mistake the road, and strangers have mentioned it as extremely disagreeable, and not unlike the smoke of Etna and Vesuvius [so a volcanic cloud of smoke from salt glazing].

Wedgwood himself had a basic education, he was literate, and then he was apprenticed to his brother. We still have his apprenticeship contract, and it says things like this: "At cards, dice or any other unlawful games, he shall not play. Taverns or alehouses he shall not haunt or frequent. Fornication he shall not commit. Matrimony he shall not contract," and so on; a great mass of negative phrases describing all the things that, as a teenage boy, he's not going to be allowed to do.

He suffered an attack of smallpox in the year 1747 when he was 17 years old, and it very nearly killed him. It afflicted his right knee very badly. Ultimately, this led to his leg being amputated in 1768. In those days, amputations were often done at home and without anesthetics except, perhaps, for a few drops of laudanum, which is a poppy derivative, like heroin. He simply sat in a chair while the doctor hacked through the bone as quickly as possible. To be a good surgeon in those days principally meant doing it as fast as possible, and a good surgeon could cut through a man's leg in two minutes. The shock and trauma must've been terrible, but he was able to survive it.

Wedgwood became an expert workman, especially working in the delicate branches of the craft, such as spouts and jug handles. This is called "stouking," the finishing work, because his bad leg meant that he couldn't use the treadle of a potter's wheel in the way that most of his contemporaries would.

After learning the trade and showing a great talent for it, he went into business on his own in the year 1759, when he was 29. One profitable element of the pottery business was repairing high-quality china that was chipped, cracked, or smashed. This gave him the opportunity to study Chinese designs, and also Meissen china from Germany and Sevres from France, two of the great styles of his era. Wedgwood taught himself how to make replacements if one cup or plate in a set had been broken, and he could often do it to almost the same standard as the originals. Grateful customers spread the word of his skill, including the local gentry—the kinds of people who were likely to own pottery of this kind—and these were the people whose patronage he always sought. He was always looking up in society, understanding that to get the patronage of high-class people would be valuable to the future of his business.

In his business correspondence, he adopts a very, very servile tone, almost groveling. Listen, for example, to a section of a letter he wrote to the Member of Parliament for Liverpool, Sir William Meredith, who was an early patron; he repaired some of Meredith's china. Wedgwood writes to him:

> You have heaped your favors on me so abundantly that though my heart is overflowing with sentiments of gratitude and thankfulness, I am at a loss where to begin my acknowledgements. I should be utterly unworthy of your further notice if I did not double my diligence in prosecuting any plan you are so kind as to lay out for me.

That's laying it on pretty thick, but presumably the aristocrats and gentlemen enjoyed being flattered by the tradesman to whom they gave patronage.

The great breakthrough in his career came in 1765, when he was in his mid-30s. He received an order from King George III's wife, Queen Charlotte, for a creamware set. Creamware is cream-colored pottery, stronger than china, but still very pale and delicate; the kind that might appeal to royalty. After completing the contract, he appealed to her successfully for permission to rename this style "Queensware," and then it became a key part of his marketing. His letterhead and his bills now carried the header "Josiah Wedgwood, potter to Her Majesty." This is what's known in Britain as the "royal warrant," and it's a system that persists right up to the present.

Once the king or queen has specifically ordered a product, the manufacturer is allowed to write "By order of His Majesty the King," or "By order of Her Majesty the Queen," which is, of course, a terrific marketing point in a hierarchical society whose apex is the monarch.

One of the things that potters found it very difficult to do in Wedgwood's era was to make two batches of pottery quite the same. In little ways, they always tended to vary; the color was a bit different, or the glaze quality, or the thickness. It remained true in the mid-1700s that many, many pots were lost in firing in the kiln. Of course, this remains true for amateur potters right up to the present. You make the pot on the wheel, decorate it, prepare it; it looks beautiful. But then when it comes out of the kiln after firing, it's cracked and broken. Wedgwood was very familiar with this and was looking for ways to prevent it from happening. He wanted to abandon the traditional ad hoc methods that had been used time out of mind, and he began to make systematic experiments with the clay, with the glazes, with the colors, and with the kiln temperatures, four of the variables he could control. He kept very, very meticulous notebooks with each batch that he fired. He kept his notebooks in code because he was afraid of industrial espionage. Wedgwood was more interested in the science of his materials than most of his contemporaries, and he was trying to discover the relevant scientific principles. In other words, why exactly does the glaze operate the way that it does? What happens to the clay while it's being fired?

Among his innovations was the invention of a high-temperature thermometer for the kilns, to take away as much guesswork as possible. Until then, the tradition had been simply that you'd stoke up the fire in the bottle kiln and let it run for a certain amount of time without quite knowing how hot it was. But Wedgwood wanted to know, and he worked out what was called a pyrometer, a very, very high-temperature thermometer, which could tell him what was going on. Because of these various experiments and his tinkering, he was able to create a stronger and more consistent creamware in which he could duplicate the color and the thickness in repeated batches, so that if a customer was to say "Could you make me some just like the type you made for this other customer?" he was able to say "Yes, I can," and could then do it.

He was willing to innovate and to try new methods, and in this sense he's very much like his other industrial pioneering contemporaries. In 1763, he bought a lathe. Lathes were designed originally for woodworking, but they were also adaptable to finishing and decorating pottery. Also like many of his contemporaries, he had to struggle continually with a recalcitrant workforce. Wedgwood was zealous for punctuality, for smart clothing, for detailed record keeping, for cleanliness, and for quality control. Rather than sell imperfect pots cheap, he'd smash them. He was a hands-on manager who would constantly prowl the workplace and chalk indignant messages on the workbenches of poor laborers. He'd write, "This will not do for Josiah Wedgwood." He aimed to make the workmen fear him and to fear dismissal if they crossed him. He's a lovely paradoxical figure: in some ways a very enlightened man, but certainly an autocrat inside the workplace.

In the pottery business, he pioneered the intensive division of labor: the mixing, the firing, the painting, and the glazing. Each job was to be specialized among a different group of men. In his works, he got rid of the old apprentice/journeyman/master system and substituted intense, repetitive specialization in the hope that each workman would become extremely proficient in one particular job without knowing all the mysteries of the craft. He studied the bottlenecks in production and tried to establish rates of work in each operation so that materials could flow evenly through the factory from start to finish, and so that he got exactly the right number of people doing each operation to make the through-flow as smooth as possible. Again, like his contemporaries, he had to fight constantly against the profound conservatism of traditional laborers who weren't used to factory hours, who wanted to celebrate Saint Monday, who expected to be able to drink at work, and who didn't understand Wedgwood's constant shifts to new styles as he tried to follow the fashions.

When his workers realized that they were making goods that sold at a high price, they demanded higher wages. Wedgwood's correspondence is peppered with his struggles to keep wages down and to keep the workmen coming in. He described one of his best workers, a modeler named John Voyez, as "vicious, fickle, and lazy," but he added that: "To live in this world, as matters and things are constituted, it is sometimes necessary to make a truce with these sensations whilst we manage a rascal that the evil stars have thrown in our way, to prevent repeated injuries he might otherwise do us." In other words, he was aware that Voyez might go into competition against him if he was fired, and that Voyez understood this perfectly and therefore abused his boss's hospitality. But eventually, the two broke up, and sure enough Voyez did go off to work with the competition.

Wedgwood also recognized the advantage of taking on children to learn his new methods as opposed to trying to convert older workers who were already set in their ways. In this sense, he's a little bit like St. Ignatius Loyola, who understood that if you get a child early, you can shape its mind and you'll have its loyalty always, whereas with older people who've learned other methods it's very, very difficult. In a letter to his business partner Thomas Bentley, they were struggling to find suitable painters to paint onto the finished pottery and finding it difficult to get suitable people. He writes to his partner:

We have stepped forward beyond the other manufacturers, and we must be content to train up hands to suit our purposes. You must be content to train up such painters as offer to you and not turn them adrift because they cannot immediately form their hands to our new style, which, if we consider what they have been doing all this while, we ought not to expect from them.

In other words, we've got to be at least a little bit considerate, bearing in mind the fact that these people have never previously done work of this kind.

This partner, Thomas Bentley, was a Liverpool merchant, an early advocate of antislavery movement, and when Benjamin Franklin from America came to visit England, his host when Franklin visited Liverpool. All of them were nonconformists; that is, members of churches other than the Church of England. They didn't conform to the Church of England. This is a point I made in the very first lecture, and it certainly is borne out when you look at the pottery business. Wedgwood himself was a Unitarian. He didn't believe in original sin, he didn't believe in the doctrine of the Trinity, and he emphasized the rational side of Jesus's teaching rather than the dogmatic or supernatural elements of Christianity. If he was rational in his religion, he was also rational in his personal life. He made a very shrewd marriage to one of his own distant cousins, Sarah Wedgwood, and she brought a big dowry to the wedding that enabled him to expand the scale of his works. His factory could get bigger with the capital that she brought to him.

He founded a factory and a workers' model village at Etruria in 1769, and it was named after the Etruscan-style ware, one of the styles that's actually made him famous. This was the era of the excavation of Herculaneum in Pompeii. The town was near Naples, which in the late Roman Empire had been buried by the explosion of the great volcano Vesuvius. As they were excavated in the 1760s and '70s, it led to a revolution in style as people became fascinated by the way of life that the Romans had lived. Some of the actual pots that they'd used had been preserved, and so a style developed in Europe to imitate them. Wedgwood himself was fascinated by all this. He got the early books about Herculaneum translated into English, he sought pictures of the excavated pottery, and he began to copy it.

The factory he built at Etruria was distinguished looking. It had a cupola and a Georgian façade. It looked like a gentleman's home, and it became the standard look of pottery factories for more than a century after that. Inside the Etruria factory, every room had a different function. Wedgwood gave each one a separate entrance, so as to keep the workers at each stage of the process as separate from each other as possible from fear that anyone who learned all the processes would carry the secret off to a rival. You can tell from this practice and from his keeping his notebooks in code that he wasn't paranoid but certainly very aware of the fact that if he wasn't careful, the advances he was making were going to be copied by others and that would make his business correspondingly less profitable. He was involved in an early example of what historians call the "deskilling" of labor. He didn't want his laborers to understand the whole process of which they were doing just one little part; he wanted to be himself the sole possessor of all the relevant knowledge.

The factory itself survived right into the 20th century, but gradually it subsided because it was built over a warren of coal mines, so eventually it sank slowly down into the ground. Having been built beside the canal, it eventually sank below canal level, and the canal banks themselves had to be shored up in order to prevent flooding.

Wedgwood, characteristically, was the first pottery master to buy a James Watt steam engine. This is something he did in 1782. He used it to turn the potters' wheels at uniform speeds; to grind colors and flint, both previously very dangerous jobs because they generated toxic dust, which had led to a characteristic ailment called "potter's rot".

On the opening day of the Etruria factory, he and Bentley, standing prominently on a wooden platform, made six vases in the Etruscan style to an interested gathering of local people. Some of these vases made on the very first day still survive. On them were painted Classical figures and the legend: "One of the first day's productions at Etruria in Staffordshire by Wedgwood and Bentley," and also the Latin phrase "Artes Etruriae Renascunter," "the Etruscan arts are reborn." One of his biographers, Robin Reilly, writes this:

> It was not only the products of the Etruria factory that were innovative. The layout of the factory and the management techniques employed there were exceptionally advanced. The finished estate included an elegant house, Etruria Hall, for the Wedgwood family and housing for many of the workers. Wedgwood insisted on strict factory discipline, but he subsidized an early form of sick-benefit scheme, and conditions for work at Etruria compared favorably with those to be found anywhere in Europe. From 1772, it was Wedgwood's policy to mark everything made at Etruria. He was the first earthenware potter consistently to mark his goods, and the first ever to use his own name, which was impressed in the clay.

Wedgwood makes a very interesting contrast with one of his principal contemporaries. The textile innovator Arkwright was a Philistine with no interest at all in culture. Arkwright was content simply to make cotton thread in huge quantities. Wedgwood, by contrast, was extremely preoccupied by questions of taste and aesthetics. He understood the importance of catering to changing ideals. He had to hire artists, get art and archaeology books translated into English, keep up with new painting techniques, and follow the London fashions as closely as possible.

His only patent was taken out in 1769 for a method of imitating Greek vases. They were red clay covered in a black glaze, but then carved through the black to create a red picture. Wedgwood's method, by contrast, was to paint the red on top of the black glaze, but the facsimile was very effective and it caught on in London and could be very sold to very high prices to members of the upper classes.

One of the reasons that Wedgwood didn't bother much with patents was that he knew how hard they were to enforce, and that very often they could enrich lawyers more than patent holders. The whole early history of industrialization is the history of patents being violated. This is one of the reasons why he favored secretiveness over patenting. He found it to be a more effective method. When Wedgwood invented what he called "jasperware"—this is one of the characteristic Wedgwood styles that's still marketed right up to the present, a characteristic blue or green matte-finish pottery with a white decoration superimposed on it in bar relief—he relied on secrecy rather than patenting to stay ahead of his rivals.

He was also a pioneer in marketing. He opened a London showroom in Soho, designed to draw in rich and leisured customers while deterring casual loiterers. It was itself a splendid place where members of the upper classes would enjoy going to look at the splendid new examples of pottery that were coming from his factory. He offered a wide inventory, frequent novelties, new products constantly coming out, and free delivery. He was even the pioneer of business ideas that have now become extremely familiar, things like "buy one, get one free" or "your money back guaranteed if you're not completely satisfied with this product." In the 1770s, this was all very, very new.

He published the first illustrated catalog of his work in 1773 so that customers could see the full range of his offerings and make orders from it. This, of course, also gave him a better sense of how demand was changing. He even tried direct mail to his regular customers two centuries before it really became commonplace. He was a very, very energetic and innovative marketing figure, and he used a sophisticated accounting system so that he could track very closely what was working and what wasn't and change his inventory accordingly.

He won a large order from Catherine the Great of Russia. This was another great coup, equal to his coup of getting the patronage of the Queen of England. In 1773, Catherine the Great ordered from him a 952-piece tea set of creamware, and she said that on every one of them she wanted the same motif of a green frog but then every single one of them had to be painted with a different landscape. That required an immense effort, and the job took more than a year. Wedgwood was required to hire a whole set of first-class landscape painters to do all the different paintings on each item. The price he charged to Catherine the Great was 3,000 pounds; that's the equivalent of more than a million pounds in today's terms. He was terrified that she might die before it was completed and that then he'd never be paid. But in the end, it all worked out fine. She did pay, and he put the whole thing on display in London before sending it off to Russia, and it caused a great sensation among London's fashionable people and again led to more orders. It was a classic story of Wedgwood's art for marketing, as well as his skill as a manufacturer.

As his business expanded, effective communications with Liverpool to the northwest and London to the southeast of Staffordshire became essential. Getting clay for the Queensware was very awkward. It was quarried in Cornwall in the extreme southwest of England, brought by ship to Liverpool, then by boat up the Mersey and Weaver Rivers, and then laboriously by wagon from Winsford in Cheshire to Etruria itself. He joined in a scheme for building an improved turnpike road. He also understood the importance of canals for bulk transport and watched with great interest the building of the first successful commercial canal, which opened in 1761. That's going to be the theme of my next lecture.

He invested in the Trent and Mersey Canal—a canal that's still there today and on which you can still sail—to link Liverpool and Manchester with the Midlands. The Mersey River flows west into the Irish Sea, and the Trent flows into the Humber and then into the North Sea, so linking the two rivers links the two sides of the country. As the canal dips southwards into the Midlands, it also establishes links with the canals that go all the way to London, so this canal system has immense positive consequences for his business. He boosted the canal. He bought shares in it. He urged family members and other pottery owners to invest, and he became the unpaid treasurer of the company itself. The canal opened in 1771, and it went right past the front of Etruria factory, not by coincidence. He'd bought up the land ahead of time into which it was going to be built with what we'd call insider knowledge of where the canal would pass. That led to a certain amount of acrimony with his rivals because they knew that he'd profited by having the early knowledge of where the canal was going to be built. But it vastly improved communications for him and for everyone else in the business and led to a startling reduction in transport costs.

Wedgwood was also a member of the Lunar Society, a group of distinguished businessmen and intellectuals who met regularly to exchange ideas. Among them were Joseph Priestly, Erasmus Darwin, and William Small, who for a while was a professor at William and Mary in Virginia, and who was the teacher of Thomas Jefferson before going back to Britain from where he'd originally come. They sometimes called themselves "the lunatics," but they were the opposite: enlightened, empirical, sensible, dedicated to the idea of human improvement in every way. They met on the Sunday of the month when the moon was nearest its fullest, to light them there and to light their way back in the days before there was any street lighting. This group of men, the Lunar Society, was strongly sympathetic to the American cause in the Revolutionary War, and many of them were anti-slavery advocates, too. Wedgwood himself made an anti-slavery cameo. It shows a kneeling black figure—in effect, a slave praying for release—on a white background. He gave these away very widely, and they caught on in fashionable society. So for a while, women would wear them around their necks on a chain or as hair pins and so on, advertising the anti-slavery cause. Wedgwood had deplored British tax policy in the foregoing years leading up to the revolution, and he anticipated the political rift. But as a businessman, he was discreet. He knew that he couldn't afford to offend his upper-class customers. Most of them certainly took the British side in the Revolutionary War dispute, so he'd only share his real views with his close friends and his Lunar associates.

In 1783, he was made a Fellow of the Royal Society—the leading scientific society in the kingdom—and he presented papers to the Royal Society on his "pyrometer," the high-temperature thermometer, and on the scientific analysis of different clay samples. I should emphasize that Wedgwood was never alone in these endeavors. He was merely the most innovative and enterprising of the pottery entrepreneurs. Among his rivals were John Turner and Josiah Spode, who imitated many of his methods and contributed to the industrialization of the pottery business. Spode carried on as a major pottery dynasty into the next centuries, as did Wedgwood. The scientific exactitude he practiced soon caught on when it became clear that it made easier the manufacture of a more dependable, durable product, and one that could be turned out reliably on a large scale.

By the time of his death in 1795, the "five towns" were the center of British pottery making, with thousands of the distinctive bottle-shaped kilns and a sooty sulphurous atmosphere from the constant firing. Characteristically for Britain, the five towns consist of six places; now they're all clustered together as Stoke on Trent. They are: Tunstall, Burslem, Hanley, Stoke, Fenton, and Longton.

Arnold Bennett made the area famous in his early 20th century novels, particularly *The Old Wives' Tale*, with convincing, three-dimensional working-class characters. Arnold Bennett was part of a generation of writers, along with H. G. Wells and D. H. Lawrence, to come from working-class backgrounds and to make the lives of working people the substance of genuine literature.

I mentioned earlier in this lecture that Wedgwood invested in the Trent and Mersey Canal. The great surge of canal-building in Britain that took place in the late 18th and early 19th centuries, and that greatly enhanced the country's internal communications, will be the subject of my next lecture.

Building Britain's Canals
Lecture 10

C anals facilitated nearly every aspect of industrialization. Britain's first commercial canal opened in 1761 and at once showed itself superior to all other methods of transport. A horse pulling a floating barge could draw almost 50 times as much weight as it could with a wagon. Canals made it possible to carry bulk solids, such as coal, iron ore, bricks, timber, clay, and grain, over long distances at relatively low cost. Building canals, especially across hilly country, proved an immense technical challenge but inspired some highly innovative technologies. Canals, which accelerated bulk transport across Britain, caught on rapidly between 1770 and the 1830s, when they were eclipsed by the faster and more efficient railways.

Improving River Transport

- Before the Industrial Revolution, roads in Britain were poor, even after the building of turnpikes. Periodic attempts to improve Britain's navigable rivers—the Thames, Severn, Mersey and Weaver, Humber and Trent—had been made for centuries. Strategies to improve the rivers included straightening curves, dredging shallow areas to deepen them, shoring up banks, and building towpaths and locks to make them navigable higher up.

- Because rivers are flowing, they shift their banks over the years, and their currents can make progress upstream difficult for draft horses, whereas canals are still-water environments.

- Sankey Brook in Lancashire was extensively broadened and deepened for coal transport from St. Helens to the Mersey River and began to carry in 1757. However, this consisted mainly of an improvement of a preexisting stream.

Britain's First Canal

- The first wholly artificial canal was projected by the 24-year-old duke of Bridgewater, the owner of coal mines at Worsley, who was looking for a method of economically shipping coal to Manchester.

  o He hired James Brindley (1716–1772) to design and build the canal. Brindley joined up with the duke and his agent, John Gilbert, and together, they confronted the vast array of new problems in making a working canal, often inventing techniques to overcome unforeseen difficulties.

  o Brindley favored the method of contouring to keep earth moving to a minimum. This meant he would take an indirect route to cut down on the number of cuttings through hills and embankments across low places—all work that had to be done by hand and was painstakingly slow. Brindley's method of *clay puddling* was key to making the bed of the canal watertight so that the area did not just become a swamp.

© Photos.com/Thinkstock.

The opening of Britain's first canal was such a success that two passenger boats were built, offering day tours along the canal.

- The single most spectacular feature of the Bridgewater Canal was the Barton Aqueduct, a structure built over the valley of the Irwell River. People flocked to the aqueduct to see the sheer strangeness of boats sailing over a bridge, high above a river. Embankments leading to the aqueduct were equally impressive as engineering feats. Intense lateral pressure exerted by the water above ground level made the banks susceptible to breaking. Brindley foresaw the possibility and worked out a method for isolating sections in the event of a breach so that the entire canal would not drain away.

- Opening of the canal halved the price of coal in Manchester and proved immensely profitable to Bridgewater. He recouped all his expenses in less than 10 years and went on to become enormously wealthy. At Worsley, the canal doubled as mine drainage, and because an ever-growing network of underground canals was built inside the mines, coal could be loaded onto barges almost at the coal face.

- Over the next 15 years, there were 52 acts of Parliament related to canal building. Parliament would authorize routes and eminent domains and specify tolls to be charged at the locks on different items carried.

Trent and Mersey Canal

- Brindley was next commissioned to build the Trent and Mersey Canal. For that, he needed a change in elevation, which meant building locks. Criticisms came from mill owners who feared that they would lose water power, from river navigation companies now facing competition and forced to cut prices, and from gentry who didn't want canals crossing their lands.

- The key to the creation of the canal was the locks. A lock is a pair of gates that can be opened and closed to control changes in water level. The system presupposes a reliable water supply at the high point, because water will not flow uphill.

- As completed, the Trent and Mersey Canal rose through 35 locks and a 3,000-yard tunnel, the Harecastle Tunnel, and four shorter tunnels. The Harecastle Tunnel took 11 years to build and was completed in 1777.

The Canal Scheme

- Canal tunnels were too small for horses, which had to be led over hilltops, while crew members "legged" the boat through the tunnel—that is, they lay on their backs and walked upside down, with the friction of their feet on the walls and their backs on the deck keeping the boat going. Some later tunnels had groups of full-time professional "leggers" waiting in huts at either end.

- The canals were built by workers with picks and shovels. At first, the builders relied on local subcontractors, who hired farm laborers during the off season, but in the 1790s, these were replaced by migratory teams of full-time builders.

- Creating lock bottoms required "clay puddling," or compressing a mixture of clay and sand into place to stop seepage into the surrounding ground. A towpath of ash and cinders for pulling horses was built beside the canal.

"Canal Mania"

- The years 1793 and 1794 were a time of "canal mania," in which 38 acts of Parliament were passed for new canal schemes. It was also a period of exaggerated enthusiasm by investors, as some routes were never destined to be profitable.

- The pros and cons of the canal system were aired in pamphlet wars. One argument in favor was that canals, by bringing prices down, promised cheaper food and, therefore, a healthier, happier population. Also, because a horse could pull 50 times as much freight by barge as by wagon, fewer horses were needed for the same amount of trade, creating savings in acreage needed for horses' fodder.

- Brindley's great successors were John Rennie, Benjamin Outram, William Jessop, and Thomas Telford. These builders were increasingly daring, creating longer and higher bridges, deeper cuttings, and straighter and more direct canals.

Thomas Telford

- Thomas Telford (1757–1834) was probably the greatest of the canal builders after Brindley. The son of a Scottish shepherd and apprenticed to a stonemason, Telford became a road surveyor, architect, and general engineer. In the 1790s, he began to specialize in canals.

- Telford recognized the benefits of iron for aqueducts. Iron aqueducts could be prefabricated offsite and weighed far less than solid stone structures. Their only drawback was that they would eventually rust, requiring sections to be replaced.

- Telford's greatest achievement was the Pontcysyllte Aqueduct in north Wales, which was 1,000 feet long and 120 feet high. Although the original plan had stepped locks down one side of the valley and up the other, with a low stone aqueduct, Telford urged investors to let him build a high iron structure instead.

- The structure was made of cast iron. Stone piers rose from the valley, but the trough was cast iron, bolted to plates on the masonry. Brass bands and cannon fire celebrated its opening, followed by a procession of barges. Sir Walter Scott said that the aqueduct was the most impressive work of art he had ever seen.

Funding the Canal System

- Canals authorized in the 1790s often struggled with inflation. A sudden demand for supplies and labor relevant to canals caused prices to rise. This was the era of the Napoleonic Wars, which also stimulated demand and contributed to rising prices.

- Acts of Parliament often specified how much money canal companies were allowed to raise. When the funds ran out because of inflation, investors suspected corruption or negligence. Many projects had repeated stops and starts as they cast around for more money.

Important Canal Routes

- The most significant canal routes were the Forth and Clyde Canal (finished in 1790), which linked the west and east coasts of Scotland, and the Leeds and Liverpool Canal (finished in 1816), which linked industrial Yorkshire and Lancashire—including an amazing crossing of the Pennines. The Kennet and Avon Canal linked Bristol and the Severn estuary with the Thames Valley.

- One of the most impressive features of the Leeds and Liverpool Canal was the Bingley Five Rise, a set of five locks in a "flight," in which the lower gate of one served as the upper gate of the next. The set of locks raised the canal 60 feet.

- As canals became larger after 1790 and crossed more high ground, the problem of keeping them full of water intensified. Dams had to be built across high streams to store enough water through the year so that it could be fed into the canals.

- Telford also worked with Jessop on the Caledonian Canal, designed to cut across Scotland from southwest to northeast, linking up the lochs. This canal route greatly shortened the stormy sea route around the north of Scotland and gave access to large ships, not just narrow barges.

- Poet Robert Southey, a friend of Telford, found the scene of a successive locks, nicknamed "Neptune's Staircase"—the longest staircase lock in Britain—particularly impressive. He wrote, "The pyramids would appear insignificant in such a situation."

- By 1830, there were 3,900 miles of canals in Britain and a new category of employment: bargemen. Bargemen led a healthier life than many of those working in the new industrial jobs. There was also a new work category of lockkeeper, who opened the gates, collected tolls, and ensured that embankments were watertight.

- Working on the canals became a way of life for hundreds of people for more than a century, only falling into decline when railways could do the work of transportation faster and more efficiently. When railway building began, however, the expertise and cumulative experience of the canal builders would be put to good use.

Suggested Reading

Burton, *The Canal Builders*.

Corble, *James Brindley*.

Crowe, *The English Heritage Book of Canals*.

Hanson, *Canal People*.

Questions to Consider

1. Why was the transportation of bulk solids so vital to industrial progress?

2. What were the greatest strengths and weaknesses of canals as a transport system?

Building Britain's Canals
Lecture 10—Transcript

Britain's first commercial canal opened in 1761, and at once showed itself superior to all other methods of transport. A horse pulling a barge could draw almost 50 times as much weight as it could with a wagon. Suddenly, it was possible to carry bulk solids like coal, iron ore, bricks, timber, clay, and grain over long distances at relatively low cost.

As we saw last time, Wedgwood grasped the benefits of canals and made sure the Trent and Mersey Canal came right past the front of his new Etruria factory. Building canals, especially across hilly country, proved an immense technical challenge but provoked some highly imaginative new technologies. Canals caught on rapidly, and between 1770 and the 1830s, when they were eclipsed by railways, canals accelerated bulk transport across Britain. They facilitated every other aspect of industrialization.

I've said it many times already in this course, but it bears repeating: The roads were nearly always terrible, even after the building of a set of turnpikes, roads you'd pay to go on that were of slightly better quality. Arthur Young, the agricultural writer whom I mentioned in Lecture 3, describes the Wigan turnpike like this:

> Let me most seriously caution all travelers who may accidentally purpose to travel this terrible country, to avoid it as they would the devil; for a thousand to one but they break their necks or their limbs by overthrows or breakings down. They will meet with ruts which I actually measured four feet deep, and floating with mud only from a wet summer; what therefore must it be after a winter.

So even the better roads were often in terrible shape.

Periodic attempts to improve Britain's navigable rivers had been tried for centuries; the Thames, the Severn, the Mersey and Weaver, the Humber, and the Trent. It was possible to straighten some of the worst curves, to dredge shallow areas to deepen them, to shore up the banks, to build towpaths beside the river along which a horse could walk, and sometimes even build locks to make them navigable higher up than they otherwise would be. But because rivers are flowing, they shift their banks over the years. They're alive. Their current can make progress upstream very difficult for draft horses. If it's rained, suddenly the flow is increased and they're hard to go, whereas canals are still-water environments which, once they're built, are far, far more manageable.

One of the most extensive river improvements in the days immediately prior to the canal age was Sankey Brook in Lancashire. It was extensively broadened and deepened for the sake of coal transport from St. Helens to the River Mersey in the Liverpool area, and it began to carry, very successfully, in 1757. But this was still mainly the improvement of a preexisting stream.

The first wholly artificial canal was projected by the 24-year-old Duke of Bridgewater, an aristocrat, the owner of coal mines at Worsley, who was looking for a method of shipping coal economically to Manchester. Worsley is now part of suburban Manchester, but then it was far enough away that getting coal into the city was pricey and difficult, and this was the problem that the Duke aimed to overcome. He hired James Brindley, who lived from 1716–1772, to design and build the Bridgewater Canal. Brindley was the son of Derbyshire farmers. He was apprenticed as a boy to a millwright, and he later set up a wheel and mill manufactory. Like many of the first generation of industrialists, he was a hands-on worker with little formal education, but with a very great gift for tinkering and finding technical solutions to awkward problems. Brindley joined up with the Duke and with his agent, John Gilbert, and together they confronted the vast array of new problems in making a working canal, often inventing techniques to overcome unforeseen problems. The Duke of Bridgewater almost bankrupted himself in the project and had no financial partners in the scheme. Because it was new, everything was being done for the first time.

Brindley himself, the engineer, favored the method of contouring. In other words, he tried to make sure that the canal simply followed the contours of the land so that there would be an absolute minimum change of altitude, even though that was going to make the canal quite a lot longer. This would keep earthmoving to a minimum. He was determined to take an indirect route to cut down on the number of cuttings through hills or embankments across low places that would otherwise be necessary, because everything had to be done with painstaking slowness by hand. Canals were built by men with shovels. He developed a method called "clay puddling," and this was the key to making the bed of the canal watertight. If you simply dug a long ditch and let the water flow into it, most of the water would flow through the bottom and simply turn into a swamp. But clay puddling, creating a clay bed for the canal, would keep the water in it.

The single most spectacular item on the Bridgewater Canal was the Barton Aqueduct, a structure built over the valley of the River Irwell. It caused a sensation at the time: The sheer strangeness of seeing boats sailing over a bridge, high above the river. People poured into the area to see it. Here's an anonymous writer in 1779, a few years after the canal had opened, describing it. He wrote:

> At Barton Bridge, Mr. Brindley has erected a navigable canal in the air; for it is as high as the tops of trees. Whilst I was surveying it with a mixture of wonder and delight, four barges passed me in the space of about three minutes. I durst hardly venture to walk on the aqueduct, as I almost trembled to behold the large river Irwell underneath me, across which this navigation is carried by a bridge.

There's a famous picture of Francis Egerton, the Duke of Bridgewater, pointing to the aqueduct below and behind him, because this became the signature object of the entire project.

From an engineering point of view, the embankments that lead to the aqueduct are equally impressive, because the intense lateral pressure exerted by the water above ground level made the banks liable to bursting. Brindley foresaw this possibility and worked out an ingenious method for isolating sections in the event of a breach so that the entire canal wouldn't then drain away through the breach made.

The opening of the canal in 1761 halved the price of coal in Manchester. It proved immensely profitable to Bridgewater himself. He recouped all his expenses in less than 10 years and went on to become immensely rich; incidentally showing other members of the aristocracy, who were sometimes skeptical, about the possibilities of improvements of this kind. At Worsely, where the mines were, the canal doubled as mine drainage; water could flow out of the mines into the canal. An ever-growing network of underground canals was also built inside the mines so that coal could be cut and loaded onto the barges almost right at the coal face, so a very ingenious and very successful project.

The canal was so popular and generated so much public interest that he had two passenger boats built to take day tours along the canal at the pace of a walking tow horse, and coffee and wine were available on board, so it's the very beginning of the kind of river cruising that goes on right up to the present.

Fifty-two acts of Parliament were passed over the next 15 years when the possibilities of canals were realized. Usually they were joint stock companies attracting investment from a wide variety of wealthy people who hoped for higher returns than they could get with government bonds, which usually yielded a steady three percent interest. It's very common in 18th- and 19th-century literature to have characters who are wealthy enough that they don't have to work, and they sometimes mention "My money is in the 3 percent," meaning they've put their money in a very, very safe place—they've invested in the government—and it yields three percent per year. But more daring investors are looking for a bigger return, and canal companies, after the Duke of Bridgewater's project, showed that this was a realistic hope.

Parliament would authorize the route by these acts of Parliament and would specify the right of eminent domain, a very important legal doctrine that said the lands across which this canal are going to be built have to be sold by their current owner. It has to be at a fair market price, but the owner doesn't have the right to deny the opportunity of the purchase. Otherwise, of course, individual landowners could indefinitely prevent the canals from ever being built. This, again, is a legal doctrine that persists right up to the present for road building and so on. Parliament also specified the tolls that would be charged at the locks and the different items that were going to be carried.

Here's a poem from the year 1766 on the benefits of canal building. The canals themselves are called "navigations." We think of navigation as the activity of plotting a course from one place to another, but originally a navigation, using it as a noun, was a canal that took you from one place to another. Here's the poem:

A fine intercourse with our principal ports
For trade must be certainly better;
When traffic's extended, and goods easy vended
In consequence things will be cheaper.

Our Commerce must thrive, and the Arts will revive,
Which are now in a sad situation,
If we follow this notion, from ocean to ocean,
To have a complete navigation.

Poems were being written to celebrate this marvelous new opportunity that's being developed.

Brindley himself went on to win the commission to build the Trent and Mersey Canal. For that, he needed changes in elevation, because this meant actually crossing the middle of the country itself. To do it that meant building locks. The Trent and Mersey Canal was the project in which Wedgwood took such an interest. He befriended Brindley, and even though he only had one leg after his amputation, he traveled widely along the route of the canal, and to Manchester, Liverpool, and Nottingham, the cities most directly affected, to raise money. As the unpaid treasurer, he also had to suppress squabbles among the investors and answer the critics who didn't want to see the canal built. The commonest criticisms came from mill owners who feared that they would lose water power. They were now using waterwheels, and they were afraid that if water was diverted from the rivers into the canals, the flow of the river would be diminished and their waterwheels would no longer work. They also faced criticism from river navigation companies, which foresaw rightly that they were going to be forced to cut their prices. Not surprisingly, they encountered criticism from gentlemen who didn't want canals crossing their lands but who knew that the eminent domain was going to force them to do so. On the other hand, Brindley and Wedgwood were able to quote the success of the Bridgewater canal, on the strength of which this looked to be a very, very lucrative project in which it made perfect sense to invest.

They key to the actual creation of the canal was the locks. Locks are beautiful devices, marvelously simple in a way but difficult to think of until they'd been invented. The way it works is this: There is a pair of gates built along the canal, and they enable a boat to go from a high level down to a low level. The gate at the low level is closed and the gate at the high level is opened so that the boat itself can sail into the lock. Then the high level gates are closed and the low level gate opened very slightly to let the water out in a controlled way, with the result that then the boat begins to sink down in the lock as its water level adjusts to the low level situation. When that's happened, the low level gates are fully opened and the boat sails out into the lower water level. It works exactly the same in reverse for going uphill: A boat comes in at the low level through the open low gates. They are then closed. Then water is let in in a controlled way from the high level, bringing the water level up and carrying the boat up with it, until the water level inside the lock is the same as the higher level of the water. The upper level gates are opened, and the boat sails out.

Of course, this system, which works beautifully with massive ships, too, in places like the Panama Canal, presupposes a reliable water supply at the high point of the system. For the canals to work there has to be a dependable source at the highest point because, of course, no water is actually going to flow uphill. Even though the boats are able to go uphill in stages through a series of locks, the water itself only ever flows down.

As completed, the Trent and Mersey Canal rises through a series of 35 locks, and then a 3,000-yard tunnel, the Harecastle Tunnel, and four shorter tunnels. Harecastle itself took 11 years to build. It wasn't completed until 1777. Although the first parts of the canal opened in 1771, the whole length of it wasn't available for another six years.

The building of the tunnel: It was dug in the same way as coal was mined. It's just a matter of men with sledgehammers and chisels chipping their way into the rock; a constant hazard of collapse, a constant hazard of flooding, and a hazard of poisoned gases. Men worked from both ends, and they also dug down in the center and moved outward from the bottom of the shaft, again like a mineshaft, so that four faces were being worked on at once. Progress was safeguarded inside by building brick arches to hold up the roof. In those days, just as they were unfamiliar with aqueducts, so they were unfamiliar with tunnels. They compared the bargemen entering the tunnels to Charon, whose mythological boat crosses the River Styx into hell.

The tunnel itself was too small for horses. In other words, the tow path on which the horses walked dragging the barges stopped at the beginning of the tunnel. They then had to be led over the hilltops by a groom or an assistant while the crew of the boat "legged" the boat through tunnel. "Legging" the boat means this: The men on board have to lay on their backs on the roof of the boat, and then with their feet over their heads they have to push the boat as though they were walking—lie on their backs and walk upside down— with the friction of their feet on the ceiling of the tunnel and their backs on the deck, keeping the boat going. Some of the later tunnels had groups of fulltime professional "leggers" waiting in huts at either end to carry the boat through; a grueling way of life, especially when the roof was left as jagged rock, slightly less bad when it was bricked.

After going through the tunnel, the Trent and Mersey Canal descended through another 40 more locks to join the River Trent at Shardlow in the middle of the country, after which you could go along the River Trent into the Humber and out into the North Sea. As I say, both ends opened before the middle because of the tunnel holdup.

These canals were actually built by men with picks and shovels. At first, the builders relied on local subcontractors, "hagmasters," who hired farm laborers during the offseason, but eventually they were replaced by migratory teams of fulltime canal builders in the 1790s. Because each canal scheme was usually called a "navigation," the men who built them were the "navigators." Again, this is a word whose meaning has changed significantly. *Navigators* was abbreviated to *navvy*, and the word *navvy* is a slang word that's still in use for an unskilled pick-and-shovel man at work anywhere in Britain. If you need somebody to dig a hole in your backyard, you'll say "I need to hire a navvy." Creating the bottoms of the locks required very high quality "puddling"; that is, pushing a compressed mixture of clay and sand into place to stop seepage into the surrounding ground. The towpath along which the horses would walk was made usually of ash and cinders, and there was plenty of ash available in newly-industrializing Britain.

Brindley himself, the great pioneer of canal building, died in 1772 before the whole length of the Trent and Mersey Canal was finished. A poem in the *Chester Courant*, a local newspaper, has this obituary offering to give: "James Brindley lies amongst these rocks. He made canals, bridges, and locks. To convey water, he made tunnels for barges, boats, and air-vessels. He erected several banks, mills, pumps, machines with wheels and cranks." A really terrible poem, but the quality of his workmanship was great, even though the eulogy at his death was terrible.

An era of "canal mania" began in 1793 and 1794, when 38 acts of Parliament were passed for new canal schemes. Investors by now had developed an exaggerated enthusiasm. Some of the routes they laid out were destined never to be profitable. Vigorous pamphlet wars took place pro and con. One of the arguments often made in favor of canals was that by bringing the prices of goods down, it promised an era of cheaper food, because transport was a major cost of the food most people bought. That would mean a healthier, happier population. Also, because a horse could pull 50 times as much freight by barge as by wagon, many fewer horses were going to be needed for the same amount of trade. That would create a big saving in the acreage needed for horses' fodder.

Brindley's great successors were John Rennie, Benjamin Outram, William Jessop, and Thomas Telford. They were daring builders: direct, building bridges longer and higher than any predecessor, cutting was deeper, and canals straighter and more direct. Stage by stage, the canal builders developed in confidence as they witnessed the success of previous schemes. Probably of all these men, Telford, who lived from 1757–1834, is the greatest of the lot. He was the son of a Scottish shepherd, raised in a one-room croft in Scotland and apprenticed to a stonemason. He later became a road surveyor, an architect, and eventually a general engineer, but in the 1790s, the era of canal mania, he began to specialize in canals. He recognized the benefits of iron for building aqueducts. As I said in an earlier lecture, iron is the great miraculous new product that's so much harder and so much more durable than the alternatives. The great advantage of building an aqueduct of iron rather than stone was that it could be prefabricated offsite and then brought to be located. It weighed far less than a solid stone structure, and only had the drawback that eventually it would rust out, requiring the sections to be replaced periodically.

Telford's greatest achievement was with the Pontcysyllte aqueduct in North Wales, carrying the Llangollen Canal across a broad valley of the River Dee. The aqueduct was built between 1795 and 1805. This, again, is one of those wonderful objects that you can go and see, and you can still sail a boat across it. It's very high and feels marvelously unexpected to be in a boat that high above the valley. It enthralled people in the 1760s, and it still enthralls people even today in the 21st century. It's 1,000 feet long and 120 feet high.

The original plan had been a series of locks stepping down the side of the valley on one side and up the other, with just a low stone aqueduct in the middle. But, of course, that would mean it would slow everything down because the locks take a long time to get through, and the building of locks is highly expensive. Telford finally urged the investors and persuaded them to let him build a high iron structure instead. He collaborated with William Jessop, the mason John Simpson, and the ironmaster William Hazeldine, and together they worked out how to make, in prefabricated sections, the iron aqueduct. It was made of cast iron. The stone piers rise from valley, but the trough itself is of cast iron, and it's bolted to plates on the masonry to keep it firmly in place. Only one man died during the construction at a time when mortality rate among navvies was extremely high, especially in things like bridge building projects.

When it opened, brass bands played and cannons fired, and then a great procession of barges crossed over the aqueduct itself. We have an eyewitness account, which says this:

> The discharge from the guns as the procession returned, the plaudits
> of the spectators, the martial music, the echo reverberating from the

mountains, magnified the enchanting scene; and the countenance of everyone present bespoke the satisfaction with which they contemplated this very useful and stupendous work.

The novelist Walter Scott, the author of *Ivanhoe*, then the most popular novelist in Britain, said "The most impressive work of art" he had ever seen. Many paintings and rhapsodic descriptions followed, and it's a much-memorialized object.

The canals authorized in the 1790s often struggled with inflation. The sudden demand for supplies and labor relevant to the canals caused the price of all these things to begin to rise. This was also the era of the Napoleonic Wars, the 1790s and the 1800s, which also stimulated demand for all kinds of things and contributed to prices rising. We're familiar with inflation today—all too familiar with it—but they weren't. The acts of Parliament had often specified how much the company was going to be allowed to raise. When the funds ran out because of inflation, the investors suspected corruption or negligence. Many of the projects had repeated stops and starts as they then cast around for more money.

But despite all this, some really significant routes were finished. Among the most significant were the Forth and Clyde Canal, finished in 1790, which linked the Clyde River, which flows through Glasgow out into the Irish Sea on the west, with the Forth River, on which Edinburgh is built and that's linked to the North Sea on the eastern side; that is to say, linking the west and eastern parts of Scotland at the point of the central lowlands, which are economically the most productive. The Leeds and Liverpool Canal, finished in 1816, linked industrial Yorkshire in the east with industrial Lancashire in the west and included an amazing crossing of the Pennine hills, high, wild country. One of its very best features, still visible, is the Bingley Five Rise, a set of five locks in a "flight" where the lower gate of one lock is also the upper gate of the next one, and it raises the canal 60 feet. As you sit at the bottom, you can actually watch boats rising bit by bit into the air ahead of you. Another important route was the Kennett and Avon Canal, which linked Bristol on the west coast in the estuary of the River Severn with the River Kennett, which flows into the Thames, the river that flows through London, again, into the east. This also has the effect of linking Britain east and west.

By 1820, a complete network linked up the various parts of the kingdom east and west, and also north and south.

As the canals got bigger after 1790, and as they crossed more high ground, the problem of keeping them full of water intensified. It required building dams across high streams to store enough water through the year that it could always be fed into the canals to keep them operative.

Telford also worked with Jessop on the Caledonian Canal to make a cut across northern Scotland from the southwest to the northeast, linking up a series of the great Scottish lochs. This had the effect of greatly shortening the stormy sea route around the north of Scotland and giving access to big ships, not just the characteristic narrow canal barges. It was a great stimulus to a depressed area of Britain. The poet Robert Southey, who was a friend of Telford, found the scene of eight successive locks on the Caledonian Canal, which was nicknamed "Neptune's Staircase," particularly impressive, and he wrote the following:

> The pyramids would appear insignificant in such a situation, for in them we would perceive only a vain attempt to vie with greater things. But here we see the powers of nature brought to act upon a great scale, in subservience to the purposes of man. One river created, another, and that a huge mountain stream, shouldered out of its place, and art and order assuming a character of sublimity.

That's a big claim, that this is even more impressive than the pyramids.

By 1830, there were 3,900 miles of canals, and they created a new way of life: the world of the bargemen, the people who actually traveled with the barges up and down the kingdom. It was a healthier life than many of the new industrial jobs. It was work out-of-doors, leading the horses, loading and unloading the brightly painted and decorated barges. The canalmen, the bargemen, would often be tanned by being out in all weathers. They were sometimes suspected of being gypsies who'd taken to the water. Bargemen were regularly accused of petty thefts in the neighborhoods they passed through. If something disappears, it's convenient to blame the bargemen. Some families did move into canal barging and stay with it through generations. By the early 20th century, families had been barging for 100 years, passing it down from father to son.

Another new characteristic job was that of lockkeepers. At the locks, many of which you can still visit, there are characteristic little lockkeepers' cottages. Their job was to open and close the gates, collect the tolls from the boats as they came through, and ensure the watertightness of the embankments in their section of the canal. This was a way of life for hundreds of people for more than a century, eventually falling into decline when railways could do the work faster and more efficiently.

When railway building began, particularly after 1830, the expertise and the cumulative experience of the canal builders would be put to good use, because in some respects they're comparable types of work.

Today, the canals are nearly all still there. They fell into disuse through the early 20th century, but now three generations of enthusiasts have revived them and turned them into a valuable part of Britain's tourist industry. They were dredged and repaired. Marinas were built. The locks were restored, and hundreds of new narrowboats were launched, modeled on the old ones. But now they're nearly all motorized, and they seem to be the epitome of an unhurried preindustrial way of life. But, in fact, they're one of the surest signs of the transformation of Britain in the late 18th and early 19th centuries. They now offer a chance to slow down from the rapid pace of life, but when they were new, they represented an incredible acceleration of commercial possibilities; so they're paradoxical places.

I've mentioned several places to which I encourage you to go when you visit industrial Britain, and there's a wonderful museum at Ellesmere Port; this is just across the River Mersey from Liverpool in Cheshire. It's the museum of the English waterways where dozens of wonderful old canal boats from every generation are gathered together, and the whole technology of the waterways is fully explained. It's as interesting in its way for people who are interested in canals as Coalbrookdale is for people interested in the iron industry.

I think it's easy to overlook the importance of the canals in the development of industrialization, partly because they feel so rustic and partly because they were quite quickly upstaged by an even better system of bulk transportation: the railways. To the history of steam engines and steam railways, we'll turn in the next two lectures.

Steam Technology and the First Railways
Lecture 11

The year 1830 was one of the great turning points in the history of transport—and, thereby, of industrialization itself. The Liverpool and Manchester Railway, which opened in 1830, was the first railway run entirely by steam-powered locomotives. Based on a long series of incremental technological improvements over the previous half-century, it brought together high-pressure steam engines, high-quality iron manufacture, and successful experiments in using rails for horse-drawn or cable-drawn haulage. Over the next 20 years, a nationwide railway system spread across Britain, privately financed and operated, immensely lucrative, and providing a stimulus for the entire British economy.

Early Steam Engines

- Steam engines went through nearly a century of improvements before being mounted on vehicles. The first steam engines, developed by Thomas Savery and Thomas Newcomen, were used mainly for mine pumping and were slow and inefficient.

- In the Newcomen engine, steam from a boiler pushed a piston up inside a cylinder. The steam valve closed, and then a jet of cold water was shot into the cylinder. It caused the steam to condense, creating a vacuum, which drew down the piston. Then, the cycle was repeated. The up-and-down motion was transmitted by a beam to a simple pump, drawing water out of the mine. Another name for an engine of this kind is a "beam engine."

- James Watt improved the speed and efficiency of Newcomen engines. Watt realized that Newcomen engines were inefficient because the cylinder had to be heated and cooled during every stroke. Most of the energy from the fuel was devoted to heating the cylinder, rather than working the engine itself. In 1764, Watt substituted a separate condenser, enabling the main cylinder to remain hot all the time and achieving far higher fuel efficiency.

- Watt, in partnership with Matthew Boulton, created a highly profitable enterprise: a factory to build steam engines. They employed John "Iron-Mad" Wilkinson to bore cylinders in a method developed for military cannons.

Precision and Innovation
- All early industrialists were plagued by poor-quality machine tools, lack of standardized parts, and lack of precision craftsmanship. Watt, Boulton, and Wilkinson all specialized in precision. Boulton and Watt sold ready-made engines or helped owners of Newcomen engines convert them, for huge savings in coal costs.

- Watt also patented the "sun and planet" motion in 1781, which converted the reciprocating stroke of a beam engine into rotary motion. That made it applicable to turning factory machinery, including at cotton mills, and increased his business.

- Watt's patent restricted other entrants into the steam engine business until 1800. After that, steam engines caught on in a huge array of businesses, speeding them up and creating new possibilities for large-scale production.

Richard Trevithick
- Horse-drawn railways, especially in coal-mining districts, were already in operation throughout the 18th century. The low-friction environment of smooth wheels on smooth rails enabled horses to pull greater weights than they could have done on roads.

- In mining areas, gravity carried full wagons down to the wharf, and then a horse or a stationary steam engine attached to a cable dragged them back up, empty. These early mine railways were usually wooden, but the engineers at the Coalbrookdale ironworks substituted iron rails as early as 1767. Iron rails proved vastly superior and caught on at other ironworks and collieries; they were not subject to rot and could carry greater weights more easily.

- In the early 19th century, mining engineers began to experiment with steam-driven locomotives. In 1801, Richard Trevithick, a Cornish engineer, created a steam-powered carriage that he nicknamed the "Puffing Devil" and ran it on the road. It worked, but the roads were very poor, and it often broke down.

- Trevithick patented the high-pressure steam engine in 1802 and made a working railway locomotive in 1804. Its weight was so great that it broke the rails. Still, he had made a crucial breakthrough by bringing together a high-pressure steam engine mounted on a trolley and running it on iron rails. This innovation would change the world.

George Stephenson
- George Stephenson was probably the single most important person in the history of railways, one whose work brought together all the necessary inventions and insights, improved them, and turned them into recognizable working railways. He and his son, Robert, built the first commercially successful railways in the 1820s.

- Stephenson was a mining engineer whose job was to look after the pumping engines at the mine. He was aware of Trevithick's experiments and began to tinker with making his own locomotive.

- In 1810, Stephenson realized the importance of the "steam blast" system—a necessary advance in making workable locomotives. Directing the exhaust steam from the cylinders into the chimney created suction to draw air into the locomotive's fire (like a bellows effect), causing it to burn hotter and more efficiently.

- Stephenson also showed skeptics that metal wheels on metal rails did provide enough friction to give traction, so long as the gradients were shallow—therefore, a rack-and-pinion system would not be necessary.

- Stephenson was commissioned to build the Stockton and Darlington Railway, partly using stationary steam engines with cables and partly using moving locomotives. The railways was 25 miles long and opened for business in 1825.

- ○ Horses pulled the passenger trains, which looked just like stagecoaches, except they were on rails. Stephenson worked out a system called the "dandy cart." When the rail gradient was uphill, the horse would pull, but when it was downhill, the horse would climb onto a cart at the back, where hay was waiting, and ride as gravity carried the train down the slope.

- ○ The locomotive engine, however, could pull a long freight train, occasionally reaching 15 miles per hour. It led to a halving of the price of coal in Darlington.

Liverpool and Manchester Railway

- Stephenson followed up by engineering and building the Liverpool and Manchester Railway, which opened in 1830. It was faster and relied entirely on moving locomotives.

- The Liverpool and Manchester Railway was financed by Lancashire industrialists impatient at the high cost and slow speeds of the canal system. Among the advantages of a railway over a canal was that it would not freeze in winter and was not susceptible to drought; further, one train could make many back-and-forth trips in the time a canal boat could make only one. It was also easier to increase the volume of traffic on a railway.

- The Stephensons defied skeptics by working out a way to cross the Chat Moss swamp, pouring in thousands of tons of rock ballast to create a firm surface.

Rainhill Trials

- In 1829, as the Liverpool and Manchester Railway was nearing completion, the board held a competition, the Rainhill Trials, to determine whether stationary steam engines or moving locomotives would be used to pull the trains. The best locomotive maker would receive £500 and the contract for the new line.

The method of heating water with a tubular boiler used in George Stephenson's *Rocket* was retained in the building of steam locomotives in Britain into the 1950s.

- Huge crowds gathered, seated in grandstands alongside the track. Locomotives had to go up and down the selected length of track 20 times, for a total of 60 miles, pulling three times their own weight.

- An early favorite was the *Novelty*, which limbered up with a solo run and astonished the onlookers by going nearly 30 miles per hour. But it was finicky and accident prone, whereas the Stephensons' locomotive, the *Rocket*, was hardy, durable, and dependable.

- The *Rocket* was the clear winner, traveling 70 miles fully laden and even going at 12 miles per hour up a gradient (much faster than the fixed-engine system could have managed).

- The *Rocket* embodied another important technical breakthrough—the tubular boiler. Rather than have a fire heating one large tank of water, water was forced through 25 copper tubes surrounded by superheated air, which boiled it and turned it to high-pressure steam far more quickly.

The First Railway Casualty

- The opening of the Liverpool and Manchester Railway was a momentous occasion, drawing national celebrities, including the prime minister. A procession of eight trains set off, pausing along the route to exhibit the railway's most spectacular achievements, such as the crossing of Chat Moss and the Sankey viaduct.

- At one point, William Huskisson, Liverpool Member of Parliament and president of the Board of Trade, who had been one of the great enthusiasts for the railway throughout its construction, walked in front of the *Rocket* as it was coming down an adjacent track. People then had no conception of how quickly a vehicle traveling at 20 miles per hour would reach them. Despite shouted warnings, the locomotive hit and seriously injured Huskisson.

- Wounded, he was put on board another of the trains, the *Northumbrian*, driven by George Stephenson himself, which set off at top speed to Manchester and the nearest hospital. The hospital couldn't save Huskisson's life, but bystanders were astonished at the train's speed in covering the ground—36 miles per hour (which shows how rapid progress had been since the Rainhill Trials of the previous year).

A Significant Leap in Industrialization

- Early railway promoters had expected the railways to thrive entirely on freight, but they discovered an unanticipated demand from passengers, as well. Ten times as many people rode the train in the first year as expected, and for the first decade, passenger transport was the most lucrative part of the whole business.

- It was clear by the early 1830s that the railway was going to upstage the canals, even though canals had been such a dramatic improvement over earlier transport. This is an excellent example of the way industrialization began to speed up traditional methods.

- It was not long after that Stephenson and many of his rivals were commissioned to build major railways between such distant centers as London, Birmingham, and Edinburgh. And already at the Rainhill Trials, representatives from the first American railroads had been in attendance to see whether the locomotives actually worked and were impressed by the outcome.

- In the next lecture, we will see how the Stephensons and many other eminent engineers set about building a great nationwide railway network, much of which is still in operation today.

Suggested Reading

Burton, *The Railway Builders*.

Dickinson, *James Watt and the Industrial Revolution*.

Rolt, *George and Robert Stephenson*.

Simmons and Biddle, eds., *The Oxford Companion to British Railway History from 1603 to the 1990s*.

Questions to Consider

1. How did Watt's improvements to the Newcomen engine make steam-powered railways possible?

2. What qualities enabled George Stephenson to succeed as a pioneer railway builder?

Steam Technology and the First Railways
Lecture 11—Transcript

The first railway run entirely by steam-powered locomotives running at 30 miles per hour was the Liverpool and Manchester Railway, which opened in 1830. Based on a long series of incremental technological improvements over the previous half-century, it brought together high-pressure steam engines, high quality iron manufacture, and experiments in using rails for horse-drawn or cable-drawn haulage. Over the next 20 years, a nationwide railway system spread across Britain, privately financed and operated, immensely lucrative, and providing a stimulus for the whole British economy. Much of the basic system built then is still in operation today.

Steam engines went through nearly a century of improvements before being mounted on vehicles. The first engines, developed by Thomas Savery and Thomas Newcomen, were used mainly for mine pumping. They were slow and inefficient. In a Newcomen engine, steam from a boiler pushes a piston up inside a cylinder. Then the steam valve closes, and then a jet of cold water is shot into the cylinder. It causes the steam to condense, creating a vacuum, which then draws down the piston. Then the cycle is repeated. The up-and-down motion of the piston in the cylinder is transmitted by a beam to a simple pump, drawing water out of the mine. Another name for an engine of this kind is a "beam engine." Newcomen-type beam engines are huge—as big as a house—but there are still a few of them running. I've mentioned several times during these lectures that at certain places in Britain it's possible to see the old textile and iron working techniques. The same is true of the oldest steam engines, and the place to go in this case is Kew in West London, very close to Kew Gardens, which are much more famous. Although to me, the most interesting thing in Kew is the Live Steam Museum, which has monster beam engines running every Sunday.

James Watt improved the speed and efficiency of Newcomen engines. James Watt was an instrument maker at Glasgow University in Scotland, and one of the very few among the first generation of industrial inventors to have any formal scientific education. After studying the Newcomen engine, he realized that it was very inefficient because the cylinder had to be heated and then cooled during every stroke. Most of the energy from the fuel was devoted to heating the cylinder rather than working the engine itself, because the injection of cold water is what creates the vacuum and draws down the piston. In 1764, Watt substituted a separate condenser for the condensation of the steam so that the main cylinder could remain hot all the time, achieving a far greater level of fuel efficiency.

His partnership with Matthew Boulton created a highly profitable enterprise. I mentioned Boulton previously in the lecture on Wedgwood, the pottery maker. Boulton was a Birmingham toymaker—that is to say, a maker of metal goods—but he understood the significance of Watt's achievement, which was patented in 1769. Boulton was so convinced of the essential rightness of Watt's invention that he sold his country estate to raise capital to build a steam engine-building factory. The two of them, Boulton and Watt, employed John Wilkinson, whom we met in the iron lecture—"Iron Mad" Wilkinson. His job was to bore the cylinders in a method patented in 1774 developed for boring out military cannons. I mentioned then that he was capable of getting a very, very accurate method for precision in cannon boring, and the same technique was applied to the drilling of the cylinders so that the absolute minimum of the steam would escape, so that the vacuum would be tight, and so on.

All the early industrialists were plagued by poor quality machine tools, lack of standardized parts, and lack of precision craftsmanship. Watt, Boulton, and Wilkinson specialized in precision. In fact, the best place to look for it at the time was in the metal goods around Birmingham, the luxury toy industry. Boulton and Watt's business model was like this: They sold ready-made engines or they helped owners of Newcomen engines that were already installed to convert them to the Watt technique, for a huge saving in coal costs (more efficient).

Watt also patented the "sun and planets" motion in 1781, which converted the reciprocating stroke of the beam engine into rotary motion. Until then, the beam had simply rocked back and forth and the motion was just up and down. It was Watts who worked out how to link it to a wheel in such a way as to cause the wheel to rotate so the up-and-down motion was now circular. Of course, that makes it possible for the engine to be applied to turning factory machines, including at cotton mills; another increase for his business.

Watt enforced his patents very rigorously and restricted other entrants into the steam engine business until the year 1800. After that, they caught on in a huge array of businesses, speeding them up and creating new possibilities for large-scale production.

Samuel Smiles, who was a mid-19th-century enthusiast for industry, eulogized the importance of steam in transforming all types of work. Here's a quotation from Samuel Smiles; he wrote:

> Steam has become the universal drudge. Coal, water, and a little oil, are all that the steam engine, with its bowels of iron and its heart of fire, needs to enable it to go on working night and day, without rest or sleep. Yoked to machinery of almost infinite variety, the results of vast ingenuity and labor, the steam engine pumps water, drives spindles, thrashes corn, prints books, hammers iron, ploughs land, saws timber, drives piles, impels ships, works railways, and, in a word, asserts an almost unbounded supremacy over the materials which enter into the daily use of mankind.

A great eulogy there to the potency of steam power, written in a time when it was still fresh and could be admired in that way.

The economist Andrew Ure, writing in 1835, compares steam engines to horses, which very often they displaced, in a similarly enthusiastic passage. Ure writes the following:

> There are many engines made by Boulton and Watt, 40 years ago, which have continued in constant work all that time with very slight repairs. What a multitude of valuable horses would have been worn out in doing the service of these machines! And what a vast quantity of grain they would have consumed. Had British industry not been aided by Watt's invention, it must have done with a retarding pace in consequence of the increasing cost of motive power, and would, long ere now, have experienced in the price of horses, and the scarcity of waterfalls, an insurmountable barrier to further advancement. Could horses, even at the low prices to which their rival, steam, has kept

them, be employed to drive a cotton mill at the present day, they would devour all the profits of the manufacturer.

Again, striking testimony to the impact that steam technology has and the recognition on the part of economic writers about just how important this transfer is.

At the same time as steam engines themselves were being developed, so were railways. Horse-drawn railways, especially in coal mining districts, were already in operation through the 18th century, and we glanced at this in the lecture on mining. The low friction environment of smooth wheels on smooth rails enabled horses to pull greater weights than they could have done on roads. In mines around Newcastle on Tyne, gravity often carried full wagons down to the wharf, then a horse or a stationary steam engine would be attached to a cable to drag them back up again empty. These early mine railways were usually made of wood, but the engineers at the Coalbrookdale iron works substituted iron rails as early as 1767. Ironically, this was during a slow spell when Abraham Darby just wanted to keep the workmen busy and use up some spare materials. But iron rails proved vastly superior, and they caught on quickly at other iron works and then at the collieries, the coal mines. They didn't rot, and they could carry greater weights more easily.

Most of the early railways were short lines, just two or three miles long each often, between coal mines and the river or the sea wharves. About 200 miles of such lines were in operation nationwide by 1800. But in the next year, in 1801, the Surrey Iron Railway was built in the southern suburbs of London, drawn by horses. It made a sensation when one horse was able to pull 55 tons of stone in wagons, whereas on a cart it could pull less than one ton. This shows straight away that railway offered the same improvement of traction as canals. A horse could pull 50 times as much in a canal boat than on a road; now it turns out that the smooth, low-friction environment of a railway is very nearly as good.

Mining engineers began to experiment with steam-driven locomotives in the early 19th century. The first of them was a man named Richard Trevethick. He came from Cornwall in the extreme southwest of England, a Cornish engineer but working in South Wales at the mines. He created a steam-powered carriage that he named "the Puffing Devil." This was also in 1801, and he ran it on the road in the town of Camborne. It worked, but the roads were terrible and it often broke down. After one such break, the crew went into the pub without extinguishing the fire, and while they were eating and drinking, the Puffing Devil caught fire and destroyed itself.

It was Trevethick who patented the high-pressure steam engine in 1802, and then made a working railway locomotive in 1804. Its weight was so great that it broke the rails. This was at the Pennydarren Iron works in Merthyr Tydfil in South Wales, and it's one of the places that can lay claim to being the birthplace of steam-powered railways. Still, though Trevethick had a lot of problems to deal with, he'd made the crucial breakthrough by bringing together a high-pressure steam engine, mounting it on a trolley, and running it on iron rails. This combination of technologies was soon going to literally change the world.

A few years later again in 1808, he built a locomotive called "Catch Me Who Can," and it was a fairground curiosity. What he did was in a site very near Euston station as it is today, he built a circle of track—a simple circle, just the thing you might lay around your Christmas tree—fenced it off from prying eyes, and then invited curious visitors to pay a shilling to come in and look at the train and to ride around in a circle pulled by his locomotive. It was a kind of fairground attraction. Trevethick himself at that point still seems not to have quite understood the enormous potential of this invention that he did so much to advance.

Probably the single most important name in the history of railroad technology is that of George Stephenson. His work brought together all the necessary inventions and insights, improved them, and turned them into recognizable working railways. He and his son, Robert, built the first commercially successful railways in the 1820s. George Stephenson was a mining engineer. He worked at Killingworth Colliery near Newcastle on Tyne. He lived in a cottage past which ran a wooden-railed, horse-drawn railway, and his job was to look after the pumping engines at the mine. George Stephenson had very little formal education; he didn't learn to read and write until he was 18. But he had a great deal of practical savvy, like so many of this first generation; not a formally educated or scientifically educated person at all.

He used to take the Newcomen engines at the mine to pieces to see how they ran, and put them back together; tinker, look for possible improvements.

Surviving letters we have from him show a man who never mastered spelling, never bothered with paragraphs or punctuation, but had a direct and accurate way of describing technical problems and how to solve them. Historians of engineering have enjoyed reading Stephenson's letters because on the one hand they seem terribly clumsy and amateurish, but are actually packed with very shrewd insight. He was aware of Trevethick's experiments, and began to tinker with making his own locomotive.

In 1810, he recognized the importance of the "steam blast" system, a necessary advance in making workable locomotives. Steam blast means this: By directing the exhaust steam from the cylinders into the chimney that carries the smoke away from the fire, it created suction to draw air into the locomotive's firebox, a bellows effect. That, of course, causes the fire to burn much hotter and more efficiently. Steam blast is one of the crucial insights to make locomotives work properly.

Stephenson also showed skeptics that metal wheels turning on metal rails did provide enough friction to give traction so long as gradients were shallow. If you think about the railways that you've seen, they're nearly always either flat or almost flat. There's enough friction to enable the metal wheels to turn on the rails, but not enough to make them climb up steep hills, and a gradient of about 1 in 50 is about the best you can manage. Anything steeper than that would need a rack-and-pinion system where a rotating wheel with teeth on the locomotive locked into a zigzag system on the rail itself. That would make everything much slower and more difficult.

George Stephenson was commissioned to build the Stockton and Darlington Railway, partly using stationary steam engines with cables to draw the wagons, and partly using moving locomotives. It was 25 miles long and it opened for business in 1825. On the Stockton and Darlington Railway, horses pulled the passenger trains, and the passenger coaches looked just like stagecoaches, except mounted on rails. Stephenson worked out a system called the Dandy Cart. When the rail gradient was up, the horse would pull, but when the gradient was down, the horse would climb onto a cart at the back where some tasty hay was waiting, and the horse would ride as gravity carried the train down the slope.

But the really important thing about the motive power on the Stockton and Darlington Railway was the steam engine he built; the locomotion. He showed that it could pull a long freight train, occasionally at speeds as high as 15 miles per hour. Characteristically, it ran at about 4 miles per hour. Children would race the locomotives, and they could sometimes win. They also enjoyed jumping aboard the moving train; harrowingly dangerous, but the kids loved it. The success of the Stockton and Darlington Railway was measured in the fact that the price of coal in Darlington fell by 50 percent. It had the same kind of impact as the Bridgewater Canal had had when it opened, carrying bulk solid commodities, coal in both cases, and making it much cheaper at its ultimate destination.

George Stephenson followed up by engineering and building the Liverpool and Manchester Railway, opened in 1830. It was faster, and after many arguments about the merits of using fixed engines and hauling on ropes, it depended entirely on moving locomotives. The Liverpool and Manchester Railway was financed by Lancashire industrialists, particularly the cotton manufacturers, who were impatient at the high cost and slow speeds of the canal. Their prospectus read, among other things:

> In the present state of trade and commercial enterprise, dispatch is no less essential than economy. Merchandise is frequently brought across the Atlantic from New York to Liverpool in 21 days, while owing to various causes of delay goods have in some instances been longer in their passage from Liverpool to Manchester.

So they come a great distance—3,000 miles in 21 days—and then it takes as long again, or more, to get up to Manchester. This is a sign, isn't it, of the rate of expectation increasing? Once, the canal had seemed marvelously fast; now, already, it's starting to seem a little bit too slow.

Among the advantages of a railway over a canal was that it wouldn't freeze in winter, bringing transport to a standstill. It wasn't susceptible to drought conditions, and one train could make many back and forth trips in the time a canal boat could only make one. It was also easier to increase the volume of traffic on a railway. Railway wagons could be built much more quickly than canal boats.

The Stephensons, father and son, George and his son Robert, whom he trained up into the business, defied the skeptics by working out a way to cross the Chat Moss Swamp. This was one of the great obstacles that the railway had to cross to link up the two cities. They poured in thousands of tons of rock ballast to finally create a firm surface. There were legends that Chat Moss was a bottomless swamp and that you could pour things into it forever and it would never become firm. They proved that to be false and were, in fact, able to lay the railway across it, at which point the crossing itself became a marvel.

They also built a long tunnel near the Liverpool end. When it was nearly finished, George Stephenson whitewashed the inside of the tunnel, hung gas lamps every 50 feet along it, and let the public pay a shilling to walk its length; a great curiosity to people who'd never before had the opportunity to walk through an illuminated tunnel.

The board of the railway held a competition called the Rainhill Trials in 1829; Rainhill is the place where the trials were held. The intention of the trials was to establish which was the best locomotive maker in Britain. The winner was going to receive a prize of 500 pounds and the contract to provide locomotives to run on the new line, so a very lucrative contract for whoever could win. Huge crowds gathered at Rainhill, and they were seated in grandstands that were set up alongside the track. Obviously, this is a shrewd commercial promotion to publicize the railway. The rules of the trials were that the locomotives that entered had to go up and down the selected length of track 20 times, for a total of 60 miles—it was a 3-mile section—and they had to be pulling three times their own weight.

The early favorite in the Rainhill Trials was a locomotive called the *Novelty*, which limbered up with a solo run and astonished the onlookers by going at nearly 30 miles per hour. When we drive at 30, especially on a good road, we feel terribly slow, and it's worth reminding yourself that in 1829 nobody had ever traveled at 30 miles per hour at all. Even a galloping horse can't go that fast. The only way anything went at 30 was as it fell, and, of course, it doesn't fall for very long. But now, suddenly, in a controlled way, people are traveling at 30. A Liverpool journalist who, like all the others, had never seen anything go so fast, became rhapsodic. Here's what he wrote watching the *Novelty*:

It seemed indeed to fly, presenting one of the most sublime spectacles of human ingenuity and human daring the world has ever beheld. It actually made one giddy to look at it, and filled thousands with lively fears for the safety of the individuals who were on it, and who seemed not to run along the earth, but to fly, as it were, on the wings of the wind. It is a most sublime sight; a sight indeed which the individuals who beheld it will not soon forget.

But the problem with the *Novelty*, actually as its name suggests, is that it was finicky and that it was accident-prone, whereas Robert Stephenson's locomotive, the *Rocket*, was hardy, durable, and dependable. By the end of the Rainhill Trials, the *Rocket* had emerged as the clear winner. It traveled 70 miles fully laden, and even went at 12 miles per hour up a gradient, much faster than a fixed engine system could have towed a cable.

The *Rocket* embodied another very important technical breakthrough: the tubular boiler. Rather than have a fire heating one big tank of water inside the locomotive, the system adopted instead was to have the water being forced through 25 copper tubes that were surrounded by superheated air, which boiled it almost instantaneously and turned it into high-pressure steam far more quickly than would be possible in one big tank. This method of the tubular boiler was retained from then on right through into the 1950s when the building of steam locomotives in the United Kingdom finally came to an end.

The *Rocket*, this locomotive, is in the London Science Museum in Kensington, which is a marvelous place to visit. It's a grimy black object that doesn't look particularly impressive, despite its significance. On the other hand, there's a beautiful replica of the *Rocket*, painted bright yellow as it was at the time of the Rainhill Trials, on display at the National Railway Museum in York. The National Railway Museum in York is also very much deserving of your time and a visit. It's a magnificent place where the most beautiful trains from every generation of English railway history have been gathered together. I often tell groups of students that if they've only got one day to spend in England, they should spend it at the National Railway Museum in York. Of course, they think I'm kidding, but I'm not.

The opening of the Liverpool and Manchester Railway was a big occasion. It drew national celebrities, including the Prime Minister, the Duke of Wellington, the war hero who'd won the Battle of Waterloo against Napoleon. He was given a silk-draped carriage to ride in, and three future prime ministers were with him: Lord Grey, Sir Robert Peel, and Lord Melbourne, who a little bit later was going to become Queen Victoria's first Prime Minister and her great friend. A procession of eight trains set off, pausing along the route to see its most spectacular achievements, such as the crossing of Chat Moss and, a bit further along, the Sankey viaduct.

At one point, William Huskisson, a Member of Parliament for Liverpool and President of the Board of Trade, a man who'd been very enthusiastic about the building of the railway and taken a great interest throughout its construction, walked towards the Duke of Wellington's train just at the moment when the *Rocket* was coming down the adjacent track. People then had no conception of how quickly a vehicle traveling at 20 mph can reach you. Despite shouted warnings from some of the onlookers, the locomotive hit and seriously injured him. Wounded, William Huskisson was then put on board another of the trains, the *Northumbrian*, driven by George Stephenson himself, which set off at top speed to carry him to Manchester, the nearest hospital. It couldn't save his life, but the bystanders were astonished at the train's speed in covering the ground. It went at 36 miles per hour, which shows that progress had been made even since the Rainhill Trials of the previous year. There's still a marker today at the spot where this accident happened, the death of William Huskisson, marring the otherwise triumphant opening of the railway.

The promoters had expected the Liverpool and Manchester Railway to thrive entirely on freight, but they discovered an unanticipated demand from passengers, too. People wanted to ride on the train; they wanted to see what it was like. Once they'd been reassured that they weren't going to die by traveling at 30 miles an hour, they took a great interest in wanting to do it if they possibly could. Ten times as many people rode the train in the first year as the directors had foreseen, and for the first decade that was the most lucrative part of the whole business.

It was clear by the 1830s that the railway was going to upstage the canals, even though they'd recently been such an improvement on earlier forms of transport. This is an example of the way industrialization began to speed up traditional methods, permitting economical and high-speed bulk transport for the first time ever. It's the railways that made the canals seem to leisurely and so rustic.

A writer in the county of Sussex describes being on a canal barge and watching a train passing by near him. He writes:

> The horse that draws our boat is quietly feeding on the banks of the canal. As we remain here, languidly waiting to be liberated from the lock, along comes "Puffing Billy" flying over the iron rails like a mad thing. "Phew" whistles the locomotive. "Puff Puff Pull" retorts the engine, and as we look round, the whole train of carriages whisks out of sight, leaving the smoke from the tunnel to slowly settle itself. The contrast is funny. While we have been fudging about in the lock, the engine has possibly flown 10 miles with its freight.

It wasn't long after that that Stephenson, and then many of his rivals, started to be commissioned to build major railways, not just between adjoining towns like Stockton and Darlington, or Liverpool and Manchester, but between distant centers like London, Birmingham, and Edinburgh. Already at the Rainhill Trials, representatives from the first American railroads had been in attendance to see whether the locomotives actually worked and, of course, they were delighted by the outcome.

1830 was one of the great turning points in the history of transport, and therefore one of the great turning points of industrialization itself. We'll see in the next lecture how the Stephensons, and many other great engineers, set about building a great nationwide railway network, much of which is still in operation right up to the present.

The Railway Revolution
Lecture 12

The advent of the railways marked one of the most decisive shifts in British history. The technical and commercial success of the Liverpool and Manchester Railway set off a boom in railway building throughout the 1830s and 1840s. Trunk lines were built between major cities, linking previously remote parts of Britain and making the transport of bulk items—and people—far quicker and cheaper than ever before. Although the railways displaced long-distance stagecoaches and threatened the canals' monopoly on inland bulk transport, they stimulated urban growth. They also created a high demand for further development in the metal industries, significantly stimulated the economy, and provided employment for tens of thousands of people.

A National Effort

- In Britain, each new railway line required an act of Parliament. The acts provided limited liability and created the right of eminent domain. Because Britain was already a densely settled country, the siting of lines meant cutting across lands owned by hundreds of individuals. Bribery of Members of Parliament, who owned estates the railways would cross, was widespread and contributed to the high cost of British railway building.

- Landowners who lacked political influence were often resentful of these forced purchases. There was also widespread opposition from people who had made their fortunes in turnpikes, stagecoaches, and canals—technologies that now faced the threat of a faster and more efficient rival.

- In the 1820s and early 1830s, financing was usually local (local mine owners and merchants), but it became national as the success of the Liverpool and Manchester line showed the immense possibilities of the technology.

Isambard Kingdom Brunel

- The Stephensons continued as major railway builders in the 1830s and 1840s, with the son, Robert, gradually displacing his father, George. Robert was a formidable witness before Parliamentary committees and had a brilliant grasp of detail in both locomotive building (the *Rocket* and many superior successors) and line planning.

- Robert Stephenson also understood the need to develop good subcontractors to build sections of the line, people who were able to handle tough gangs of unruly workers, master complicated tasks in building cuttings and embankments, drive tunnels, and handle money.

- Other major figures came on the scene, many of whom had been apprentices under George Stephenson. The greatest of these newcomers was Isambard Kingdom Brunel, chief engineer of the Great Western Railway.

- Brunel used a seven-foot railway gauge for greater comfort and luxury. (Gauge defines the spacing of the rails on a railway track.) However, a seven-foot gauge made the line more costly to build, enforced shallower curves, and prevented interchangeability of rolling stock.

London and Birmingham Railway

- Robert Stephenson built the London and Birmingham Railway at the usual gauge of four feet, eight and a half inches, which became the standard for most of the world (mainly because British contractors built many of the first railways in other countries).

- Before the work even started, the company spent £32,000 on legal expenses to maneuver the bill through Parliament and £750,000 on land purchases (the equivalent of several billion pounds today). On the first presentation of the bill, the House of Lords rejected it, reflecting a greater skepticism about railways in the south of England than in the north. But the bill passed in 1833, and work began on this 112-mile line, the longest ever attempted.

- Robert Stephenson was only 29 when the work began, but he was a daunting personality with unrivalled experience. Stephenson divided the whole length into sections of about six miles and contracted them out. All sections were built simultaneously. To have 20,000 people working on one project simultaneously was a new jump in scale over the kind of organization the factories, mines, and foundries had achieved in the previous decades.

- The London and Birmingham Railway was laid out to exacting standards and was extremely flat, with no sharp curves; thus, it has remained usable as a high-speed line even today, without much reengineering. It opened in 1838, having a cost £5.5 million—more than double the anticipated amount.

A Stimulus to Economic Growth

- English railway architecture shows the Victorian spirit at its most euphoric, and some of the finest structures in Britain are related to railways. The London and Birmingham Railway and others boasted elegant stone stations, triumphal arches, and classical tunnel facades.

- Some stations, built in the Gothic Revival style, were designed to look like medieval cathedrals. These buildings, while overdone, still conveyed the general sense of excitement and pride generated by railways.

- Railways stimulated economic growth both directly and indirectly. Communication between cities was quicker and easier than ever before, as was bulk transport of low-value items, such as coal, iron ore, and cotton.

- Railways under construction were a major stimulus to the iron and steel business, contractors, brickworks, and mining. By 1850, all the largest companies on the London stock exchange were railways, and they were far more highly capitalized than even the biggest manufacturers.

St. Pancras Station in London was completed in 1868; with its adjoining hotel, it resembles a medieval castle.

A Major Employer

- Railways also became major employers in their own right. The actual building of the lines was done by tens of thousands of migratory workers, with the basic tools of pick, shovel, and wheelbarrow. The workers were called "navvies"—a holdover term from when these kinds of teams worked on the canals, or "navigations." In the late 1840s, 300,000 were at work building railways, and 60,000 more worked on the completed lines.

- Railway workers transformed the landscape with cuttings, embankments, bridges, and tunnels of a kind and scope never previously seen. By 1850, there were 6,000 miles of track in operation, with main line average speeds of 40 miles per hour.

- By 1873, railways had 275,000 permanent employees, making them a central component of the economy. Several new towns, such as Crewe, Swindon, Middlesbrough, and Wolverton, grew up solely as railway building and repair centers.

Cheaper and Faster Postal Service

- In 1840, Rowland Hill's innovation, the "penny post," was made possible by the railways. Hill was an inventor and social reformer who wrote an influential study of the postal system in 1837, urging reform of waste, slowness, inefficiency, and high cost.

- Until then, delivery of letters had been expensive and slow, and payment was made on delivery (the recipient could look at the letter and decide not to take it). Costs varied according to distance and were high. The General Post Office accepted Hill's proposals. Making mail delivery cheap and prepaid by the sender was a calculated risk that paid off; business and personal communication became far easier and cheaper, and the move contributed to economic growth and business security.

- The General Post Office delivered 76 million letters per year in 1839 and 863 million per year by 1870. Next-day delivery was available anywhere in the United Kingdom. Easy communication by rail combined with cheap post was another milestone in the history of industrialization and economic growth.

New Management Challenges

- Stagecoach lines' fears that railways would displace them were well founded, but the demand for short term horse-drawn transport actually accelerated, and the number of horses and carriages in Britain continued to rise as cities grew and citizens' wealth increased.

- Railways created a new class of managers, remote from their employers, who had to take responsibility for the safe working of the railways. Most industries until then operated all in one place, under the supervision of the owner or overseer, but railways, by their nature, were dispersed. Managers had to show the right blend of subordination and initiative to prevent crashes and to keep the system running smoothly and according to schedule.

- Companies also recognized the need for long-term worker loyalty and tried to make working for the railway a lifetime proposition with security and dignity. Railways built by private enterprise meant owners did not have to contend with bureaucratic national planning, wasteful duplication, nonstandardization, and unprofitable lines.

- More railway lines were projected than were ever built, and some lasted only a few years before falling into bankruptcy. After the astonishing success of the Liverpool and Manchester Railway, a great surge of enthusiasm in 1836–1837 led to a bubble, with some unwise overinvestment in railways by people who lacked the necessary detailed knowledge.

- The diversity of private ventures also led to the building of 13 separate London termini but no general exchange, which created severe transshipment problems and remained a weakness of the system into the 20th century.

Limited Government Involvement

- While government largely kept a hands-off attitude, an 1844 act of Parliament established minimum safety standards for trains, brakes, and signals. It also specified that every line should run at least one cheap passenger train per day (the "parliamentary trains") to enable ordinary people to ride.

- Parliament reserved to government the right to take over private lines after they had been in operation for 21 years (although when it came to that point, in the 1860s, government did not—until 1947). The threat of takeover was important in discouraging abuse of a natural monopoly position and probably helped keep prices down for shippers and passengers.

- A period of consolidation reduced the number of companies, all of which agreed in 1892 to move to standard gauge. Steam locomotives ran on British rails for 140 years, the last ones being withdrawn in 1968. The railway system, much of it, is still present, with the original track beds laid out by Stephenson, Brunel, and others still in use.

- In the next lecture, we'll study more closely one of the great railway builders, Isambard Kingdom Brunel. After distinguishing himself as chief engineer of the Great Western Railway, he went on to pioneer another of the significant new industrial technologies: oceangoing steamships.

Suggested Reading

Barman, *Early British Railways*.

Gourvish, *Railways and the British Economy, 1830–1914*.

Kirby, *The Origins of Railway Enterprise*.

Lewin, *The Railway Mania and Its Aftermath, 1845–1852*.

Questions to Consider

1. What were the benefits and drawbacks of leaving railway development in private hands rather than instituting a government planning policy?

2. In what ways were railways clearly superior to canals as bulk transportation devices?

The Railway Revolution
Lecture 12—Transcript

The technical and commercial success of the Liverpool and Manchester Railway set off a boom in railway building through the 1830s and 1840s. Trunk lines were built between the major cities, linking previously remote parts of Britain and making the transport of bulk items and of people far quicker and cheaper than ever before. They displaced long-distance stage coaching, they threatened the canals' monopoly on inland bulk transport, but they stimulated urban growth. They also created a high demand for further development in the metal industries, provided employment for tens of thousands of men, and created new managerial challenges.

Each railway line needed an Act of Parliament. There was a great deal of bribery of Members of Parliament, because they were often the landowners whose estates the railways would cross. The bribery was widespread to persuade them to vote in the right way. This contributed to the high cost of British railway building. Britain was already a densely settled country, and the siting of lines meant cutting across lands owned by hundreds of individuals. The acts provided limited liability and created the right of eminent domain, the ability of the railway company to compulsorily buy the lands it needed. Landowners who lacked political influence were often resentful of these forced purchases. Parliament required a detailed land survey for every line, but didn't grant automatic entry to the lands in question, so the surveyors often found themselves forced to trespass. One of the dodges they resorted to was to go on Sunday mornings to lands where they knew they were going to be unwelcome because then the local land owners, the gentry and the clergy, were sure to be in church.

In his wonderful novel *Middlemarch*, written in the 1870s but set in the 1830s, George Eliot recreates a typical scene, where the railway surveyors are chased off lands that they're measuring because suspicious local people regard them as a threatening presence from outside their closed little world. Caleb Garth, the surveyor and the local estate manager, calms the peoples' fears and persuades them not to attack the surveyors. He tells them that in the long run the railway will benefit rather than harm their community, although at the time, in the early 1830s, that was a point over which there was a great deal of disagreement.

The opposition came from people who were, in fact, likely to lose out by the coming of the railways; people who'd had made their fortunes in turnpikes, in stagecoaches, and in canals, the technologies that had already improved communications in Britain but now faced the threat of a much swifter rival. They threw as many obstacles in the way of the railways as they possibly could, particularly in the south of the country, which was less industrialized in the 1830s and slower to catch what was called "railway fever."

In the 1820s and 1830s, when it was a matter of building the Stockton and Darlington Railway and the Liverpool and Manchester line, before the credibility of railways had been fully established, the financing usually came from local sources, local mine owners and merchants. But it started to become national as the success of the Liverpool and Manchester line showed the immense possibilities of the technology.

George and Robert Stephenson continued as major builders in the 1830s and 1840s, with the son gradually displacing his father. Robert Stephenson was a formidable witness before parliamentary committees. He had a brilliant grasp of detail in both locomotive building—he was the man who'd built the *Rocket* and many of its superior successors—and in line planning. Robert Stephenson also understood the need to find and develop good subcontractors to build the sections of the line; men who had to be able to handle tough gangs of unruly navvies, master the complicated tasks in building cuttings and embankments, driving tunnels, and handling the huge sums of money that were involved in every one of these processes.

Other major figures came on the scene, many of whom had been apprentices with George Stephenson, including Joseph Locke, one of the most distinguished of the second generation of railway builders. The technology historian L. T. C. Rolt, himself a very colorful figure, wrote this:

> The post of Engineer-in-chief to a great trunk line of railway called for abilities of quite a new order; for outstanding technical skill allied with a capacity for organization and powers of sheer physical

and mental endurance that must be almost superhuman. In such an exacting race, the spoils went to the young and the swift: to Robert Stephenson, Joseph Locke, Charles Vignoles and Isambard Brunel, while an older generation of engineers, including George Stephenson himself, lost ground.

The greatest of these newcomers was Isambard Kingdom Brunel, the chief engineer of the Great Western Railway, and he's going to be the subject of our next lecture. He decided that he was going to make the gauge of the Great Western Railway seven feet. In other words, the two rails on which the train runs, instead of being four feet, eight-and-a-half inches apart, which was George Stephenson's standard gauge, he put them seven feet apart for greater comfort and greater luxury. But seven-foot gauge made the line more costly to build. It enforced shallower curves and, of course, it prevented the interchangeability of rolling stock. It means that every vehicle designed for the Great Western Railway could run only on that railway.

Robert Stephenson built the London to Birmingham Railway at the usual four feet, eight-and-a-half inch gauge, which became standard for most of the world. If you go to the United States, or to Spain, or to France, or to Germany, or the Netherlands, or to Japan, in all those places you find that the rails are four feet, eight-and-a-half inches apart. Why? Because that's how far they were apart in the old New Castle collieries where George Stephenson started out, the system he then adapted to the metal railways in England and that's continued as an acceptable compromise between all the various relevant factors ever since. Of course, it was British contractors who built many of the first railways in the many countries of the world.

Before the work even started on the London and Birmingham Railway, the company spent 32,000 pounds on legal expenses to maneuver their bill through Parliament, and then they spent another three-quarters of a million pounds on land purchases. That's really the equivalent of several billion dollars in today's terms, and it had the same kind of massive financial implications that the biggest contemporary projects also have. Despite all this careful preparation, on first presentation of the bill, the House of Lords rejected it. Legislation to go through Parliament has to be accepted first by the House of Commons, then by the House of Lords, and then signed by the

King or Queen. The fact that the Lords rejected it shows a greater skepticism about railways in the south of England than in the north. But after more parliamentary maneuvering, it finally passed in 1833, at which point work began on this 112-mile line, the longest one ever attempted in world history up to that point.

Robert Stephenson was still only 29 years old when the work began, but he was a daunting personality with unrivaled experience, and carried within himself a great deal of prestige because of the success of his work on the Liverpool and Manchester project. He divided the whole length of the line into sections of about six miles each, and then he contracted them out to subcontractors. All the sections of the line were built simultaneously. He reckoned afterwards that he'd walked the entire length of the whole railway 15 times, monitoring all aspects of the work.

To have 20,000 men working on one project simultaneously was a new jump in scale over the kind of organization that the factories, the mines, and the foundries had achieved in the previous decades. They'd gathered together large numbers of workers, but not on anything like the scale that the railways were now attempting. Also, the workmen on the railway were spread out rather than all being concentrated in one place.

The London and Birmingham Railway was laid out to very high standards. It was extremely flat and with no sharp curves, so it's remained usable as a high-speed line without much reengineering right up to the present. It finally opened after five years' hard work in 1838, having cost 5.5 million pounds, more than double the original anticipated amount. It included elegant stone stations, triumphal arches, Classical tunnel facades, common on this line and many of the others, all of which were gratuitously unnecessary, escalated the costs, but made it look splendid. In fact, English railway architecture shows the Victorian spirit at its most euphoric, and some of the finest structures in Britain are railway-related. Some of them, built in the Gothic Revival style, which was then coming very much into vogue, are designed to look much older, like medieval cathedrals, so that they simultaneously bring to mind the Middle Ages and what was then the cutting edge new technology.

My personal favorite is the immense iron and glass station enclosure at St. Pancras Station, where the London, Midland, and the Scottish Railway has its London terminus, and the adjoining hotel, the Midland Hotel, which looks like a medieval robber baron's fantasy castle. It's as magnificent as Mad King Ludwig's castle in South Germany. George Gilbert Scott, the architect of St. Pancras Station, said it was almost too good for a mere railway hotel. He was a man who was never short of self-confidence. To my mind, anyway, it's one of the three or four most striking buildings in London. It was despised by modernist architects in the early 20th century—they favored clean lines and concrete—but now, luckily, it's been given its due once more.

These buildings, and the triumphal arch at Euston Station, which sadly was demolished in the 1960s when Euston was rebuilt, were far more than necessary, but they conveyed the general sense of excitement that was being generated by the railways. You couldn't go through the Euston Arch without feeling that you were setting out on a journey that had immense important. It was a way of conferring a feeling of privilege on everybody who went through it.

The railways stimulated economic growth directly and indirectly. Communications between cities became quicker and easier than ever before. Bulk transport of low-value items like coal, iron ore, and cotton became far easier and more economical. Railways under construction were a major stimulus to the iron and steel business, to contractors, to brickworks, and to mining. All the largest companies on the London stock exchange by 1850 were railways, and they were far more highly capitalized than even the biggest manufacturers. They became a major employer in their own right, another economic stimulus. The actual building of the lines was done by tens of thousands of navvies, seminomadic workmen, with the basic tools of a pick, a shovel, and a wheelbarrow. You may remember I call them "navvies" from their earlier work on canals or "navigations." Just to give you an idea of the scale of this work: In the late 1840s, 300,000 men were at work building railways, and 60,000 more men were working on the lines which had already been completed.

The railways transformed the landscape with cuttings, embankments, bridges, and tunnels of a kind never previously seen. Because the trains have to run on a relatively flat surface, if they come to a rise, the rise has to be cut through, and hence the creation of cuttings. Very often the earth and rock that are taken out of these cuttings are then placed in areas where embankments need to be built up to keep the line level in places where otherwise the land would be too low. The combination of bridges, cuttings, and embankments, and then sometimes tunnels, means that the lines make a very, very distinctive mark on the landscape and change the look of many places throughout England.

Charles Dickens describes the Camden Town cutting of the London and Birmingham Railway. As the railway makes its way north out of London, this is what the scene looked like when it was being built. Dickens writes:

> The first shock of a great earthquake had rent the whole neighborhood to its center. Traces of its course were visible on every side. Houses were knocked down, streets broken through and stopped, deep pits and trenches dug in the ground, enormous heaps of earth and clay thrown up; buildings that were undermined and shaken, propped by great beams of wood.

Dickens talks about the way in which very often streets would suddenly come to a stop because now the cutting is in the way, and so until a bridge can be built across it, the street simply ends there.

Six thousand miles of track were in operation by 1850, and by now main line average speeds had reached 40 miles per hour, a significant increase even over the Liverpool and Manchester Railway. Two hundred seventy five thousand permanent employees worked on the railways by 1873, making it a central component of the economy in its own right.

As with the canals, so with the railways: Tunnel building presented severe technical and safety challenges. Robert Stephenson struggled with the Kilsby Tunnel on the London and Birmingham Railway. At a mile and a half in length, it was the longest tunnel yet attempted and proved extremely difficult to complete. It was so long that skeptics were afraid that the passengers and the engine drivers would suffocate from locomotive fumes inside the tunnel—the train would go into the tunnel, it would be in there for a long time, and the smoke would asphyxiate everybody—so massive ventilation shafts had to be built to draw out the smoke. The work was hamstrung by quicksand and by flooding. Four years' work and a constant escalation of cost was necessary before Kilsby was finished, and yet today you flash through this tunnel at nearly 100 miles per hour in about one minute. You don't have to labor at it at all, because they did: 1,250 men and 200 horses worked on the tunnel, the men subject to wild fits of drunkenness after every payday, living in temporary shantytowns, mounting dog fights after a hard day's work. They were extremely rough, tough men.

Several new towns were founded by the railway companies, such as Crewe, Swindon, Middlesborough, and Wolverton. They grew up solely as railway building and railway repair centers, quite often at midpoints along the railways so that people could move out from these places to take care of problems on the railway itself.

One of very few books we have written by a railway worker to describe his way of life is a book by Alfred Williams called *Life in a Railway Factory*. He was a metalworker in the works at Swindon, one of these new towns, a town on the Great Western Railway, who left a vivid and moving account of his work and his way of life. Here's what he says about his workshop:

> To view it from the interior is like looking around the inner walls of a fortress. There is no escape for the eye; nothing but bricks and mortar, iron and steel, smoke and steam arising. It is ugly; and the sense of confinement within the prison-like walls of the factory renders it still more dismal to those who have any thought of the hills and fields beyond.

Williams also describes the incredibly high levels of pollution for men working among toxic fumes and smoke all day, every day. He says at one point that men become slightly inebriated by the poisonous environment and start taking crazy risks that they'd never take if they were in their right minds. He describes a world full of the most astonishing pollution, which we'd regard as absolutely intolerable today. But even he was taken by the romance of the railway, as well as by the hardships faced by its workers.

For example, he writes a wonderful rhapsodic passage on some old railway wagons now being used as storage bins. Here's what he says of them:

> What miles these old wagons have gone. What storm and stress they have endured. What burdens they have borne. East and west, north and south, over hills and bridges, through valleys, past miles upon miles of cornfields and meadows, green and gold, red and brown by turn, in rain and snow, winter frost and summer sunshine, by day and night, year after year together. These wagons, if they could speak, would tell you they have visited every station and town on the system. Now all these things are at an end. They have run their race, and grown old in the service. They have fulfilled their period of usefulness on the line and, like old veterans returned from the war, they have come back to their native town to end their days.

These are just the wagons that they're using as dumps.

There's always been a romance to railways; the dual sense that they're imprisoning and liberating, modern but having a chivalric dash and elan because of their speed and grace. The railway companies themselves were certainly proud of them, and so were the men who worked on them. They decorated the locomotives magnificently. The same impulse that led to the grand architecture also led to a beautifully high level of maintenance. The country railway stations would have gardens; they'd be beautifully laid out. They became proud display places that reflected the grandeur of the railway as a whole.

They also led to other innovations such as Rowland Hill's "penny post," of 1840, which was made possible by the existence of the railways. Rowland Hill was an inventor and social reformer who wrote an influential study of the postal system in 1837, urging a reform of its wastefulness, its slowness, its inefficiency, and its high cost. Until then, letters had been very expensive and slow to send. The way it worked was that you'd write a letter to your friend and send it, and payment was made by the recipient rather than by the sender. In fact, the recipient was even allowed to take a look at the letter and then decide not to take it, in which case he or she wouldn't pay the fee. Costs varied according to distance, and they were high. The General

Post Office accepted Rowland Hill's proposals. He said to make the letters really, really cheap to send, and let them be prepaid by the sender. This was a calculated risk, but it paid off brilliantly, because it made business and personal communication far easier than before and again contributed to economic growth and business security.

The famous first stamp was called the "penny black" of 1840. This was the stamp with which the modern postal service began, and also the world's first adhesive stamp. It's become a very valuable collectors' item, treasured by philatelists for its rarity and also for its symbolic importance.

The post office delivered 76 million letters per year in 1839, but 863 million per year by 1870. Rowland Hill's gamble pays off, and the post office expands enormously. By the 1870s, it was possible to get next-day delivery anywhere in the United Kingdom, and very often on the same day. Even when I was a kid, I remember my mother could send a letter to her friend across town and have a letter back from her on the same day; this was before we all had telephones. Easy communication by rail with cheap postal service was another milestone in the history of industrialization and economic growth because it made possible the efficient exchange of information on which a growing industrial economy depends.

The stagecoach lines' fears that railways would displace them were well founded. Stagecoaches went into decline once the railways were well-established between cities. But the demand for short-term horse-drawn transport actually accelerated, and the number of horses and carriages in Britain continued to rise as cities grew and as citizens' wealth increased. Obviously, the trains can only go the station, and after that goods need to be taken elsewhere, and horse-drawn vehicles remained the way of doing that for another 60 or 70 years.

The railways created a new class of managers, remote from their employers. They had to take responsibility for the safe working of the railways. Most industries until then had operated all in the same place under the supervision of the owner or the overseer, the factory manager, but railways, by their nature, were decentralized and dispersed. The managers had to show the right blend of subordination and initiative. They had to follow the rules, but if necessary they had to act decisively to prevent crashes and to keep the system running smoothly and according to timetable. They overcame seasonal variations and ran according to the same schedule whatever the month. Once the railways invested so much money in the system, they couldn't afford to make it stop, so whereas most activities in Britain up to that time had been highly seasonally inflected, the railways had timetables and they always ran to the same time, and also tried to make themselves famous for good timekeeping.

The separation of managers from owners, which is very, very common in industrial concerns today, began with railways. Of course, managers and owners don't always have quite the same interests. The managers are more concerned with their own job security than they are with creating high dividends for the owners. Of course, the managers often know best exactly what's actually happening and how to use the industry they work for to advance their own interests. The development of management really begins with railways and then spreads to other activities from there.

The companies themselves also recognized the need for long-term workers' loyalty, and they tried to hold workers over their lifetimes, promoting from within, offering seniority pay and benefits to people who stayed with the company for a long time, and tried to make working for the railway a lifetime proposition with the benefits of security and dignity, so that you'd begin your work as a young man, perhaps working as an apprentice fireman, go on to be promoted to fireman, then to train driver, and perhaps eventually to station manager.

The fact that the railways were built by private enterprise meant a lack of national planning, sometimes wasteful duplication, sometimes non-standardization, as we saw with the example of the Great Western, and some lines that never made a profit. As with the canals, so with the railways: More lines were projected than were ever built, and some of them lasted for only a few years before falling into bankruptcy. England today is absolutely honeycombed with railways that ran for a few years and then failed, or that were laid out but never even went into use.

After the astonishing success of the Liverpool and Manchester, a great surge of enthusiasm in 1836–1837 led to a bubble—railway fever—and to some very unwise overinvestment in railways by people who lacked the necessary detailed knowledge. The diversity of private ventures also led to the building of 13 separate major stations in London—the multiple termini—but no general exchange, and that created severe trans-shipment problems and remained a weakness of the system into the 20th century. Lines ran from every province into London, but if you wanted to get the Great Western Railway to carry something to East Anglia, there wasn't a line that bypassed London and went to East Anglia, and there wasn't a place in London where the two lines linked up. That surely was a weakness.

The government largely kept a hands off attitude, though an Act of Parliament of 1844 established minimum safety standards for trains, brakes, and signals. It also specified that every line should run at least one cheap passenger train per day—these became known as the "parliamentary trains"—to enable ordinary people to ride by the railway. The Act of Parliament also reserved to the government the right to take over private lines after they'd been in operation for 21 years, although when it came to the point, in the 1860s, the government didn't do it. That didn't happen until the nationalization of the entire system in 1947 by Clement Attlee's socialist labor government, but the threat of a takeover was important in discouraging the abuse of a natural monopoly position, and it probably helped to keep the prices down, both for shippers and for passengers.

The density of railway lines all over Britain and the availability of alternative routes had very beneficial effects—for example, during the Nazi Blitz in 1940 and 1941 when railway yards were targeted by the German bombers—but it was nearly always possible to reroute trains and take them on alternative lines. A period of consolidation reduced the number of companies, all of which agreed in 1892 finally to move to standard gauge, four feet, eight and a half.

Britons were fascinated by railways, and they came to play an important part in British literature and paintings. The novelist Anthony Trollope, who himself worked for the post office setting up branch post offices all over England, writes novels about vicars and bishops riding on the trains and checking their timetables in novels of the 1850s and 1860s, showing that very rapidly they'd become a standard part of the lives of significant people in the kingdom.

The idea that a train journey was like the journey one takes through life could also take on very interesting religious overtones. Let me read to you the grave marker in Ely Cathedral commemorating an 1845 train crash in which the engineer was killed. It's another of these rather corny poems, but it comes from the heart. Here's what it says:

> The line to Heaven by Christ was made,
> With heavenly truth, the Rails are laid. ...
>
> God's word is the first engineer,
> It points the way to heaven so dear. ...
>
> God's love the fire, His truth the steam,
> Which drives the engine and the train. ...
>
> In first, and second, and third class,
> Repentance, Faith, and Holiness. ...
>
> Come then, poor sinners, now's the time,
> At any station on the line,
> If you repent, and turn from sin,
> The train will stop and take you in.

The train that's going to heaven.

Contemporaries realized that the coming of the railways marked one of the most decisive shifts in British history. The novelist Thackeray, author of *Vanity Fair,* wrote in 1860:

> We elderly people lived in that pre-railroad world, which has passed into limbo and vanished from under us. I tell you, it was firm under our feet once, and not long ago. They have raised those railroad

embankments up, and shut off that old world that was behind them. Climb up that bank on which the irons were laid and look to the other side. It is gone.

Steam locomotives ran on British rails for 140 years, the last ones being withdrawn in 1968. The railway system, much of it is still there, with the original track beds laid out by Stephenson, Brunel, Locke, and the others, many of them still in use. What's more, dozens of societies of enthusiasts have rescued steam locomotives from the scrapyards, reconditioned them, bought up disused lines, and continue to run them. One of the most delightful and distinctive of British pastimes today is to ride on a steam train, or tinker with them in order to keep them in working order.

In the next lecture, I'll move on to study more closely another of the great railway builders, Isambard Kingdom Brunel, who I mentioned several times in this lecture. After distinguishing himself as engineer of the Great Western Railway, he went on to pioneer another of the great new technologies: oceangoing steamships.

Isambard Kingdom Brunel—Master Engineer
Lecture 13

H istorians enjoy arguing about which is more important, great
individuals or broad social and economic forces. Of course, both
are significant influences, but it can be helpful for historians to
single out particular figures who epitomize historical trends—for example,
Arkwright's work in textiles, Wedgwood in potteries, Brindley in canal
building, and the Stephensons in railways. Once we get to Isambard
Kingdom Brunel, the temptation to emphasize the life and work of a
particular individual becomes impossible to resist. He was a Promethean
figure, intellectually and technologically daring, who pushed new
possibilities further than any of his contemporaries.

A Talented Father

- Isambard Kingdom Brunel (1806–1859) was a notable figure in
  the Industrial Revolution, effecting key innovations in oceangoing,
  steam-powered, iron-hulled ships. The son of an engineer, Brunel
  learned much of his trade from his talented father, Marc Brunel.
  Marc Brunel was a royalist officer in the French navy, who fled to
  the United States during the French Revolution and worked for five
  years as chief engineer to the city of New York.

- Back in Britain by 1799, Marc Brunel pioneered the mass
  production of rigging blocks for the Royal Navy and
  won a contract to mass-produce boots for the Duke of
  Wellington's army, which won the Battle of Waterloo in 1815
  against Napoléon.

- Young Isambard Brunel helped his father build the first tunnel
  under the Thames River. Two earlier attempts had failed, one
  nearly drowning the railway pioneer Richard Trevithick. The
  tunnel was finally finished in 1842, and Marc Brunel was knighted
  by Queen Victoria.

Great Western Railway

- In 1833, at age 27, Isambard Kingdom Brunel was appointed chief engineer of the Great Western Railway and built it to a higher level of quality and comfort than any rival line.

- After riding on the Liverpool and Manchester Railway, Brunel decided it was uncomfortable and instead built the Great Western Railway to seven-foot gauge. That meant that curves had to be shallower, the right-of-way broader, tunnels wider, and all locomotives and rolling stock larger. He planned the line as flat and straight as possible—with minimal gradients. He fought an intense battle to get parliamentary approval that cost nearly £90,000 in legal and other fees.

- There were constant problems with the project because no one had worked with seven-foot gauge before. The most difficult section was from Bath to Chippenham, where huge embankments, cuttings, and a long tunnel were needed. The tunnel had to be blasted through hard rock, using a ton of gunpowder per week for three years.

- The entire line of the Great Western Railway opened in 1841. Brunel's biggest mistake was ordering locomotives that were too small and underpowered. He was forced to admit his error and subsequently bought superior ones from George and Robert Stephenson.

"Battle of the Gauges"

- The Great Western Railway also hired a brilliant 21-year-old, Daniel Gooch, who had been apprenticed under Stephenson. Gooch soon began custom building far better locomotives, well fitted to the Great Western Railway.

- Gooch was quiet, businesslike, and puritanical—the personal opposite of Brunel, who was characterized by his Byronic swagger. But Brunel, who knew Gooch had been right about the locomotives, came to trust the young man implicitly.

- The years 1845–1846 saw the "battle of the gauges," in which most of the other railway companies tried to get parliamentary approval of the railway gauge of four feet, eight and a half inches, as the national standard. Although Brunel's locomotives could run faster, there were already more than 2,000 miles of standard-gauge track, as opposed to 240 miles of seven-foot gauge. In 1892, the Great Western Railway gave up and converted to standard gauge.

The Atmospheric Engine

- When Brunel was asked to extend the line down into Devon, he made another mistake, overreaching by trying a daring new technology—the "atmospheric engine." Instead of having a heavy locomotive pulling coaches, a stationary steam engine would create a vacuum in a pipe laid along the track. A piston attached to the train would fit snugly in the pipe, and the vacuum would suck the train along. The train would be quiet, and the system would achieve significant fuel economy.

- Brunel had worked out that a large percentage of the energy used by a locomotive at high speed was consumed in moving itself against wind resistance; thus, if the engine was stationary, there would be a significant savings in fuel.

- Although the system was sound in theory, it didn't work well in practice; such a system depended on a tight, permanent seal, which proved impossible to create. The system dried out in summer, froze in winter, and needed so many workers to maintain it that it cost more than conventional locomotives. Brunel realized in 1848, after just one year of operation, that the atmospheric engine was a flop.

The Royal Albert Bridge and Paddington Station

- Another great achievement by Brunel was the Royal Albert Bridge over the Tamar River. For this structure, two massive wrought iron trusses were placed on the piers when they were just above the waterline. These trusses were then jacked up a bit at a time as the brickwork of the piers was built under them until the whole bridge was high enough to satisfy Royal Navy requirements of 100-foot clearance.

- At first, the least interesting station of the Great Western Railway was Paddington, its London terminus. It was utilitarian because of the directors' bottom-line concerns.
  - Brunel, who served on the design committee for the 1851 Great Exhibition, was delighted by Joseph Paxton's design for the Crystal Palace, constructed of iron framing and plate glass.

  - Inspired, Brunel used the same idea for Paddington Station, using prefabricated sections, which were strong and light and enabled rapid construction.

S.S. *Great Western*
- Brunel's next monumental achievement was to transform shipbuilding. In the early days of the Great Western Railway, Brunel had suggested to its directors that passengers could eventually take a Great Western train from London to Bristol, then get on a ship of the same name and sail it all the way to New York. The directors took Brunel seriously, and he collaborated with several experienced marine engineers to create the S.S. *Great Western*, a steamship that could cross the ocean.

- The current theory was that such a machine would take up all available space with coal, leaving none for passengers and cargo. Brunel disagreed, realizing that bigger ships would have far larger cargo space and room for cabins. Brunel also recognized that the limiting factor for ships' speed is their length; thus, a longer ship would be faster.

- At 236 feet, the S.S. *Great Western* was the longest ship ever built up to that time. Launched in 1838, it used a combination of sails and steam-powered paddle wheels. Brunel hoped it would be the first steamship to cross the Atlantic Ocean.

- However, a rival ship, the *Sirius*, set off first. The *Great Western* then suffered a fire in its engine room, which delayed departure. Even so, the crossing was a success. Although the *Great Western* narrowly lost to the *Sirius*, it used far less coal and crossed in a shorter time (15.5 days). In fact, the *Sirius* had run out of coal and had to burn some of its cargo to complete the voyage. The *Great Western* became the first regular trans-Atlantic passenger steamer.

S.S. *Great Britain*

- Brunel's second great achievement in marine technology came with the S.S. *Great Britain*. Ever since John "Iron-Mad" Wilkinson's iron barge, the possibility of metal ships had been accepted, but Brunel built his on an incomparably grander scale. The largest to date was 500 tons; Brunel's was 3,000.

- When the hull was half built, Brunel decided to switch to the new propeller technology, instead of paddle wheels. That offered cleaner lines, more fuel efficiency, and greater speed. The *Great Britain* finally set off on her maiden voyage in 1845 and knocked another 36 hours off the crossing time to New York (now just 14 days).

- The ship went aground a year later off the Irish coast, and the owners were afraid it would have to be abandoned. Brunel finally found a way to lift it off the reef on a high tide in 1847 and bring it back to Liverpool for repairs. It spent the next 24 years carrying emigrants from Britain to Australia.

Transforming Shipbuilding

- Brunel's third ship, the S.S. *Great Eastern*, begun in 1854, was still more innovative. It was large enough to travel nonstop to Australia, powered with propellers, paddle wheels, and sails. Six times the volume of any current ship, it needed only a small crew. It was designed with many new features, including uniform metal plates and a double hull and bulkheads for strength and watertightness.

- The ship was nearly impossible to launch. The river was not wide enough, which meant that the ship had to be built for sideways

Many features of Brunel's *Great Eastern* would later become standard in shipbuilding, such as uniform metal plates and a double hull and bulkheads.

launch. The first and second attempts to launch, in 1857, failed. Brunel finally got it into the water in January 1858 with massive hydraulic rams. The launch alone had cost £120,000.

- By the time the *Great Eastern* was launched, Brunel was on his deathbed. The ship finally sailed the Atlantic in the summer of 1860 and was acclaimed in New York. It hit a reef in 1862, but it did not sink because of the double hull. Sold in 1865, it was used to lay trans-Atlantic cable in 1866—facilitating almost instantaneous transoceanic communication.

- The Stephensons, Brunel, and the other great Victorian engineers were able to build accurate, efficient locomotives and steamships because they had access to something none of their predecessors had enjoyed—high-quality machine tools. Late-18th-century and early-19th-century craftsmen learned how to make more accurate and more durable lathes, stamps, taps, dies, and all the other devices essential for turning out precision machinery. These machine-tool innovators will be the subject of the next lecture.

Suggested Reading

Bagust, *The Greater Genius?*

Brindle, *Brunel.*

Christopher, *Brunel's Kingdom.*

Vaughan, *Isambard Kingdom Brunel.*

Questions to Consider

1. When did Brunel's fearless individuality hinder rather than help his projects?

2. What were the benefits of steam-powered, iron-hulled ships in comparison with the wooden, sail-powered alternative?

Isambard Kingdom Brunel—Master Engineer
Lecture 13—Transcript

Historians enjoy arguing about which is more important: great individuals or broad social and economic forces. Like most historians, I believe in the importance of both, but as a history teacher I've always found it helpful to single out particular figures who represent or epitomize important historical trends. There's much to be said for emphasizing the work of Arkwright in textiles, Wedgwood in potteries, Brindley in canal building, and the Stephensons in railways. It helps us realize that these were actual people making decisions, overcoming difficulties, and, of course, these were people whose lives were full of colorful incidents.

Once we get to Isambard Kingdom Brunel, the temptation to emphasize the life and work of a particular individual becomes impossible to resist. He was a promethean figure, intellectually and technologically daring, who pushed new possibilities further than any contemporary, especially by building oceangoing, steam-powered, iron-hulled ships. He lived from 1806–1859. He was the son of an engineer and learned much of his trade from a talented father. Marc Brunel, the father, started out in life as a royalist officer in the French navy. He fled to the United States during the French Revolution, and worked for five years as the chief engineer to the city of New York. Marc Brunel then emigrated back to Britain in 1799, where he pioneered in the mass production of rigging blocks for the Royal Navy. Then he won a contract to mass produce boots for the Duke of Wellington's army that won the Battle of Waterloo in 1815 against Napoleon.

Young Isambard Brunel, the son, helped his father to build the first tunnel under the River Thames. As London grew bigger, it became more and more necessary to have more ways of getting across the river. The one big bridge and the ferries were no longer good enough. Two earlier attempts to build a tunnel had failed. One of them nearly drowned the railway pioneer Richard Trevethick. The bottom of the river was a mixture of mud and gravel, but for centuries, debris and sewage had been flowing into the river and there was a lot of uncertainty about what the conditions were going to be beneath the river. How far below the bed would they have to dig the tunnel in order for it to be safe and firm?

The son, Isambard, was already the chief site engineer on the project by the age of 20. He encountered foul air, all the usual mining hazards, plus the knowledge of the river above them, which at any moment might come through and flood the entire tunnel. There were constant anxieties relating not just to the drilling, but to the pumping as well. Twice he was very nearly drowned by the roof caving in, and the work had to be abandoned in 1829 because no more money was available and the work was only half-finished. The British government finally gave enough in 1836 to resume the work and the tunnel was completed in 1842, at which point Isambard's father, Marc Brunel, was knighted by Queen Victoria.

Young Isambard then won a competition to design a suspension bridge across the Avon Gorge on the outskirts of Bristol. He submitted four distinct designs to the design competition committee and beat out Thomas Telford, the builder of the famous Welsh canal aqueduct and the Menai Straits Bridge, which was then the longest suspension bridge in the world. The Avon bridge project was also plagued by delays and financial crises, and was finally finished only in 1864, five years after Brunel's death. But it's still there, still in use, and still a spectacular sight, 200 feet above valley and 630 feet across.

Isambard Brunel was then appointed chief engineer of the Great Western Railway in the year 1833 at the age of 27, and he built it to a higher level of quality and comfort than any rival line. After riding on the Liverpool and Manchester Railway, which opened in 1830 built by the Stephensons, he decided it was too uncomfortable and resolved to build the Great Western Railway to seven-foot gauge instead. I mentioned this in an earlier lecture; that meant that the two rails were seven feet apart instead of four feet, eight-and-a-half inches. This meant that the curves had to be shallower, the right of way had to be wider, the tunnels had to be wider, it meant a lot more drilling, and all the locomotives and rolling stock had to be bigger.

He planned it as flat and straight as possible. The gradient of the Great Western was nowhere more than 1 in 500—in other words, one foot of rise for every 500 feet of travel—and mainly it was less than that. Much of it is absolutely level. Intense battles took place to get Parliamentary approval, costing nearly 90,000 pounds in legal and parliamentary fees. The canal companies and the stagecoach companies both knew that they were going to lose by the creation of the railway and lobbied very hard against it. Once it was approved, he traveled ceaselessly along the route in a modified stagecoach, which he called his Britzka. It was a kind of traveling office; a horse-drawn predecessor to the recreational vehicle, but highly practical.

Brunel encountered constant problems because nobody had previously worked with seven-foot gauge before. There was already a fund of experience in England for working with four-feet, eight-and-a-half gauge. Although it was a new technology, it wasn't brand new; but Brunel was turning his back on much of the accumulated experience by the mid-1830s in order to head out on his own. He was constantly encountering unexpected difficulties. In a letter to a friend, he wrote this:

> If ever I go mad, I shall have the ghost of the opening of the railway walking before me, or rather standing in front of me, holding out its hand. And when it steps forward, a little swarm of devils in the shape of uncut timber, half-finished station houses, sinking embankments, broken screws, absent guard plates, unfinished drawings and sketches, will, quietly and quite as a matter of course and as if I ought to have expected it, lift up my ghost and put him a little further off than before.

The completion seemed to be receding before him.

The most difficult section of all was from Bath to Chippenham, near the western end of the line, where huge embankments, cuttings, and a long tunnel, the Box Hill Tunnel, were needed. The Box Hill Tunnel had to be blasted through hard rock using a ton of gunpowder per week for three years, and a combination of mining accidents and flooding caused 100 deaths among the workforce just on that tunnel.

Brunel himself was more interested in grandeur than in profitability, and he often had to be restrained by the directors and investors who were much more interested in the bottom line. He wanted it to be a monument to himself, among other things. The entrances to the tunnels and the stations were magnificent. Going into one of the tunnels was like entering an ancient castle. The station at the western end, Bristol Temple Meads, was built in the style of Tudor Gothic. It was far, far more elaborate than it needed to be. It's still a wonderful place to go to, right up to the present.

One of Brunel's many biographers, Stephen Brindle writes this:

> Even the most humble structures were to offer delight and evoke pleasant associations. Small stations and trackside buildings were to capture the atmosphere of picturesque garden pavilions, Tudor lodges or fashionable villas, while stations were to be designed in the manner of picturesque country houses. Greater works—tunnels and viaducts—designed to conjure up images of ancient Rome or medieval ruins were to impress travelers with a satisfying sense of awe and the sublime. It was a most charming idea and typical of Brunel: a wonderful marriage of the functional and the fantastic, of art with science.

The whole length of the line from Bristol to London was opened in the year 1841. Brunel's biggest mistake at this point was ordering locomotives that were too small and underpowered for the job they had to do. Although he hated to do so, he was forced to admit his mistake and then buy much better ones from George and Robert Stephenson, who were, of course, his great rivals.

The Great Western Railway also hired as chief engineer a brilliant 21 year old named Daniel Gooch, who'd been apprenticed under Stephenson up in Northumberland. Gooch soon began custom building far better locomotives, well fitted to the Great Western Railway, at their works in Swindon, which was a purpose-built railway town. It's striking, I think, to find out how young so many of the principal people were in these enterprises. It's comparable to the way in which, in our generation, the great computer breakthroughs have often come from some very, very young and brilliant entrepreneurs. That's how it was with what was then the new technology of railways. Daniel Gooch was the personal opposite of Brunel. He was quiet, businesslike, and puritanical, as opposed to Brunel's Byronic swagger. But Gooch also knew how to stand up for himself, and Brunel knew that he'd been right about the locomotives. He came to trust Daniel Gooch implicitly.

In 1845 and 1846 took place what's remembered by historians as the "battle of the gauges" in which most of the other railway companies tried to get Parliamentary approval of the four-foot, eight-and-a-half-inch as the national standard. Although Brunel's locomotives could run faster, there were already over 2,000 miles of standard-gauge track, as opposed to about 240 miles of seven-foot gauge. The Great Western was on the defensive from then on, and in 1892 it finally gave up and converted to standard gauge. From 1892 up to the present, standard gauge has prevailed throughout the whole of Britain.

Although there were some things to be said in favor of seven-foot gauge, the analogy we need to think of is with typewriter keyboards. The earliest ones were written "QWERTY," partly to slow down operators who'd otherwise use them too rapidly and jam the works. The QWERTY system makes no sense anymore, but it's already there and everybody knows it, which makes it much more likely that it'll persist. In other words, the sheer fact of the existence of standard gauge made it that much more likely that it would carry on existing, and that's exactly what's happened.

When Brunel was asked to extend the line from Bristol down into Exeter, into Devonshire, and into Cornwall, he made another mistake, overreaching in the name of trying a daring new technology. This was what Brunel called the "atmospheric engine." Instead of having a heavy locomotive pulling coaches, the standard method by then, his idea was that a stationary steam engine would create a vacuum in a long pipe that was laid along the track. A piston attached to the train would fit snugly inside the pipe, and then the vacuum would suck the train along the track. This means, of course, that the train would be quiet and the system would achieve a big fuel economy. He'd worked out that a large percentage of the energy used by a locomotive at high speed was consumed in moving itself against wind resistance, so if the engine was stationary there would be a big saving in fuel. And, of course, the atmospheric train would be much cleaner because the passengers weren't showered in soot and sparks, which was one of the characteristics of early train travel.

The atmospheric railway was good in theory but not in practice, because it depended on a tight permanent seal inside the pipe, and that proved impossible to create. Brunel, as so often in his life, was pushing ahead of the technological possibilities then available to him. It tended to dry out in summer, it tended to freeze in winter, and it actually needed so many men to maintain that it cost more rather than less than conventional locomotives. Brunel realized in 1848, after just one year of operation, that it was a flop. At that point, he converted this section of line to conventional locomotives, at which point it began to work much better and finally became one of the most scenic railways in England because it hugs the south coast, notably at the little town of Dawlish, where it runs right along the beach, which has become a classic place for English railway photographers.

Another great achievement on that section of line was the Royal Albert Bridge over the River Tamar, built between 1852 and 1859, which takes the railway into Cornwall. The Tamar marks the boundary between these two counties; it's very close to the port of Plymouth. The two massive wrought iron trusses of the bridge were placed on the piers when they'd been built just above the waterline, and then they were jacked up a little bit at a time as the brickwork of the piers was built under them until the whole thing was high enough to satisfy the Royal Navy's requirement of a 100-foot clearance so that the biggest Navy ships could sail under the bridge while the trains went over the top.

At first, the least interesting station of the Great Western was Paddington, its London terminus. It was at first very utilitarian because of the directors' concerns with the bottom line. But as it happened, Brunel was invited to become a member of the design committee for the 1851 Great Exhibition. This was the world's first trade fair. He was delighted by the winning submission, submitted by Joseph Paxton: the design for the Crystal Palace. It was an iron frame filled in with great sheets of plate glass, built in 1851 in Hyde Park, and one of the sensations of its time; the Crystal Palace. It was quick to build, as well, from prefabricated sections; strong, and light. Brunel adapted the idea for Paddington itself, creating a series of iron frames covered with glass, and it still stands today. It became all the more famous because of the Paddington Bear stories, the story of the bear that was found on Paddington Station and then named after it, written by Michael Bond starting in 1958.

Throughout his life, Brunel was always acutely aware of his social status. He was intensely proud of his wealth and success, and of his possessions. He was the son of an immigrant who'd struggled in early life before achieving fame, and he wanted to outdo his great father. He married, in 1836, a woman who we'd probably describe as a trophy wife. Adrian Vaughan, another of his biographers, describes her like this:

> She had neither the talents nor the money which Isambard had once thought essential in a wife. She was narrow-minded, strong-willed, bigoted, snobbish, and bossy, yet submissive to Isambard. However, without talents she constituted no threat to his ego, for Isambard admitted to no equals except Robert Stephenson. She was publicly acknowledged to be very beautiful, which would be a feather in his cap, and she came from the right class in society, so she would not be a bar to his progress.

Brunel's next great project was to transform shipbuilding. In the early days of the Great Western Railway, Brunel was chatting with the directors and suggested that passengers could eventually take a Great Western train from London to Bristol, then get onto a ship of the same name, and sail it all the way to New York; the Great Western trip from London to New York. They took him seriously, and he collaborated with several experienced marine engineers to actually create a ship called the *Great Western*.

Robert Fulton's steamboat had run up the Hudson River from New York to Albany starting in 1807; this is something we'll explore in one of the later lectures about American industrialization. But nobody had yet built a steamship that could cross the ocean. The theory was that it would take up all the available space with coal and have no space left for passengers or cargo. Brunel disagreed with that. He understood that the increased size of the hull in square feet translated into increased capacity in cubic feet, so that bigger ships would have far larger cargo space and plenty of room for cabins as well as fuel. He also recognized that the limiting factor for ships' speed is their length. The longer a ship is, the faster it can go, so a longer ship than ever before would be faster than any before. At 236 feet length, the *Great Western* was the longest ship ever built up to that time and therefore no longer constrained by considerations of materials. A combination of sails and steam-powered paddle wheels were its method of moving through the water.

The *Great Western* was launched in 1838. Brunel hoped that it would become the first steamship to cross the Atlantic. But a rival ship called the *Sirius*, which had been designed and built for crossings of the Irish Sea, a much, much shorter distance, set off first, rising to the challenge. The *Great Western* then suffered a fire in its engine room, which delayed its departure. All but 7 of the 50 booked passengers, hearing about the fire, then canceled their passages. At first it looked as though everything was going to go wrong, but, in the event, the crossing was a success. It narrowly lost to the *Sirius*, which arrived after a 19-day voyage, but the *Great Western* used far less coal and did it in shorter time, just 15 ½ days. In fact, the *Sirius* had run out of coal and it had to burn some of its cargo before it could complete the voyage, whereas the *Great Western* had 200 tons left on arrival, and it became the first regular transatlantic passenger steamer.

A second great jump in marine technology came with Brunel's next big ship, the *Great Britain*. Ever since John Wilkinson's iron barge, the possibility of metal ships had been accepted, but Brunel built his on incomparably grander scales. The biggest to date was 500 tons; here was a ship that was 3,000 tons. When the hull was half built, he suddenly decided to switch to the new propeller technology, recently patented in 1836 by Francis Pettit Smith, instead of paddlewheels. The great thing about propellers is that they're completely submerged and they propel the ship from the back. They make the ship more streamlined, they give it greater fuel efficiency, and they make it faster. These were the kinds of things that were bound to appeal to an innovative engineer like Brunel; he was always looking around to see what new things had become available. But the engine builder, Francis Humphreys, who was suddenly confronted with the fact that he needed to shift the propulsion system from paddlewheels to propeller shafts, was so horrified at this last-minute change when the ship was already half-built that he collapsed and died.

When it was about to be launched by Prince Albert, the Queen's husband, in 1843, Brunel discovered that modifications to the Bristol dockyards hadn't been made as promised, and he then had to wait for another year while the changes enabled the ship to move out into the Severn estuary. It was simply too big otherwise to be accommodated. The *Great Britain* finally set off on its maiden voyage in 1845, and it knocked another 36 hours off the crossing time to New York, now just 14 days. One thing to bear in mind about this is that so long as the ships had been sail-powered, they were forced to often sail a very indirect route following the great circulation of the winds in the north Atlantic, the clockwise circulation; they couldn't sail direct. But a steamship captain could simply set course and sail directly back and forth, which itself made timetabling of such voyages possible, really for the first time.

The *Great Britain* went aground a year later off the Irish coast, and the owners were afraid that it would have to be abandoned. Brunel sailed out to see it, and he was appalled at the company's defeatist attitude. He was sure it could be saved. He was also delighted to see how well it withstood the pounding of the sea, and in a letter he wrote this:

> The finest ship in the world is lying like a useless saucepan, kicking about on the most exposed shore you can imagine. As to the state of the ship, she is as straight and as sound as she ever was, as a whole, beautiful to look at, and really how she can be talked of in the way she has been I cannot understand. It is positively cruel. It would be like taking away the character of a young woman without any grounds whatsoever.

Men have always talked about ships as "she," and there's a lovely example of it.

He finally worked out a way to lift it off the reef on a high tide in 1847 and bring it back to Liverpool for repairs. The *Great Britain* spent the next 24 years carrying emigrants from Britain to Australia. It was finally sold as a coal-carrying ship, and then ultimately wrecked in the Falklands Islands in 1886. For years, it remained there as a moldering hulk on the Falklands, but finally was towed back to Britain in 1970 and then very, very carefully and lovingly restored in Bristol, where it had started its life, and can now be visited. The *Great Britain* is a source of great pride to the city of Bristol itself.

Brunel's third great ship, the *Great Eastern*, begun in 1854, was even more innovative. It was big enough to go nonstop all the way from England to Australia; that is, as far away from Britain on the planet as you can get before you start getting closer again. It was powered by propellers, paddlewheels, and sails and had six times the volume of any current ship, yet needed only a small crew. If you put side-by-side diagrams of the *Great Western*, the *Great Britain*, and the *Great Eastern*, you could see an enormous expansion of scale. No bigger ship would be built in Britain until the *Lusitania* in 1907. It was far ahead of its time, and with many new features that later became standard; for example, standardized metal plates from which the hull could be assembled, a double hull and bulkheads for strength and for watertightness. The building of it kept 2,000 men busy at work hammering rivets for four years. It was a huge undertaking. In the building of the *Great Eastern*, there was an immense clash of wills between the shipbuilder John Scott Russell, in whose London yards it was actually fabricated, and Brunel himself. Both of them were huge egotists, both very talented, and there's been a kind of battle of the biographers ever since, with each man enjoying champions and vilifiers.

The most famous photograph of Brunel was taken at the *Great Eastern's* dockside. There he is, standing in front of immense chains, with a top hat and smoking a cigar, and looking supremely self-confident and purposeful, even in the midst of all his troubles. This was a period when there were very angry letters back and forth between Russell and Brunel, because Brunel was always busy with many other projects, too, and could never devote all of his time to just one of them. Scott Russell ended one letter "Your obedient servant," to which Brunel replied, "I wish you were my obedient servant; I should begin with a little flogging." Scott Russell eventually went bankrupt, and for months the almost-completed ship lay silent. It was almost impossible to launch. The river wasn't wide enough, so it had to be built for sideways launch; very hazardous and not much practiced up to that time. The first attempt at a cautious controlled launch on the third of November, 1857, failed. A second attempt two weeks later also failed. By then, the *Great Eastern* had drawn an enormous amount of press attention, and a lot of scornful remarks were being made that Brunel had outstripped even his own great abilities. *Mechanic's Magazine* wrote the following editorial:

Mr. Brunel has presented the world with the greatest and most costly example of professional folly that was ever seen. It was, in our judgment, an altogether unnecessary display of self-confidence in Mr. Brunel to build the ship where she is, particularly as the narrowness of the river and the populousness of its banks rendered a rapid launch extremely dangerous.

He finally got it into the water in January, 1858, with massive hydraulic rams. The launch alone had cost 120,000 pounds, which you need to multiply by 30 or 40 to get a sense of that price in contemporary terms. By the time it was launched, Brunel himself was on his deathbed, suffering from Bright's disease, a kidney ailment, but also from exhaustion. Never for a moment did he stop the hectic pace of his life.

During its trials in the English Channel, a massive explosion blew the first of the *Great Eastern's* funnels high into the air and killed five of the boiler stokers. But it finally sailed the Atlantic in the summer of 1860, just before the American Civil War, and was acclaimed in New York. It hit a reef in 1862, but didn't sink because of the double hull. It was sold in 1865 to become a cable layer, and it laid a transatlantic cable in 1866. One such cable had been finished in 1858, linking up Britain and America by telegraphy, but had very soon failed. The next one laid by the *Great Eastern* endured, facilitating almost instantaneous transatlantic communication, another great leap forward in industrial society.

The pattern of Brunel's life was one of constant overreaching, terrific blunders, and then great ingenuity to put things right. He had many of the likeable and many of the horrible characteristics of most of the great industrial innovators. By now, he's become an icon in British life and history. Aptly, at the London Olympic Games, the opening ceremony in 2012, whose symbolism must've mystified many watchers all over the world, figures dressed as Brunel wearing top hats and tailcoats played a prominent role, presiding over the great smoking chimneys that represented industrial Britain of the 19th century.

Stephenson, Brunel, and the other great Victorian engineers were able to build accurate, efficient locomotives and steamships because they had access to something none of their predecessors had enjoyed: high-quality machine tools. Late 18th century and early 19th century craftsmen learned how to make more accurate and more durable lathes, stamps, taps and dies, and all the other devices essential for turning out precision machinery. These machine-tool makers will be the subject of my next lecture.

The Machine-Tool Makers
Lecture 14

W hen we study spectacular innovations, such as steam locomotives and oceangoing ships, it is essential to remember that their makers required a wide array of special tools and materials. This lecture is a history of the pioneer tool makers who improved precision, accuracy, strength, and uniformity in the treatment of metals, on which all subsequent technologies depended. The higher standard of machine-tool making they established enabled engineers to build high-pressure steam engines to minute tolerances. It also laid the groundwork for the mass production of identical parts, which would be crucial for a later stage of the Industrial Revolution.

John "Longitude" Harrison

- A long tradition of skilled craftsmanship in metals contributed to the development of high-quality machinery. Among the preindustrial craftsmen, clock makers and watchmakers were the most skilled. The quest for accurate marine chronometers challenged a generation of clock makers, of whom the most distinguished was John "Longitude" Harrison (1693–1776).

- Sailors in Columbus's day could already compute latitude accurately with readings from the stars and sun, but longitude was much more difficult. An extremely accurate clock could help: If you knew the time in London and knew your latitude, you could work out your longitude.

In developing his marine chronometer, John Harrison worked out methods to compensate for the motion of ships, humidity, and variations in temperature.

- The challenge of making a clock that accurate took most of Harrison's lifetime. Harrison aimed to win a prize of £20,000, offered by the Admiralty in 1714. The prize was offered in the wake of a disaster at sea, in which an English fleet whose navigators had miscalculated their longitude foundered on the rocks; 2,000 men were lost.

- Harrison set out to compete for the prize while still a young clock maker. His first model, H1, went on a navy expedition to Portugal in 1736 and proved far more accurate than the ad hoc methods used by the ship's captain. Harrison worked out processes to compensate for the ship's rocking, humidity, and unevenness in temperature.

- In a 1761 trial of an improved model, the longitude estimated was accurate to within one nautical mile. Although squabbles at the Navy Board held up the prize, Parliament gave Harrison £8,750 in 1773, when he was 80. His clocks used diamonds, improved steel, bimetallic strips, and other materials enhanced over the course of the century.

- Captain James Cook loved the Harrison chronometer. Cook was the British mariner, explorer, and cartographer who circumnavigated the globe, located and mapped a large part of the Australian coast, charted the two islands of New Zealand, mapped much of the Alaskan coast, and discovered Hawaii. If anyone needed a good chronometer, it was Cook; thus, his endorsement was extremely persuasive.

Joseph Bramah

- Another important group of innovators were the locksmiths, who developed intricate and powerful mechanisms and advanced the possibilities of craftsmanship in metals.

- Joseph Bramah (1748–1814) was the most illustrious of these. The son of a Yorkshire farmer, he was apprenticed to a cabinetmaker. In 1778, he received a patent for a toilet-flushing system with a ball and flapper—essentially the same system we still use today. In 1784, he obtained the first lock patent.

- In 1801, Bramah built a lock so complicated that he promised a reward to whoever could pick it. It had 470 million possible combinations and was finally broken only in 1851, at the Great Exhibition, by an American locksmith, who took 51 hours to pick the lock.

Henry Maudslay

- The next of these great precision tool makers was a man who worked for Bramah, Henry Maudslay (1771–1831), who greatly increased accuracy in instrument making.

- Maudslay grew up as a "powder monkey," assembling explosives at an arsenal, then moved on to work as a blacksmith, where he showed a gift for detail work. He perfected metal lathes, making it possible for one precision tool to duplicate itself and to make other devices to exact specifications. Although earlier lathes had been made mainly of wood, Maudslay made his entirely of iron, for greater stability and durability.

- Maudslay linked his lathes to a steam engine to get a regular rotation rate. He adapted and improved a variety of earlier devices to hold the tool against the wood or metal being worked—in effect, serving as mechanical hands. He and his successors made these mechanical hands increasingly sophisticated, guided by fine screw threads, in ways that could be duplicated to make standardized items.

- Maudslay's employer, Bramah, patented the device in 1794 and enjoyed many of the benefits. It was now possible to make lock parts by machine rather than (slowly and laboriously) by hand.

- In 1797, Bramah refused to give Maudslay a pay raise, prompting him to strike out on his own in business—an act of mean-spiritedness Bramah came to regret. Maudslay prospered and eventually employed 80 men in his own workshops.

Precision and Uniformity

- Maudslay spent much of his later career making steam engines for ships, including the first ones to be installed in ships of the Royal Navy, presaging the end of its long sailing tradition.

- Maudslay improved micrometers to an accuracy of almost $\frac{1}{10,000\text{th}}$ of an inch. An invention of James Watt's in the 1760s also depended on improvements of fine screw threads.

- Nearly all the prominent engineers and tool makers of the next generation worked for a time as Maudslay's apprentices or assistants. One was Joseph Clement, who later built Charles Babbage's calculating machine, which is now regarded as the world's first computer.

- Maudslay perfected the making of screws, nuts, and bolts with uniform pitch (the angle at which the thread is set)—a vital improvement for high-pressure engines. The principles had been understood since Leonardo da Vinci's day, but production was only possible on Maudslay's precision lathes. Until then, each individual nut and bolt had had to be marked as partners in disassembly. Maudslay created sets, along with the taps and dies for cutting them to standard sizes.

James Nasmyth

- Maudslay's last assistant was James Nasmyth (1808–1890), who shared his mentor's perfectionism and went on to develop new machines, including the steam hammer. The son of an artist in Edinburgh, Nasmyth loved tinkering and building moving models.

- He realized early on that the key to high-quality engines is accurate machine tools. In a trip to London, Nasmyth showed Maudslay a working model of a high-pressure steam engine that impressed Maudslay so much, he took on Nasmyth as his assistant.

- In the 1830s, Nasmyth built and ran a factory halfway between Liverpool and Manchester, adjacent to the Liverpool and

Manchester Railway and to the Bridgewater Canal. (That location is surely as good a candidate as any for the symbolic center of the Industrial Revolution.)

- Nasmyth found high-quality machines much more reliable than many of his workers and wrote of his machines that they "never got drunk, their hands never shook from excess, they were never absent from work; they did not strike for wages, they were unfailing in their accuracy and regularity."

- Nasmyth developed the steam hammer to help Brunel build the S.S. *Great Britain*'s massive drive shafts.
  - The steam hammer operator could control the force of the hammer descending on an object or could rock an entire building with a power-reinforced fall.

  - The steam hammer was the central instrument for making forgings (shaped iron and steel) from then on. In 1843, Nasmyth also developed and patented the pile driver—a closely related device that was vital for metal bridge building then going on across Britain.

- Nasmyth wrote an excellent autobiography, in which he emphasized the importance of hands-on work for aspiring engineers, enabling them to get a feel for the metals, machines, and techniques. He also believed that workers involuntarily responded to the energy that they witnessed when machinery was working properly.

Joseph Whitworth

- Joseph Whitworth (1803–1887) was the most famous of Maudslay's assistants. Plane technology was vital for accuracy and was developed by several of Maudslay's assistants and a few independent engineers before Whitworth. These included James Fox, who began as a butler to a country clergyman but who went on to build high-quality looms for Arkwright and Strutt textile mills, and Richard Roberts, the son of a shoemaker who ended up in Maudslay's workshops.

- Whitworth, a fanatic for improving quality, took the achievement of absolute flatness about as far as it could go before the development of microtechnology in the late 20th century.

- Beginning in 1841, Whitworth campaigned successfully for all British manufacturers to standardize screw and bolt sizes, thread pitch, and depth. Prior to that, every manufacturer had different standards, which led to waste and complexity when repairing machines. Whitworth created the British Standard Whitworth (BSW) system, which persisted for the next century.

- Whitworth also rejected the tradition of decorative frames and casings for his machine tools, in favor of massive functional designs, as heavy and stable as possible. And, unlike his predecessors, Whitworth specialized in making and selling machine tools—they were the heart and center of his business, rather than incidental to creating other tools.

- High-quality machine tools furthered the goals of the Industrial Revolution and allowed for the development of production engineering and mass production. The next time you have to replace a nut on a bolt you already possess, or the next time you need a standardized part for your car, give a moment's thought to Bramah, Maudslay, Nasmyth, and Whitworth, whose ingenious and innovative work laid the foundations for accurate, standardized, rapid machine manufacture.

Suggested Reading

Musson and Robinson, *Science and Technology in the Industrial Revolution.*

Sobel, *Longitude.*

Whitworth, *On An Uniform System of Screw Threads.*

Woodbury, *Studies in the History of Machine Tools.*

1. Why was precision so essential to industrial progress?

2. What are the advantages of standardization?

The Machine-Tool Makers
Lecture 14—Transcript

When we study spectacular innovations like steam locomotives and oceangoing ships, it's easy to forget that their makers required a wide array of special tools and materials in order to make them. Nuts and bolts are humble objects, but unless they're available and unless they work properly, the machinery will never work. Who made the nuts and bolts? Who invented the machines on which the nuts and bolts were made?

This lecture is a history of the pioneer toolmakers who improved precision, accuracy, strength, and uniformity in the treatment of metals, on which all subsequent technologies depended. They had a mania for accuracy. They knew each other, and each built on the achievements of his predecessor. A long tradition of skilled craftsmanship in metals contributed to the development of high-quality machinery. Among the preindustrial craftsmen, clock and watchmakers were the most skilled. The quest for accurate marine chronometers challenged a generation of clockmakers, of whom the most distinguished was John Harrison, who lived from 1693–1776, and his nickname was John "Longitude" Harrison.

Sailors by Columbus's day in the late 1400s could already compute their latitude accurately with readings from stars and sun. Latitude is the distance between the Equator and the North Pole or the South Pole. But their longitude, how far west or east they were from a certain point, how far around the world they were, was much more difficult to compute. A really accurate clock could help. If you knew your latitude, and if you knew what time it was in London, and if you knew what day of the year it was and what time of day the sun would rise, then you could time dawn or sunset where you were and work out your longitude by the number of hours behind or ahead of the London dawn.

The challenge of making a clock that accurate took most of Harrison's lifetime, and it's the subject of a terrific book, *Longitude*, by Dava Sobel. This section of the lecture is drawn heavily from her insights. Harrison aimed to win a prize of 20,000 pounds that was offered by the admiralty in 1714. They offered the prize of 20,000 to anyone who could work out a method of computing longitude really accurately. The reason they offered the prize was because they recently experienced a terrible disaster: the Scilly Isles disaster of 1707, when an English fleet, whose navigators had miscalculated their longitude, foundered on the rocks. The fleet's commander, Sir Cloudsley Shovell, and 2,000 men were lost in the disaster, one of the most painful and expensive accidents in Royal Navy history. Pendulum clocks weren't accurate enough. In rough seas, the pendulum would slow down or speed up. Also, temperature and barometric pressure variation affected the regularity of operation of ordinary clocks. The challenge Harrison confronted was how to make a mechanism that was immune to these vagaries and absolutely exact, but also one that was durable and tough enough to withstand long ocean voyages.

Harrison set out to compete for the prize while still a young rural clockmaker. His first model, called the H1, went on a navy expedition to Portugal in 1836, and straight away proved far more accurate than the captain of the ship's ad hoc methods. War with Spain prevented a second one from being risked out at sea; it's too valuable to be captured. Harrison, meanwhile was working out methods to compensate for the ship's rocking, for the changes in humidity, and for unevenness in temperature as ships went to different latitudes.

The trial of a greatly improved model took place in 1761 on a voyage from England to the Barbados and back, and it was accurate to within one nautical mile. In other words, he'd almost satisfactorily solved the problem. The squabbling at the Navy Board over which method was, in fact, the best way of setting about computing longitude still withheld the prize from him, although Parliament did give him 8,750 pounds—a little bit less than half of the prize in 1773, by which time he'd reached the age of 80. But he never did get the full prize, although it's pretty clear in retrospect that, justly, he should've done.

Harrison's clocks used diamonds, improved steel, bimetallic strips, and other materials that were steadily being improved by metalworkers over the course of the century. One of the people who loved these chronometers was Captain James Cook. Captain Cook was the British mariner, explorer, and cartographer who circumnavigated the world. He located and mapped a large part of the Australian coast, he sailed all around and mapped the two islands of New Zealand, he mapped much of the Alaskan coast, and he was the person who discovered Hawaii, where eventually he was killed by some of the native peoples. If anybody needed a good chronometer, it was Cook, so his endorsement was extremely persuasive and he thought it was magnificent.

Just to give you a sense of the value of a Harrison chronometer: Its price was about a third the price of the ship itself, the *Resolution* on which Cook sailed; an immensely valuable item. This is the exact opposite of the kind of mass-produced goods brought about by industrialization whose price would steadily fall.

A second very important group who paved the way to high quality machine tool manufacture was the locksmiths. In the 18th century, they developed intricate and powerful mechanisms and advanced the possibilities of craftsmanship in metals. The most distinguished of them was Joseph Bramah, who lived from 1748–1814. He was the son of a Yorkshire farmer and started out in life as an apprentice to a cabinetmaker. In 1778, he was issued a patent for a toilet flushing system using a ball and flapper very, very similar to the ones that we still use today. One of its virtues was it prevented the freezing up of the system. But then he got interested in making locks.

In 1784, he got his first lock patent. Here's part of the language of the patent itself. "For a lock constructed on a new and infallible principle, which, possessing all the properties essential to security, will prevent the most ruinous consequences of house robberies and be a certain protection." In 1801, he built a lock so complicated that he challenged all comers to pick the lock, promising a reward of 200 guineas. Let me just explain that for a second. English currency by then had two forms: pounds, which were based on silver, and guineas, which were based on gold, which had become slightly more valuable. So 200 guineas means 200 pounds and 200 shillings, and luxury items were usually sold in guineas rather than pounds. It was a way, actually, of paying more than you thought you were going to have to. Anyway, this one lock was displayed in Bramah's shop window along with the challenge: "We'll give you the guineas if you can pick the lock." It had 470 million possible combinations, and was finally broken only in 1851 at the Great Exhibition, which I mentioned in the previous lecture, by an American locksmith named Charles Hobbs. But he took 51 hours to do it before finally getting the award money, and this, of course, was long, long after Bramah's death. Any lock picker that has to spend 51 hours on the job clearly can't break into the house.

The next of these great precision toolmakers was Henry Maudslay, who lived from 1771–1831. He worked for Bramah at first, and greatly increased accuracy in instrument making. Maudslay's father was wounded as a soldier and then got work in the Woolwich arsenal, where weapons for the English Army were made. The son grew up as a "powder monkey"; that is, assembling explosives at the arsenal itself. Then he moved on to work as a trainee blacksmith, where he showed great promise, a gift for detailed work.

Maudslay perfected metal lathes, making it possible for one precision tool to duplicate itself and to make other devices to exact specifications. Earlier lathes throughout the history of the world had been made mainly of wood, which rattles and wears out rapidly. He made them entirely of iron, his first one probably in 1790, with much greater stability and durability. Lathes had been around since the ancient world, as had potters' wheels. I spoke about them briefly in the lecture on Wedgwood and the developments in the pottery industry, which were also taking place in the later half of the 18th century. But the way in which lathes and potters' wheels traditionally worked was this: Usually the operator held a tool by hand against the wood or against the pottery and shaped the device by hand. The power source historically was a foot treadle that couldn't easily run at exactly the same speed for long periods, so the work was an approximation based on the skill of an individual operator.

But Maudslay linked his lathes to a steam engine to get an absolutely regular rotation rate, right down to the exact number of revolutions per minute. He adapted and improved a variety of earlier devices to hold the tool against the wood or the metal that was being worked. In effect, what he was doing was replacing human hands with mechanical hands that could duplicate their work exactly. He and his successors made these mechanical hands increasingly sophisticated, guided by fine screw threads in ways that could be duplicated to make standardized items.

These improvements in lathe technology were patented by Bramah, his employer, in 1794, and it was Bramah who enjoyed much of the benefit. His interest in it was principally as a locksmith. It was now possible to make the lock parts by machine rather than slowly and laboriously by hand. Of course, once they could be machine-generated, they could be made more quickly and accurately and, again, come down in price while rising in accuracy.

A momentous moment came in 1797 when Bramah refused to give Maudslay a pay raise. Maudslay had married one of the servant girls who worked at Bramah's shop. He was earning 30 shillings a week, but he didn't think that was enough for his growing family, so Maudslay left Bramah and struck out on his own in business. This was an act of mean-spiritedness on Bramah's part, which he later came to regret. Maudslay was so talented, so skillful, and so capable in every aspect of the business that he prospered, eventually employing 80 men of his own in workshops with a very, very lucrative business. He spent much of his later career after 1800 making steam engines for ships. He was one of the first marine engine builders in Britain, including the very first ones to be installed in ships of the Royal Navy, presaging the end of its long sailing tradition. Maudslay didn't patent his own improvements in machine tools, and he didn't try to sell them. He was secretive—in this sense rather like Wedgwood, who also kept his innovations to himself—but it's really clear that if Maudslay had decided to actually go into the machine tools business, he could have made a fortune doing so. Instead, he profited mainly from the sale of high-quality marine engines.

Among his many other interests, he improved micrometers to an accuracy of almost a ten thousandth of an inch. A micrometer is to measure extremely short distances. The first micrometers had been invented by James Watt, the University of Glasgow instrument maker, in the 1760s. But the improvements that Maudslay was able to make over Watts's invention itself depended on improvements of fine screw threads. Maudslay's very best micrometer was called "the Lord Chancellor," a nickname. The Lord Chancellor was right at the top of the British legal system, so the idea is if you need a judgment about exactly how thick something is, use the very best micrometer ever. Its name is the Lord Chancellor.

Maudslay's workshop near Oxford Street in central London became a center for inventions and improvements in the metal and machine-tool trades. Nearly all the prominent engineers and tool makers of the next generation worked for a time as his apprentices or assistants. One of them was Joseph Clement, who later built Charles Babbage's calculating machine, the difference engine, which is now regarded as the world's first computer. It was never completely finished. Babbage promised it to the government, but could never actually get the thing built. Even so, he created a lot of the breakthroughs which made computer technology possible.

An interested visitor to Maudslay's workshops wrote:

> The sight of his workshops astonished me. They excelled all that I had anticipated. The beautiful machine tools, the silent smooth whirl of the machinery, the active movements of the men, the excellent quality of the work in progress, and the admirable order and management that pervaded the whole establishment, rendered me tremblingly anxious to obtain some employment there, in however humble a capacity.

So very, very impressed by the techniques he sees at work.

Maudslay perfected the making of screws, nuts, and bolts with a uniform pitch. The pitch of a screw thread is the angle at which the thread is set relative to the axis of the screw itself, the angle. This was a vital improvement for high-pressure engines because they had to be bolted together very, very tightly. The principles of screw threads had been understood at least since Leonardo da Vinci's day, but production of good quality nuts and bolts was only possible on Maudslay's precision lathes. Until then, each individual nut and bolt had had to be marked as partners and then disassembled. There were no standards. Maudslay's innovation was to create sets and to create standards, along with the taps and dies for cutting them to standard sizes so that they could be duplicated again and again and reliably fit each other. One bolt that he made was five feet long, with 50 threads to the inch, and it engaged a nut with 600 threads; in other words, a screw-thread device of extraordinary intricacy. It won a prize of 1,000 pounds from the admiralty, which understood perfectly well how valuable such devices were going to be as it became a more mechanized organization.

One of Maudslay's collaborators was Marc Isambard Brunel, father of the famous shipbuilder about whom the last lecture was given. For Marc Brunel, Maudslay built block-making machines, and he provided some of the equipment for the building of the treacherous Thames Tunnel that we heard about last time. Brunel, Sr., the father, had a contract with the Navy to make the blocks that were needed for the miles of rope on every sailing ship in the Napoleonic-era Navy. Until then, they'd been made by hand. Brunel, Sr. got a contract to make them by machine, but it was Maudslay who actually made the machines themselves, 44 of them over the space of six years, all of them up and running and working very reliably by 1809, and they carried on working throughout the rest of the century until the complete phasing out of sailing ships from the Royal Navy itself.

Maudslay's last assistant was James Nasmyth, who lived from 1808–1890, and he shared Maudslay's perfectionism. He went on to develop several new machines of his own, including the steam hammer. Nasmyth was the son of an artist living in Edinburgh in Scotland. As a boy, he loved tinkering and building moving models. In fact, he turned his bedroom into a foundry and cast miniature metal parts at white heat for working miniature steam engines, which he then sold to admirers for 10 pounds each as a kid making steam engines. Despite having witnessed the great fire of Edinburgh of 1824, which destroyed much of the city, his mother's only comment was "I hope all this metalworking won't be bad for your health." You might think she'd be more alarmed about the fire hazard and having a little forge going in the bedroom.

Nasmyth realized that the key to good engines was good machine tools. He wrote:

> I had, on many occasions, when visiting the works where steam engines were employed, heard of the name and fame of Maudslay. I was told that his works were the very center and climax of all that was excellent in mechanical workmanship. These reports built up in my mind at this early period of my aspirations an earnest

and hopeful desire that I might someday get a sight of Maudslay's celebrated works in London. In course of time, it developed into a passion.

His father finally took him to London by ship to meet Maudslay. At this meeting, Nasmyth showed Maudslay a working model high-pressure steam engine that he'd built himself. It so impressed Maudslay that he agreed to take on Nasmyth as one of his assistants.

In the 1830s, Nasmyth built and ran a factory. It was situated halfway between Liverpool and Manchester, and it was adjacent to the Liverpool and Manchester Railway, then brand new. It was also at the place where the Bridgewater Canal flowed by, the famous first commercial canal. I think that location is surely as good a candidate as any for an award as symbolic center of the Industrial Revolution. The Bridgewater Canal, the Liverpool and Manchester Railway, and Nasmyth's factory, all in the same place.

Nasmyth loved machines. He found high-quality machines much more reliable than boozy workmen, and he wrote that his machines "never got drunk, their hands never shook from excess, they were never absent from work; they did not strike for wages, they were unfailing in their accuracy and regularity." In his autobiography, he describes visiting one of his customers in 1838, an iron maker. He himself was 30 years old at the time. He fell in love with the man's 21-year-old daughter, Anne Hartop, on the spot, proposed to her after knowing her for one day, and she accepted. Then, he says, they were happily married for 50 years. In this, as in all things, he was a very decisive fellow.

Nasmyth developed the steam hammer, one of his important inventions, to help Brunel, the son, build the S.S. *Great Britain*'s massive drive shafts. One of the issues ship builders, particularly Brunel, had to come to terms with was this: Once you've installed a great steam engine inside the hull of the ship, how do you then make an effective drive shaft to carry the power from the engine either to the paddlewheels or to the propellers? The scale of the ship was so big that the drive shaft itself had to be massive. Nasmyth developed the steam hammer specifically to enable Brunel to get shafts of the right size. The operator of a Nasmyth steam hammer could control the force of the hammer descending on the object. One of Nasmyth's boasts was that it could be used so gently that it would be possible to put an egg in a shallow glass and bring the steam hammer down with just enough hardness to break the egg without harming the glass. On the other hand, he said, we can rock the whole building with a power-reinforced fall where the hammer doesn't just fall with the weight of gravity, as had been the case until then with such devices, it's actually forced downwards by steam pressure. Steam hammers became one of the central, most important instruments for making forgings—which is to say shaped iron and steel objects—from that time forward.

Nasmyth also developed and patented the pile driver in 1843. This is a closely related device. It gives a very, very powerful downward hammering stroke, and it's extremely important because so much bridge building was going on all over Britain as the railway network was being built up. This is a device that enables them to drive the piles down, for example, into the ground or into the river beds.

Nasmyth himself wrote an excellent autobiography in the early 1880s describing his childhood in Edinburgh, his friendships, and his achievements. He emphasizes very strongly the importance of hands-on work for aspiring engineers; doing it for yourself, getting the feel of the metals, the machines, and the techniques. He writes:

> The truth is that the eyes and the fingers—the bare fingers—are the two principal inlets to sound practical instruction. They are the chief sources of trustworthy knowledge in all the materials and operations which the engineer has to deal with. No book knowledge can avail for that purpose. The nature and properties of the materials must come in through the finger ends.

He also believed that workers involuntarily responded to the energy that they witnessed when the machinery was working properly. He describes how he once improved the steam engine at the workshop of one of his friends. He wrote:

> The result of my labours was a very efficient steam engine, which set all the lathes and mechanical tools in brisk activity of movement.

It had such an enlivening effect upon the workmen that George Douglass afterwards told me that the busy hum of the wheels, and the active, smooth, rhythmic sound of the merry little engine had, through some sympathetic agency, so quickened the stroke of every hammer, chisel, and file in his workmen's hands, that it nearly doubled the output of work for the same wages.

Reflecting on this incident later, he added, "We all know the influence of a quick merry air, played by fife and drum, upon the step and marching of a regiment of soldiers. It is the same with the quick movements of a steam engine upon the activity of workmen."

The next of these great instrument makers was Joseph Whitworth, who lived from 1803–1887, and he was the most famous of Maudslay's assistants. Plane technology—that is, creating absolutely flat surfaces for accurate measurement—was vital for accuracy and was developed by several of Maudslay's assistants and a few independent engineers before Whitworth perfected it. One of them was James Fox from Derby, who started life as butler to a country clergyman before being drawn into the world of technology. He went on to build very high quality looms for the Arkwright and Strutt textile mills. Also Richard Roberts, a man who came from a toll house on the Welsh border, son of a shoemaker, who also ended up in Maudslay's workshops, drawn there by this sort of magnetic appeal that he seemed to exercise.

L. T. C. Rolt, who wrote the first history of machine tools, writes:

It is strange that so many of the leaders of Britain's industrial revolution were drawn to the new workshops from remote rural areas, not by the pressure of necessity or by the influence of their surroundings or parental example, but by a mysterious aptitude for and love of mechanics. But is this, after all, any stranger than the inexplicable flowering of poetic or artistic genius? For the truth is, surely, that these pioneer engineers were the artists of their profession, whose careers were determined by the artist's compulsive need to fulfill his creative endowment.

Whitworth was a fanatic for quality improvement, and he took the achievement of absolute flatness about as far as it could go before the development of micro technology in the late 20th century. Beginning in 1841, he also campaigned successfully for all British manufacturers to standardize their screw and bolt sizes, the thread pitch, and the depth. Maudslay had done it within his own workshops, and Whitworth says, "let's make it a nationwide standard," because at that time every manufacturer had different standards, which, of course, led to waste and complexity when repairing machines. Unless you got parts from the same manufacturer, you couldn't be confident that a bolt of a given diameter would fit a nut of the same diameter. In an 1841 pamphlet, Whitworth described this problem. He writes:

> The screw threads, which form the subject of this paper, are those of bolts and screws used in fitting up steam engines and other machinery. Great inconvenience is found to arise from the variety of threads adopted by different manufacturers. The general provision for repairs is rendered at once expensive and imperfect. The difficulty of ascertaining the exact pitch of a particular thread, especially when it is not a submultiple of the common inch measure, occasions extreme embarrassment. This evil would be completely obviated by uniformity of system, the thread becoming constant for a given diameter.

It was he who created the BSW standard, which means British Standard Whitworth, and it persisted for the next century. Just as the railway companies eventually agreed on standard gauge in 1892, so BSW is the standardization of machine tools across the whole country.

Whitworth also rejected the tradition of decorative frames and casings for his machine tools in favor of massive functional designs, as heavy and as stable as possible. Unlike his predecessors, Whitworth actually specialized in making and selling machine tools. They were the heart and center of his business, rather than being incidental to the making of other things, as they had been for Maudslay.

It's ironic, I think, that the work these men did has enabled us to forget them. Next time you have to replace a nut on a bolt you already possess, or next time you need a standardized part for your car, give a moment's thought to Bramah, Maudslay, Nasmyth, and Whitworth, whose ingenious work laid the foundations of accurate, standardized, rapid machine manufacture. The higher standard of machine tool making they established enabled the engineers—men like Stephenson and Brunel—to build good high-pressure steam engines to minute tolerances. It also laid the groundwork for the mass production of identical parts, which would be crucial for a later stage of the Industrial Revolution in sewing machines, bicycles, guns, cars, and other consumer goods.

Up to this point in the course, I've concentrated on the manufacturers and the inventors who found new and better methods of making things. In the next lecture, I'm going to turn to an equally important matter: the lives of the men and women who worked for them. The working conditions of these early generations would be regarded as intolerable today. They worked for long hours in dangerous conditions, breathed toxic air in a workplace without safety equipment. They didn't grow rich. The condition of their lives, and their sufferings, make it easy for us to understand why industrialization, right from the outset, never lacked for critics.

The Worker's-Eye View
Lecture 15

For more than 200 years, journalists, politicians, sociologists, and other interested observers have debated the effect of industrialization on the English working class. Important questions include whether wages actually fell for the men and women drawn into the new factories, forges, and coal mines and whether the working class was growing steadily poorer or their lives were actually better than the rural poverty from which they came. Economic historians have concluded that there was a slight fall in real wages from the 1760s to about 1820, followed by a steady rise thereafter into the era of mid-Victorian prosperity. These are, however, just trends, which conceal the particular realities of individual families' experiences.

The "De-Skilling" of Workers

- The shift to industrial work often entailed "de-skilling" of workers. The traditional sequence of apprentice, to journeyman, to master was displaced by a situation in which employees performed a single job. Many of these jobs, in mining, shipbuilding, and iron and steel working, required great physical strength, which gave advantage to younger men. Miners and shipyard workers sometimes worked in gangs of different ages, partly as a way of protecting their older members.

- As strength and eyesight deteriorated, older workers were often forced into lower-paying situations. In the industrial era, older workers were extremely vulnerable; there was no vestige of a welfare state until the early 20th century and certainly no state-supported pension schemes to care for elderly workers.

- While employers sought control over their workers, working people in many trades struggled to retain some sense of autonomy. Mine workers owned their own picks and shovels, for example, and paid to have them kept sharp by the blacksmith. Shoemakers had their own tools, as did coopers (barrel makers).

Swings in the Business Cycle

- An odious tradition was paying workers in "truck"—that is, not with real money but with tokens that could be redeemed only at a store owned by the employer. Prices were often higher than in other shops, and food was sometimes adulterated by unscrupulous owners. Its American equivalent, a little later, was the company store.

- Even workers paid in money usually had to patronize shops where they were generally charged high prices. They were too poor to buy anything in bulk and could never enjoy economies of scale. Those who worked a six-day week were often unable to shop until Saturday night, and late-night markets became a feature of industrial towns. Saturday night markets had a social function, as well.

- When work was available, most trades' workers maintained a fragile solvency; however, seasonal unemployment and underemployment were widespread. Textile markets would sometimes be glutted, leading to layoffs. Swings of the business cycle could lead to years of accelerated work, followed by months of idleness, confronting working people with crisis conditions.

- Traditionally, there had been a clear connection between willingness to work and prosperity. By the early 1800s, it was becoming obvious that the business cycle took no account of individual decency. Before the Industrial Revolution, people went hungry when harvests failed. Now, some were hungry in the midst of what otherwise looked like prosperity—a baffling new reality.

Separation of Work from Home Life

- The New Poor Law of 1834 was a harsh measure to minimize social welfare. Those who had no work and no family to care for them were forced to go to the workhouse. This system also made it more difficult to travel to areas where work was available, because this relief was available only in the parish where one was registered as living.

- Workers shared the middle-class ideal that the man should work and his wife should stay at home to look after the children. On farms, women had traditionally worked as long and as hard as their husbands, but after migration to the towns, the separation of work from home created a new ideal.

- The reality of low wages often made fulfilling the ideal impossible, forcing married women into the workforce,

Workhouses, made famous by Dickens's novel *Oliver Twist*, were designed to be similar to prisons; only the desperate would rely on this form of "relief."

where they were vulnerable to pay discrimination. Some industries excluded women from all but the lowest-paid and least-skilled work.

- Cities had always been unhealthy places, and they remained so—or deteriorated—as industry caused their immense growth—often with no planning for adequate sanitation or water supply and with no minimum standards embodied in building codes.

Friedrich Engels

- Friedrich Engels's *The Condition of the Working Class in England* is one of the classic accounts of working conditions. In 1842, as a young man, Engels came from Germany to manage his father's textile factory in Manchester. He traveled widely and wrote a searing account of the wretchedness of workers' lives. He combined his personal observations with those of journalists, magistrates, and reformers.

- Engels noted that workers' houses in Manchester were built so shoddily and carelessly that they were never warm or dry and began to fall to pieces as soon as they were inhabited, yet landlords charged exorbitant rents. The homes were overcrowded, often with two or three families to a house, all sharing the same rooms. There was no running water, only communal wells and communal latrines.

- Such areas were centers of the periodic outbreaks of cholera that terrified everyone after 1830. They were also chronic sources of intestinal and respiratory diseases. Photographs of the towns confirm written descriptions that these cities were full of choking smoke, smog, and sometimes acidic fog.

- Engels also noted in the 1840s that a bad situation was being made worse by the arrival of numerous Irish immigrants.
  - He seems to have shared a widespread prejudice against the Irish, seeing them as prone to drunkenness and recklessness and having such low living standards that they would force down wages for everyone else.

  - On the other hand, Engels said that the Irish were more fiery than the phlegmatic English, and he speculated that they might provide the spark for revolutionary class consciousness that would lead to reform.

- Engels's book came out in Germany and impressed Karl Marx, who became his lifelong friend and collaborator. They anticipated that conditions would continue to worsen and that the workers would finally be goaded into collective revolutionary action.

- Equally horrified was the French liberal Alexis de Tocqueville, who after seeing Manchester, famously remarked: "Civilization works its miracles and civilized man is turned back almost into a savage." An American writer for the *Whig Review* of 1849 noted, "Every day I live I thank heaven that I am not a poor man with a family in England."

Workers' Protections

- An obvious way for the workers to react to poor wages, job insecurity, and dangerous working conditions was by creating trade unions—strength in unity. However, fear of the French Revolution prompted Parliament to pass the Combination Acts of 1799 and 1800, making it illegal for workers to conspire in this way.

- Only "friendly societies" were allowed, in which workers paid weekly sums with the promise of sick pay or a decent burial if they died in a work accident.

- Workers' legal protections were also weakening. Since the late Middle Ages, Parliament had legislated minimum wages and fixed prices for many crafts and trades. After 1800, it began to repeal these laws in response to manufacturers' lobbying and a new attitude toward economic growth and changing technology.

- Workers who had earlier been protected by these laws now found themselves more vulnerable. Courts had previously upheld workers' complaints against innovations but now generally sided with the employers instead.
    - One response was intimidation of employers by workers. Another response was Luddism, a violent, destructive protest against labor-saving machinery. Luddites were named for "Ned Ludd," a semi-mythical figure, comparable to Robin Hood, who stood up for the poor by attacking symbols of their oppression. Luddism began during the economic crisis conditions of 1811–1812 in Nottinghamshire.

    - Hosiery employers were using new looms and unskilled labor; the Nottingham workers responded by smashing the machines. Luddism then spread to northern areas, where hand workers were threatened with displacement by machinery. This panicked the government, which devoted huge resources to stamping out Luddism. Eventually, the movement was repressed.

Methodism

- A significant force in moderating radicalism was the influence of Methodism. Growing since the mid-18th century, the religion of Methodism caught on widely among working-class people who were alienated from the Church of England. The religion, which emphasized decency, restraint, temperance, moderation, and respectability, was particularly influential in Welsh mining villages and Lancashire textile towns.

- E. P. Thompson, in his 1963 book *The Making of the English Working Class*, suggests that the widespread adoption of Methodism in Britain, which had no counterpart in France, accounts partly for the orderliness of British industrial life in comparison with the repeated revolutionary upheavals in France. That moderation, as opposed to the tradition of riots and machine breaking, contributed to the later English trade unions' emphasis on dignity and restraint.

- Thompson also emphasized that one of the consequences of industrialization was the recognition by the people who worked in these new mines, factories, and workshops that they all had something in common. He wrote, "In the years between 1780 and 1832, most English working people came to feel an identity of interests as between themselves, and as against their rulers and employers." Consider his title, "the *making*" of the working class— created partly by pressures on them, partly by their reaction to those pressures.

- Thompson pointed out that these were real people, faced with difficult and often dangerous situations as they struggled to come to terms with a new reality. They were never passive but contributed to this new world—sometimes through protest and violence.

Suggested Reading

Belchem, *Industrialization and the Working Class*.

Engels, *The Condition of the English Working Class in England*.

Hobsbawm, *Industry and Empire*.

Thompson, *The Making of the English Working Class*.

Questions to Consider

1. Why were urban conditions so squalid in the first industrial cities, and why was government slow to remedy the situation?

2. How did old traditions of work persist into the new industrial environment and with what consequences?

The Worker's-Eye View
Lecture 15—Transcript

For more than 200 years, journalists, politicians, sociologists, and other interested observers and historians have debated the effect of industrialization on the English working class. Did wages fall for the men and women drawn into the new factories, forges, and coalmines? Were the horrible living conditions that Frederick Engels found in Manchester in the early 1840s signs that the working class was getting steadily poorer, paving the way, as he and Karl Marx believed, for an explosion of revolutionary violence? Or were these conditions actually better in some ways than the less visible but chronic rural poverty from which the workers had come?

Generations of economic historians, usually working with great ingenuity and using incomplete data sets, have concluded that there was a slight fall in real wages from the 1760s to about 1820, followed by a steady rise thereafter into the era of comparative mid-Victorian prosperity. These are, however, just trends that conceal the particular realities of individual families' experiences, in which there were winners and losers, and periods of intense crisis. Quite apart from their material struggles, how did working people understand what was happening to them? How did they interact with their employers? What was the texture of their everyday lives?

The shift to industrial work often entailed "deskilling" of workers. The old apprentice, journeyman, master sequence through which you could hope to have mastered one of the old mysteries through life and become your own employer, was displaced by employees doing one simple job, and very often they became more and more monotonous as the work was more and more subdivided. Many of these jobs in mining, shipbuilding, iron, and steel required great physical strength, which gave an advantage to younger men. Miners and shipyard workers sometimes reacted to that reality by working in gangs made up of men of different ages, partly as a way of protecting their older members. The young men could do more work for the moment knowing that eventually they'd need to be protected, too. Very often, this would be groups of men who were related to one another. Also, workers very early learned how to deliberately restrain the pace so that the disparities between the young and the old would not be too great.

As men's strength and eyesight deteriorated over the course of their life cycle, older workers were often forced into lower-paying situations. One 79 year old worker in London told the investigator Henry Mayhew, who was fascinated by all these things and whose information is pricelessly valuable to historians today:

> We try to hide our want of great strength and good sight as long as we can. I did it for two or three years, but it was found out at last, and I had to go. In most shops, the moment a man puts his glasses on it's over with him. It wasn't so when I first knew London. Masters then said, "Let me have an old man, one who knows something." Now it's "Let me have a young man. I must have a strong fellow. An old one won't do."

In this era, long before the creation even of a vestigial welfare state, old workers were extremely vulnerable. There was no vestige of a welfare state until the early 20th century, and certainly no state-supported pension schemes to care for elderly men, even after a lifetime of hard work.

While employers wanted to control them as much as possible, working men in many trades struggled to retain some sense of autonomy. They didn't want to feel their lives had been taken over in every respect by the boss. For example, mine workers often owned their own picks and shovels, and they paid to have them kept sharp by the blacksmith. Shoemakers had their own tools, as did the coopers; that is, the barrel makers. The mule spinners inside the factories often hired assistants of their own and paid them out of their own wages. It was a partly of holding on to the feeling that they had some autonomy over the work process.

Payday in most industrial occupations was usually Saturday. Some industries had a tradition of paying the workers not at the factory, but at the local pub, encouraging or even coercing the men into drinking before they could actually lay hands on their wages. As I've said in some of the earlier lectures, drink had a very long tradition in English life—I mentioned the old Saint Monday tradition, for example—and it remained right at the center of working men's sociability. For that matter, it's remained there right up to the present. For example, there was a tradition in many trades that a newcomer to the workshop or the factory would have to buy drinks for all the men in his workshop. Or that an apprentice, on finally reaching the end of his apprenticeship, would have to treat the master and all the journeymen to drinks on a particular day. Publicans, the men who owned the pubs, would promote cockfights, dog fights, and boxing matches to draw in big crowds. The publicans were often retired boxers who'd won enough in prize money to set up businesses of their own. This was a rough, tough, brawling, boozy, and coarse world. Occasionally, historians sentimentalized working-class life, but there's no question that it was a tough and violent one.

Some employers exploited this tradition, becoming pub owners as well. It was very much the minority, people like Titus Salt, the creator of Saltaire, who tried to create an alternative environment by setting up a teetotal world. It was his factory where the arch said "Abandon beer all ye who enter here." For many people that meant they'd never dream of working there. For others, this possibility of industrial work along with sobriety started to become a possibility.

Another of the odious traditions was employers who paid the men in "truck," as it was called; in other words, not by giving them real money, but by giving them tokens that could be redeemed only at a store that was owned by the manufacturer. Prices were often higher than in other shops, and the food was sometimes adulterated by unscrupulous owners. Its American equivalent, a little later, was called the company store, but the same principle in both places was widespread.

Even workers who were paid in actual money usually had to patronize small corner shops where they were generally charged high prices. They were too poor to buy anything in bulk, and they could never enjoy economies of scale. Those who worked a six-day week were often unable to go shopping until Saturday night, and late-night markets became a feature of many of the industrial towns. Often, the poor leftovers of food sold in the better neighborhoods earlier in the day ended up at the Saturday night markets.

But these markets had a social function as well as a commercial one. One observer of a Saturday night market in Manchester describes the bands and the buskers playing music, and adds this:

> Boys and girls shout and laugh and disappear into the taverns together. Careful housewives—often attended by their husbands, dutifully carrying the baby—bargain hard with the butchers for a hay-penny off the pound. The pawnbroker is busy, for pledges are being rapidly redeemed, and flat irons, dirty pairs of stays, candlesticks, Sunday trousers, tools, blankets and so forth are being fast removed from the shelves. From byways and alleyways and back streets, fresh crowds every moment emerge. Stalls, shops, cellars are clustered round with critics and purchasers. Cabmen drive slowly through the throng, shouting and swearing to the people to get out of the horse's way, and occasionally perhaps the melodious burst of a roaring chorus, surging out of the open windows of the Apollo Theater, resounds loudly above the whole conglomeration of street noises.

So this is a kind of weekly festival, in which it's part entertainment and part shopping.

As this quotation shows, the pawnbrokers were very important in working-class districts. It was common for families to pawn items of any value so that they could raise ready money during the week, and then to redeem their pawned items after payday; for example, so that the family could wear its Sunday best clothes during their one day of leisure. Pawnbrokers were often trusted locally among people who didn't have any experience with bank accounts. Some working people would leave their best clothes with the pawnbroker even when they weren't actually pawned for safekeeping. The pawnbrokers themselves, because their shops were full of goods, had the best locks, and so families would say to the pawnbroker, "Let me trust you with my clothes until I get them back." This is a world of such poverty that the theft of ordinary clothing was very common and people had to look out for the danger that their most basic things would be stolen.

When work was available, most trades' workers could maintain a fragile solvency. But seasonal unemployment and underemployment were very widespread. For example, in the coalmining districts, demand was very high in the winter, but less so in the summer. Often the miners would work very hard all through the winter months, but then there wouldn't be much demand and they'd be on short time or off altogether in the summer. The textile markets would sometimes be glutted, leading to layoffs. Swings of the business cycle, first overproduction then underproduction, could lead to years of accelerated work followed by months of idleness, confronting working people suddenly with crisis conditions because they are hardly ever earning enough, even during the good times, to build up very much surplus.

Traditionally, there had been a clear connection between one's willingness to work and one's ability to prosper. But by the early 1800s in the industrial towns, it was becoming obvious that the business cycle took no account of individual decency. Before the Industrial Revolution, people went hungry when the harvest failed. But now, some people were hungry in the midst of what otherwise looked like prosperity, and that was a baffling new reality with which it was very difficult to come to terms.

The New Poor Law, passed by Parliament in 1834, was a harsh measure to minimize the cost of social welfare, and also to make it as odious as possible to its recipients. People who had no work and no family to care for them were forced to go to the workhouse. The workhouse was made famous, or infamous, by Charles Dickens's novel *Oliver Twist.* Oliver himself starts out in the workhouse, and that's where he dares to ask for a little bit more gruel. As Dickens portrays it, it's a cruel and heartless place. Workhouses were gender-segregated and did have many of the characteristics of prisons. They were mortifying by design, and the idea was that only the desperate would succumb.

In my home town of Derby, a former workhouse was turned into a hospital in the early 20th century when the whole system was finally abandoned. It was named The Manor Hospital, but many older people, knowing what it had once been, knowing that it had once been the workhouse, absolutely refused ever to pass through its doors. The doctors in the neighborhood became familiar with the fact that if you were sending an elderly person to the hospital, it was no good trying to persuade them to go to the Manor Hospital, no matter how good the treatment there might actually have been by then.

There was an extraordinary importance laid on human dignity for members of the upper working class. They were determined to differentiate themselves from the people who might fall destitute, the lower working class. Even within what we might think of as one social grouping, there were very important social distinctions, and the possibility of ever becoming vulnerable to the workhouse was certainly one of them.

The workhouse system, not only was it cruel, it also was impractical. It made it more difficult than previously to travel to areas where work was available, because even workhouse relief was only available in the parish where one was registered as living.

In places where workers lived in houses that were provided by their employers, they often had to continue to find the rent even when no work was available. In other words, it was a dangerous bargain to accept workers' housing provided by the boss because it increased your dependence on the boss, and if he was unscrupulous or capricious, you'd feel yourself in a very vulnerable situation.

Most working people in the 1800s shared the middle class ideal that the man should work and his wife should stay at home to look after the children. On farms, women had traditionally worked as long and as hard as their husbands, but the separation of work from home after the migration to the industrial towns created a new ideal. The reality of low wages often made the fulfillment of this ideal impossible, forcing married women into the workforce where they were particularly vulnerable to pay discrimination. Some industries jealously excluded women from all but the very lowest paid and least skilled work, which kind of had the effect of helping the man but very often could harm the family as a whole, because pay discrimination against women was entirely legal.

Cities had always been unhealthy places, and they remained so, or even deteriorated, as industry caused them to grow rapidly, often with no planning for adequate sanitation or water supply, and with no minimum standards embodied in building codes. Engels's book *The Condition of the Working Class in England*, from the mid-1840s, is one of the great classic accounts of such conditions. As a young man, Engels came from Germany in 1842 to manage his father's textile factory in Manchester. He was lively, alert, and eager to explore. He traveled widely and wrote a searing account of the wretchedness of English workers' lives. In the book, he also combined his personal observations from his wide travels with those of newspaper stories, of magistrates when cases came to court, and even of conservative reformers—Tory reformers—with whom he was politically out of sympathy, but whose accuracy in describing the terrible conditions he greatly admired. Listen, for example, to his famous description of the workers' housing in Manchester near the River Irk. He wrote:

> These streets contain unqualifiedly the most horrible dwellings which I have yet beheld. In one of these courts, there stands directly at the entrance, at the end of the covered passage, a privy without a door, so dirty that the inhabitants can pass into and out of the court only by passing through foul pools of stagnant urine and excrement. Below it on the river, there are several tanneries which fill the whole neighborhood with the stench of animal putrefaction. At the bottom flows the River Irk, a narrow, coal-black, foul-smelling stream, full of debris and refuse, which it deposits on the lower right bank. In dry weather, a long string of the most disgusting blackish-green slime pools are left standing on this bank, from the depths of which bubbles of miasmatic gas constantly arise and give forth a stench unendurable even on the bridge forty or fifty feet above the surface of the stream.

The book is full of bravura passages like that in which the description is mixed with an intense moral revulsion. Engels noted that many of these houses were recently built, but so shoddy and careless in construction that they were never warm or dry, that they began to fall to pieces as soon as they were inhabited, and yet that they exacted exorbitant rents from the poor inhabitants. Many of them were overcrowded, often with two or three families to a house, all sharing the same room. There was no running water. Communal wells and communal latrines were used out-of-doors, and poor families often had little furniture. It often went to the pawnbroker. It's not surprising, is it, that such areas were the centers of the periodic outbreaks of cholera that terrified everyone after 1830? Also, chronic sources of intestinal and respiratory diseases. You couldn't get properly warm or dry. It was difficult to get a sufficiently good fire. The insulation was bad. Everything leaked. We have pictures of these towns, and they confirm the written descriptions that they were full of choking smoke, smog, and sometimes acidic fog, too. English cities then were as bad or worse than Mexico City or Beijing are today.

Engels also noted in the 1840s that a bad situation was being made worse by the arrival of numerous Irish immigrants. He seems to have shared a widespread prejudice against the Irish, seeing them as particularly prone to drunkenness, wild, reckless, willing to live with pigs literally in their houses, go barefoot, and have such low living standards that they'd force down wages for everyone else. Here's another passage from the book:

> The Irishman loves his pig as the Arab his horse, with the difference that he sells it when it is fat enough to kill. Otherwise, he eats and sleeps with it, his children play with it, ride upon it, roll in the dirt with it, as anyone may see a thousand times repeated in all the great towns of England. The filth and comfortlessness that prevail in the houses themselves is impossible to describe. The Irishman is unaccustomed to the presence of furniture: a heap of straw, a few rags, utterly beyond use as clothing, suffice for his nightly couch. When he is in want of fuel, everything combustible within his reach, chairs, doorposts, mouldings, flooring, finds its way up the chimney.

They're literally tearing the houses to pieces internally to feed the fire. That passage is also a timely reminder to us that towns in those days were full of animals; thousands of horses, but also pigs, too, cows for milk, and so on. We think of animals as living strictly outside town, but in those days they didn't.

Engels does say that there's one offsetting virtue to the Irish: that they're more fiery than the phlegmatic Englishmen. He speculated that they might provide the spark for revolutionary class consciousness that was otherwise clearly absent.

Engels also described the way in which a series of major roads led from the suburbs of Manchester into the center, the business district, so that the middle classes, who lived further out in the suburban neighborhoods, could travel to and from the city without being directly aware of the horrible workers' districts, which were behind these main arteries and therefore were kept out of sight. Many of the other English cities lacked this kind of geographical segregation so that the rich and the poor lived right next to each other, as they still often do today in cities like Johannesburg in South Africa or Sao Paolo in Brazil.

This book, *The Condition of the Working Class in England*, came out in Germany and it greatly impressed Karl Marx, who became his lifelong friend and collaborator. Marx and Engels anticipated that conditions would continue to worsen and that the workers would finally be goaded into collective revolutionary action. In this expectation of what was going to happen in the future, they were wrong. But still, Engels's book remains a superb source for understanding not only the urban conditions, but also the moral indignation that was felt by the early generation of socialists. When you read the book, you'll feel it too, and it's still very useful to us for helping us feel the moral objection to capitalism, which burned so brightly from the early 19th century until the mid-20th.

Equally horrified by these urban conditions was the French liberal Alexis de Tocqueville. He wrote a very famous book called *Democracy in America*, but he also went to visit England and shrank with distaste from the living conditions in Manchester. He wrote this: "Civilization works its miracles and civilized man is turned back almost into a savage." Similarly, an American writer for the *Whig Review* of 1849 wrote: "Wretched, defrauded, oppressed, crushed human nature, lying in bleeding fragments all over the face of society. Every day I live, I thank heaven that I am not a poor man with a family in England."

An obvious way for the workers to react to poor wages, job insecurity, and dangerous working conditions was by creating trade unions, because a trade union creates strength through unity. However, fear of the French Revolution prompted Parliament to pass the Combination Acts in 1799 and 1800, making it illegal for working men to conspire in this way. The only form of workers' association that was allowed was a "friendly society," and a friendly society is an organization in which all the members give a penny or two every week so that if one of them becomes sick, that will be a source of sick pay, or if one of them dies—and many of them did die prematurely—they'd be promised a decent burial if it was a work-related accident. It was a simple kind of do-it-yourself insurance scheme.

Workers' legal protections were weakening in this period. Ever since the late Middle Ages, Parliament had legislated minimum wages and fixed prices for many crafts and trades. But after 1800, it began to repeal all these laws in response to manufacturers' lobbying and a new attitude to economic growth and changing technology. The whole point about industrial manufacturing is that you make things in much greater volume and then sell them for a far lower price than previously. The manufacturers said that it's appropriate that just as the prices are now fluctuating, so should the wages depending on market conditions; a new way of thinking about wages and prices. Workers who'd earlier been protected by these laws now found themselves more vulnerable. The courts had previously upheld workers' complaints against innovations, but now they generally sided with the employers instead; that is, the government itself was committed to the idea of dynamic economic growth.

Another possibility short of trade unionism, or different from it, was intimidation of the employers. A group of Wiltshire cloth workers warned their employer, who was planning to mechanize part of the business in 1799, by sending him this letter: "If you follow this practice any longer, we will keep some people to watch you about with loaded blunderbusses or pistols. And will certainly blow your brains out. It is no use to destroy the factories but put you damned villains to death." That's about as frank as you can get in threatening the boss and giving him an incentive not to mechanize the works.

Another connected response was Luddism or machine breaking. This is named for "Ned Ludd," who's a semimythical figure, comparable to Robin Hood, who stood up for the poor by attacking the symbols of their oppression. Luddism began in the economic crisis conditions of 1811–12 in Nottinghamshire. In fact, one legend said that Ned Ludd, like Robin Hood, actually lived in Sherwood Forest. Hosiery employers using new looms and unskilled labor were cutting costs and, according to the workers, cutting quality as well. The Nottinghamshire workers responded by smashing the machines, and Luddism, machine breaking, spread to northern areas where hand workers were threatened with displacement by machinery. Luddism panicked the government, which devoted huge resources to try to stamp it out. Twelve thousand troops were raised; that's more than the Duke of Wellington had taken to Spain in his battle against Napoleon. Because the French Revolution was recent, the memory of it, there was terrible fear among the British upper classes that a comparable kind of revolution might take place in England and that they, the upper classes, would be executed just as the French leaders had been. The leading Luddites were put on trial in York in 1813. Many of the leaders were condemned to death, and others to transportation for life to Australia, which was then a prison colony.

Repression of this kind brought Luddism to an end, but another thing that was significant in moderating radicalism was the influence of the Methodist Church. It had been growing since mid-18th century, and it caught on very widely among working-class people who were alienated from the established Church of England. But the Methodists were puritanical. They emphasized decency, restraint, temperance, moderation, and respectability. Methodism was very strong in the South Wales mining villages and in the Lancashire textile towns.

One of the best and most influential history books ever written is *The Making of the English Working Class* by E. P. Thompson, a book published in 1963 and almost universally acclaimed by historians in the English language. It's a book in which he suggests that the widespread adoption of Methodism in Britain, which had no counterpart in France, accounts partly for the orderliness of British industrial life and protest by comparison with the repeated revolutionary upheavals in France. E. P. Thompson himself, the author, had been raised by zealous Methodist parents. He didn't like the religion—in fact, for many years he was a member of the English Communist Party—but he did recognize its immense influence in the trend towards respectability. That respectability, at war with the tradition of rioting and machine breaking and riotous drunkenness, contributed to the later English trade unions' emphasis on dignity and restraint. Once the Combination Acts were repealed, many unions were restrained.

Thompson also urged historians to realize that one of the consequences of industrialization was the recognition by the people who worked in these new mines, factories, and workshops that they all had something in common. He wrote: "In the years between 1780 and 1832, most English working people came to feel an identity of interests as between themselves, and as against their rulers and employers," hence his title, *The Making of the Working Class*. He said what's happening is that this group of people is becoming aware of itself as a social class, partly by the pressures on them and partly by their reaction to these pressures. He pointed out that these were real people, faced with difficult and often dangerous situations as they struggled to come to terms with a new reality and a new way of life. They were never passive, but contributed to this new world, sometimes by protest, sometimes even by fighting back.

Warning against other historians' tendency to read later events back into earlier ones, Thompson wrote:

> I am seeking to rescue the poor stockinger, the Luddite cropper, the "obsolete" handloom weaver, the "utopian" artisan from the enormous condescension of posterity. Their crafts and traditions may have been dying. Their hostility to the new industrialism may have been backward-looking. Their communitarian ideals may have been fantasies and their insurrectionary conspiracies may have been foolhardy. But they lived through these times of acute social disturbance and we did not.

In other words, says Thompson, take them on their own terms and try to see how they understood their situation, even if in the long run they couldn't succeed.

In this lecture, I quoted extensively from Engels. In the next, I'll introduce the literary response to industrialization from a wider range of writers, some of them in favor of industry, some of them against it, and a few making responses to aspects of the new industrial scene that now just seem to us quirky and strange.

Poets, Novelists, and Factories
Lecture 16

Industrialization changed the appearance of the world and its social organization. It had tremendous intellectual implications, as well, affecting political and economic thought, poetry, fiction, painting, and aesthetics. This lecture is a look at how poets and novelists responded to industrialization, whether praising it for its material achievements; condemning it for its noise, ugliness, and pollution; or puzzling over the vast disparities it generated between rich and poor. Industrialization is an inexhaustible topic for literature. Although it is not literally true, literature is—figuratively and symbolically—more emotionally intense than economic, technical, or political writing on the same topics.

A Human Enhancement of Nature

- For more than a century, critics have emphasized literary condemnations of industrialization, but there was actually a great deal of excitement and admiration for the new technologies and the changes they inspired.

- In a 1754 poem, John Dalton described the Thomas Savery steam engine, then in use to keep mines from being flooded. Impressed by its combination of fire, steam, iron, great wooden beams, and ability to pump water, he celebrated this machine as better than anything the Romans had built.

- Equally impressed with steam power was Erasmus Darwin (grandfather of Charles Darwin), who anticipated the wonders it would achieve in a lengthy 1792 poem called *The Economy of Vegetation*. Already before the invention of first steam train, Darwin glimpsed the possibility of powered flight and aerial warfare.

- Steam engines fascinated poets and novelists because machines never grew tired or discouraged and could do so much more work than individual people. Ebenezer Elliott, around 1830, pointed out that Watt's steam engine, though very powerful, was constructive, whereas tyrants' powers were all destructive.

- Wordsworth makes a similar point in the poem "Steamboats, Viaducts, and Railways," from 1833. Although Wordsworth was critical of the misuse of industrial power and was horrified when a railway line was built in the beautiful mountains of the Lake District, he also admitted that steam engines were a superb achievement, a kind of human enhancement of what nature had offered.

Dark Satanic Mills

- One response to industrialization was the belief that, as different parts of the world were brought closer together through railways and steamships, the bad old days of war would cease and universal peace would take its place. Charles Mackay was a newspaper writer and editor (the London *Times*'s reporter in New York during the American Civil War), who in "Railways, 1846," voiced the hope that railways would bring peace and harmony.

- When we look at a steam locomotive, we see something old, something deserving of preservation. To 19th-century writers, however, locomotives were brand new. The temptation for artists was to compare them to something older, such as horses, which they were replacing.

- One of the most common reactions, especially among poets, was to criticize industrialization for making England uglier than it used to be and making nostalgic comparisons of past and present. In the 1868 poem "The Earthly Paradise," William Morris, socialist and craftsman, condemns contemporary England for its ugliness, in favor of a happier, cleaner, imaginary past.

- For some artists, this comparison took on a philosophical or religious undertone.
  - For example, William Blake detested Newton and Locke; he saw them as attempting to unravel the delightful mystery of life and to put in its place barren mechanisms.

- Blake's poem "Jerusalem," written in 1808, speculates that Jesus once came to Britain and contrasts a glorious religious utopia in the past with the contemporary industrial horror. He asks, "And was Jerusalem builded here / Among these dark Satanic Mills?" In fact, "dark satanic mills" entered English from this poem as a standard phrase condemning the ugliness of industrialization.

A New Utopia or Hell on Earth?

- The idea of factories as fiery pits of hell is another common image from the literary critics of industrialization. The poet Ernest Jones, in "The Factory Town," from 1855, argued that people were being tortured in factories, just as they were once tortured on the rack by the Spanish Inquisition.

- Many writers had a special indignation about child labor. Frances Trollope suspected that middle-class people didn't know, and didn't want to know, what was actually going on around them; Trollope believed that literature was the medium for exposing evils.

- Depending on whom you read, you could conclude that industrialization was either building a new utopia or creating a hell on earth. Skillful writers were able to imply both ideas at once.

Charles Dickens

- One of the great ages of British fiction coincided with the Industrial Revolution. In 1854, Charles Dickens drew a deeply unflattering picture of the new industrialists in *Hard Times*.
  - Mr. Thomas Gradgrind is the pitiless representative of the industrial system, who has made a fortune in the hardware business and tries to bring up his children according to strict utilitarian principles. He spends his time tabulating data on people as though they were just pieces of machinery.

  - The representative working man in the book is Stephen Blackpool. Hardworking and honest, he refuses to join a trade union because he rejects the concept of class conflict. In the book, Dickens implies that both sides of the industrial system corrupt and degrade people.

- Dickens himself as a child had been taken out of school and forced to work in a factory at the age of 12. The place swarmed with rats, and his job, for 10 hours a day, was to stick labels on bottles of boot polish. His father was in debtors' prison at the time, which meant that Charles's education had come to an abrupt end.

- Dickens was always a searing critic of child labor and of the feeling of monotony and helplessness characteristic of long hours of factory labor.

© Photos.com/Thinkstock.

Charles Dickens, along with Charlotte Brontë, Elizabeth Gaskell, Charles Kingsley, and other great writers, offered vivid portraits of life during the Industrial Revolution.

Elizabeth Gaskell

- Elizabeth Gaskell depicted sympathetic industrial characters in *Mary Barton*, but her version of their employers was much less satirical. Her husband was a Unitarian minister in Manchester who actually met many of the central figures and knew firsthand what was happening.

- A famous passage in *Mary Barton*, from 1848, contrasts the households of the poor and rich. The poor workers' house has hardly any furniture, is infested with vermin, and smells terrible. In the gloom are "three or four little children rolling on the damp, nay wet, brick floor, through which the stagnant, filthy moisture of the street oozed up." By contrast, the house of the local factory owner has a roaring fire, plenty of food for everyone, fine carpets, and even cut flowers.

- Gaskell's *North and South*, published in 1855, went further in arguing both sides of the great industrial question.
  - Margaret, a 19-year-old girl, leaves the rural south of England with her parents and goes to work in a textile mill. She befriends a working-class family, whose father is a militant worker, preparing to lead a strike. At first, Margaret sympathizes openly with the workers and despises the factory owner, Mr. Thornton. She chides him for not looking after the workers better and, by calling them "the hands," dehumanizes them.

  - He responds that the workers put in their hours at the factory and are then free to do whatever they want; he refuses to become a paternalist. Thornton also points out to Margaret that in order to compete with his rival manufacturers, he cannot pay wages as high as he might like, or else will go out of business.

  - The ending shows Margaret accepting Mr. Thornton's offer of marriage. By then, the militant factory worker has come to recognize that on crucial questions, he and his employer agree: Their common foe is dishonesty, laziness, and backward-looking obstructionism. Margaret, too, has come to share this view and to reject the idea that there is an essential antagonism of interests between capital and labor.

Industrialization Overlooked
- Perhaps equally striking, however, is how many of the Victorian novelists said little or nothing about industrialization. Anthony Trollope's dozens of immense novels take place in London and all over the English provinces, but there is never so much as a mention of industrialization. Only the fact that his characters travel by train demonstrates that the world has recently changed.

- George Eliot just once, in *Felix Holt*, created a politically engaged working man, whereas William Thackeray had none. That's a reminder that large areas of Britain—particularly in the south—remained relatively unaffected by the industrial transformation.

- Of course, industry is always present in the background, creating fortunes for some, making others poor, and both sharpening and challenging class distinctions.

D. H. Lawrence
- In the late 19th and early 20th centuries, a new generation of novelists with working-class backgrounds achieved success, especially Arnold Bennett and D. H. Lawrence.

- Bennett's novels are all set in the "five towns," the potteries district where Josiah Wedgwood created the first modern pottery factories.

- D. H. Lawrence came from the Nottinghamshire coal fields. His autobiographical novel *Sons and Lovers*, from 1913, describes his early life growing up as a coal miner's son. The father is a tyrannical, hard-drinking man made coarse and desperate by life underground, and the hero's mother, who has come to hate her husband, is determined that her son shall not suffer the same fate.

Suggested Reading

David, *The Cambridge Companion to the Victorian Novel*.

Gallagher, *The Industrial Reformation of English Fiction*.

Warburg, *The Industrial Muse*.

Webb, *From Custom to Capital*.

Questions to Consider

1. How did authors' social class position affect their literary interpretation of the Industrial Revolution?

2. Why do the acceleration of industrial life and the growing gulf between rich and poor make such compelling themes for fiction and poetry?

Poets, Novelists, and Factories
Lecture 16—Transcript

Industrialization changed the appearance of the world and its social organization. It had huge intellectual consequences, too, affecting political and economic thought, poetry, fiction, painting, and aesthetics. This lecture is a look at how poets and novelists responded to industry, sometimes praising it for its material achievements, sometimes condemning it for its noise, ugliness, and pollution, and sometimes puzzling over the vast disparities it generated between the rich and the poor.

Literary critics for more than a century have emphasized the condemnations of industrialization made by contemporary writers, and there were plenty of them. But to look a little closer is to find a great deal of excitement and admiration for the new technologies and the changes they provoked.

Before the year 1800, efforts simply to describe the new techniques and equipment were quite common. Here, for example, is a poem written in 1754 poem by the Reverend John Dalton, describing the Thomas Savery steam engine, which was then in use to keep mines from being flooded. This is the first generation of steam engine. The Reverend was very impressed by its combination of fire, steam, iron, great wooden beams, and its ability to pump water, either for urban water supply, or its principal use of pumping the water out of coal mines. He says, "This is better than anything the Romans gave us." Here's the poem, and he's addressing Thomas Savery, the inventor, directly.

> Sagacious Savery! Taught by thee
> Discordant elements agree,
> Fire, water, air, heat, cold unite,
> And listed in one service fight;
> Pure streams to thirsty cities send,
> Or deepest mines from floods defend.
> Man's richest gift, thy work will shine;
> Rome's aqueducts were poor to thine!

Equally impressed with steam power was Erasmus Darwin. This is the grandfather of Charles Darwin, and I mentioned Erasmus Darwin previously. He was a friend of Wedgwood and a member of the Lunar Society. He anticipated the wonders that steam was going to achieve in a poem called "The Economy of Vegetation" from 1792. Already, before invention of first steam train, he glimpsed the possibility of powered flight and even aerial warfare. In this poem, which is addressed directly to the power of steam, he anticipates steam-powered aircraft:

> Soon shall thy arm, unconquered Steam! afar
> Drag the slow barge, or drive the rapid car;
> Or on wide-waving wings expanded bear
> The flying-chariot through the fields of air.
> Fair crews, triumphant, leaning from above,
> Shall wave their fluttering kerchiefs as they move;
> Or warrior-bands alarm the gaping crowd,
> And armies shrink beneath thy shadowy cloud.

Aerial armies and steam-powered aircraft.

Steam engines fascinated poets and novelists because they never got tired or discouraged, and they could do so much more work than an individual man. Ebenezer Elliott, in about 1830, pointed out that James Watt's steam engine, though very powerful, was constructive, whereas tyrants' powers throughout the ages had always been destructive. His poem is addressed directly to Watt, or to the engine:

> Engine of Watt! unrivalled is thy sway.
> Compared with thine, what is the tyrant's power?
> His might destroys, while thine creates and saves.
> Thy triumphs live and grow, like fruit and flower;
> But his are writ in blood, and read on graves!

Nobody but English literature antiquarians has ever even heard of Ebenezer Elliott, but William Wordsworth, a very famous Romantic poet who went on to become Poet Laureate, makes a similar point in his poem "Steamboats, Viaducts, and Railways" from about 1833. Wordsworth was critical of the misuse of industrial power, and he was horrified when a railway line was built into the beautiful and mountainous Lake District where he lived and that he eulogized. But Wordsworth could also admit that steam engines were a superb achievement, a kind of human enhancement of what nature had offered, and he anticipated that although the ones in his generation were ugly, they promised a better tomorrow. Here's a little fragment of Wordsworth's poem addressing the steam engine directly. He declares:

> In spite of all that beauty may disown
> In your harsh features, Nature doth embrace
> Her lawful offspring in Man's art; and Time,
> Pleased with your triumph o'er his brother Space,
> Accepts from your bold hands the proffered crown
> Of hope, and smiles on you with cheer sublime.

In other words, nature itself is paying tribute to this justified improvement of what it offers.

As a young man, the first time Wordsworth ever saw a steam engine, he was hiking with his sister Dorothy and his friend Coleridge, another of the great Romantic poets. This is in the Lake District, at the edge of which is a coal field, and this was a mine-pumping engine, a Newcomen Beam engine. They saw the mine-pumping engine, and Dorothy describes what happened next:

> It heaved upwards once in half a minute with a slow motion and seemed to rest to take breath at the bottom, its motion being accompanied with a sound between a groan and "jike." There would have been something in this object very striking in any place, as it was impossible not to invest the machine with some faculty of intellect. It seemed to have made the first step from brute matter to life and purpose, showing its progress by great power. William made a remark to this effect, and Coleridge observed that it was like a giant with one idea.

A related response was to believe that as different parts of the world were made closer through railways and steamships, the bad old days of war would cease and universal peace would take its place. Charles McKay was a

291

newspaper writer and editor. In fact, later on he was going to be the *London Times's* man in New York during the American Civil War in the 1860s. But in his poem "Railways," from the year 1846, he voices this hope that railways will bring peace and harmony to the world:

> Lay down your rails, ye nations, near and far—
> Yoke your full trains to Steam's triumphal car;
> Link town to town; unite in iron bands
> The long-estranged and oft-embattled lands. ...
>
> Blessings on Science, and her handmaid Steam!
> They make Utopia only half a dream;
> And show the fervent, of capacious souls,
> Who watch the ball of Progress as it rolls,
> That all as yet competed or begun,
> Is but the dawning that precedes the sun.

When we look at a steam locomotive, we see something old, even sentimentally old and deserving of preservation. To 19th-century writers, the steam engines were brand new. The temptation for them was to compare them to something that was older, such as horses, which they were gradually replacing. Listen to a passage from this poem by Dante Gabriel Rossetti from the 1850s. Rossetti, we know him mainly as one of the pre-Raphaelite artists, but he'd written a lot of poetry as well. In one he writes: "The steam / snorts, chafes, and bridles, like three-hundred horse / And flings its dusky mane upon the air." In other words, the smoke pouring out of the engine is like the horse's mane as it tosses its head. There were also a great number of poetic comparisons of steam with lighting, comets, and dragons, all fire-breathing monsters that go fast.

One of the commonest reactions, especially among poets, was to criticize industrialization for making England uglier than it used to be, and then to make a nostalgic comparison of the wonderful past and the nasty, ugly present. This is the other side of the poetic evocations of industrialization. William Morris was one such poet, and influential craftsman and a socialist writer, a wonderful, fascinating person. In his poem, "The Earthly Paradise," written in 1868, he condemns contemporary England for its ugliness in favor of a happier and cleaner past, although one that's actually largely imaginary. He writes:

> Forget six counties overhung with smoke,
> Forget the snorting steam and piston stroke,
> Forget the spreading of the hideous town;
> Think rather of the pack-horse on the down,
> And dream of London small, and white, and clean,
> The clear Thames bordered by its garden green.

There's a lovely shifting of mood in that poem, but it's not really very accurate. Packhorses were insanely inefficient, and London itself had been supplied with coal from Newcastle for 300 years by then. You have to go a very long way back in history to find it small and gentle and green and clean.

For some poets, this comparison of the good old world and the nasty new one can take on philosophical or religious overtones. For example, William Blake, the artist and poet: He detested people like Isaac Newton and John Locke. He saw them as attempting to unravel the delightful mystery of life and to put in its place barren mechanisms. That's how he thinks of industrialism: as something barren, mechanical, and heartless. Blake's poem "Jerusalem," from 1808, speculates that Jesus once came to Britain, and he contrasts a glorious religious utopia in the past with the contemporary industrial horror:

> And did those feet in ancient time
> Walk upon England's mountains green?
> And was the Holy Lamb of God
> On England's pleasant pastures seen?
>
> And did the Countenance Divine
> Shine forth upon our clouded hills?
> And was Jerusalem builded here
> Among these dark Satanic mills?

This little phrase, "dark Satanic mills" entered English from this poem as a standard phrase condemning the ugliness of industry, the "dark Satanic mills."

The idea of factories as fiery pits of hell is another common image from the literary critics of industrialization. Because they were often flaming and smoking, the furnaces, the idea of hell was what seemed like an apt metaphor. Here's the poet Ernest Jones and his poem "The Factory Town" from 1855. He argues that people are being tortured in factories, just as they were once tortured on the rack by the Spanish Inquisition. Part of his poem goes like this:

> The night had sunk along the city,
> It was a bleak and cheerless hour;
> The wild winds sang their solemn ditty
> To cold grey wall and blackened tower.
>
> The factories gave forth lurid fires
> From pent-up hells within their breast;
> E'en Etna's burning wrath expires,
> But *man's* volcanoes never rest.
>
> Women, children, men were toiling,
> Locked in dungeons close and black,
> Life's fast-failing thread uncoiling,
> Round the wheel, the *modern rack*!

Some lovely images there: the rack; it's like hell; it's like volcanoes. But at least volcanoes eventually give up, whereas this volcanic torment goes on and on.

There was a particular indignation among middle class writers about child labor. Frances Trollope—that is, the mother of Anthony Trollope, the more famous son of this pair—wrote a novel in 1840 called *Michael Armstrong, the Factory Boy*, and it's a condemnation of conditions in the factories. In the preface to the book, Frances Trollope says that her role is "to drag into the light of day, and place before the eyes of Englishmen, the hideous mass of injustice and suffering to which thousands of infant labourers are subjected, who toil in our monster spinning mills." She suspected that reading middle class people didn't know, and that they didn't want to know, what was actually going on around them, and she believed that literature was the ideal medium for exposing it. This is very similar on the English side of the Atlantic to Harriet Beecher Stowe with *Uncle Tom's Cabin*, written 12 years later on the other side of the Atlantic. Harriet Beecher Stowe wanted everyone to know, "This is what slavery is like. You can't turn your eyes away from it, because it's real and it's happening here in our country."

You see from the foregoing examples that, depending on whom you read, you can conclude that industrialization was making a new utopia or that it was creating a hell on Earth. Skillful writers were able to imply both ideas at once; Thomas Carlyle, for example, in his book *Signs of the Times* from 1829. Critics have disagreed about what Carlyle is getting at because of his ambiguity. He's certainly very critical of utilitarianism, the philosophy of Bentham and Mill with its fact-based, down-to-Earth calculus of pleasures and pains, but its description of new processes could be taken in a positive light as well as a negative one. Here's a passage from Carlyle's *Signs of the Times*. He says:

> Were we required to characterise this age of ours by any single epithet, we should be tempted to call it the Mechanical Age. It is the Age of Machinery, in every outward and inward sense of that word; the age which, with its whole undivided might teaches and practises the great art of adapting means to ends. Nothing is now done directly. Our old modes of exertion are all discredited and thrown aside. On every hand, the living artisan is driven from his workshop to make room for a speedier, inanimate one. The shuttle drops from the fingers of the weaver and falls into iron fingers that ply it faster. The sailor furls his sail, and lays down his oar. Men have crossed oceans by steam. There is no end to machinery. Even the horse is stripped of his harness, and finds a fleet fire-horse invoked in his stead.

Carlyle appears to regret the mechanical ideas about all sorts of other things are spreading. For example, that the right political machinery will give us a good society rather than, as Carlyle believed, goodness in the souls of men.

One of the great ages of British fiction coincided with the Industrial Revolution. Charles Dickens, Charlotte Brontë, Elizabeth Gaskell, Charles Kingsley, Benjamin Disraeli, Harriet Martineau, and George Eliot all responded by offering vivid portraits of this new life that was springing up in England. From their works, we can get a sense not just of what was happening, but of how these acutely observant people understood and explained it.

Charles Dickens drew a deeply unflattering picture of the new industrialists in his novel *Hard Times* from 1854. Mr. Gradgrind is the pitiless representative of the industrial system. He's made a fortune in the hardware business, and tried to bring up his children according to strict utilitarian principles. Hardware is just right, isn't it? I noticed when I read the first volume of the Harry Potter series that Harry in his early life lives with Mr. Dursley, and you know that Mr. Dursley is a bad man when you find out that he runs a drill factory. Drills and hardware; they're pitiless. Anyway, Mr. Gradgrind is an MP and spends his time tabulating data on people as though they're just pieces of machinery. He's emotionally stunted and he's tried to stunt his children's emotional growth, too. There's something of a parody in this of James Mill, the philosopher, who brought up his son, John Stuart Mill, with an intensive education from a very early age, but that led to his son feeling emotionally bereft and having a nervous breakdown at the age of 19.

The schoolteacher in *Hard Times* is called Mr. M'Choakumchild, and, again, as soon as you hear the name, you know what sort of person he's going to be. He squeezes all the joy out of learning and he's interested only in hard calculation. Mr. Bounderby is a self-made man; successful, complacent, and rich but he's also disgusting. He's the perfect discredit of the rags-to-riches idea, and at the end of the book he turns out also to be a liar and a fraud. It's not just the people in *Hard Times*, but it's the place as well. Here's how *Hard Times* begins, with the description of the town called Coketown:

> It was a town of red brick, or of brick that would have been red if
> the smoke and ashes had allowed it. It was a town of machinery and
> tall chimneys, out of which interminable serpents of smoke trailed
> themselves for ever and ever. It contained several large streets, all
> like one another, inhabited by people equally like one another, who

all went to do the same work, and to whom every day was the same as yesterday and tomorrow.

You saw nothing in Coketown but what was severely workful. If the members of a religious persuasion built a chapel there—as the members of 18 religious persuasions had done—they made it a pious warehouse of red brick. Fact, fact, fact, everywhere, in the material aspect of the town; fact, fact, fact everywhere in the immaterial.

The concept of *fact*, the word, keeps on showing up, and it's always something negative. For example, Mr. Bounderby wants to marry Gradgrind's daughter, Louisa. Gradgrind tells his daughter of the proposal, and she answers her father: "Do you think I love Mr. Bounderby?" This is how her father replies: "Confining yourself rigidly to fact, the question of fact you state to yourself is: Does Mr. Bounderby ask me to marry him? Yes, he does. The sole remaining question then is: 'Shall I marry him?' I think nothing can be plainer than that." He then goes on to convince her with a show of statistics that the marriage makes sense. In the end, Louisa's unhappy marriage to Bounderby forces Gradgrind to admit that his system is inadequate, and he begins to understand the need for a richer emotional life as well. Again, this corresponds with a section of John Stuart Mill, who says that after he recovered from his nervous breakdown, he began to understand the importance of a rich affective and emotional life as well, and how he came to value that poetry and art.

The representative working man in *Hard Times* is Stephen Blackpool. He's very hard-working and honest, and he refuses to join a trade union. In other words, he rejects the concept of class conflict, which was then catching on as one way of interpreting what's happening. On the other hand, he also refuses to spy against the trade union for Bounderby. Dickens implies that both sides of the industrial system corrupt and degrade men. Blackpool almost alone has an exemplary character, but he's unhappily married to a drunkard and he comes to a tragic end. Dickens offers us no easy outlet there for a virtuous character.

For Dickens himself, there's an autobiographical element in all this. As a child, he'd been taken out of school and forced to go to work in a factory at the age of 12. The place swarmed with rats, and his job for 10 hours every day was to stick labels on bottles of boot polish. Dickens's father was in debtor's prison at the time, so Charles's education had come to a very abrupt end, and he felt this contrast perhaps even more than kids born with no alternative than hard, joyless work. Dickens was always a searing critic of child labor and of the feeling of monotony and helplessness that's characteristic of long hours spent at work in factories. The vision of an alternative world in this book comes from a girl called Sissy Jupe. She was raised at the circus, and the circus represents play, generosity, bright colors, amusements; all the things that are missing in the world of Coketown and its endless work.

The novelist Elizabeth Gaskell, who was a near contemporary of Dickens, depicted sympathetic industrial characters in her novel *Mary Barton*, but her version of the employers was much less satirical than Dickens's; she didn't caricature either side. Her husband was a Unitarian minister in Manchester, and he actually met many of the central figures in the textile revolution and knew firsthand what was happening in the factories and in the communities around them. One famous passage in *Mary Barton*, which was published in 1848, contrasts the household of the poor and the household of the rich. When old Ben Davenport is sick with typhus and can't go to work, his family becomes destitute. Two other sympathetic working men go to see him and try to help the family. The house has hardly any furniture. It's infested with vermin, and it smells horrible. In the gloom, the men see "three or four little children rolling on the damp, nay wet, brick floor, through which the stagnant, filthy moisture of the street oozed up." From there, from this scene of suffering and disease, one of the men goes straight to the Carson household—and Carson is the local factory owner—where there's a roaring fire, plenty of food for everyone, fine carpets, good clothes, and even plenty of money to spend on buying cut flowers, money of the kind that could rescue Ben Davenport's family. Mrs. Gaskell, the novelist, emphasizes that the boss doesn't even know how severely his own employees are suffering.

Her novel *North and South*, published in 1855, seven years later, went further in arguing both sides of the great industrial question. What happens in *North and South* is that Margaret, a 19 year old girl, leaves the rural south of England with her parents and goes to live in a town called Milton, which is obviously meant to be Manchester. There she discovers the textile factory system in full swing. She befriends a working class family. The mother has died. One of the daughters has contracted tuberculosis from inhaling contaminated air in the cotton mill. The sick girl's father is a militant worker who's preparing to lead a strike of the factory hands. At first, Margaret sympathizes openly with the worker and despises the factory owner, Mr. Thornton. She chides him for not looking after the workers better, and by calling them "the hands." She says, "By calling them 'the hands,' you make it sound as though that's the only part of their bodies that matter. It dehumanizes them." Mr. Thornton responds that they put in their hours at the factory and then they're free to do whatever they want, and he absolutely refuses to become a paternalist. He doesn't want to meddle in every part of their lives. He also points out to her that in order to compete with his rival manufacturers, he can't pay wages as high as he might like or else he'll go out of business and they'll all be in a worse situation than before.

Several set pieces in this novel, *North and South*, show the cogency of these different points of view. I find it a very useful book to teach to students for exactly this reason when we're studying Victorian Britain or the Industrial Revolution. The ending shows Margaret, the young woman, accepting Mr. Thornton's offer of marriage after rejecting an offer from a Southern lawyer. By then, the militant factory worker has come to recognize that on crucial questions he and his employer agree, and that their common foe is dishonesty, laziness, and backward-looking obstructionism. Margaret, too, has come to share this view and to reject the idea that there's an essential antagonism of interests between capital and labor. Her education in industrial realities is cemented by her marriage to the employer, whom she now thinks of as enlightened.

But perhaps equally striking is how many of the Victorian novelists said little or nothing about industrialization. Anthony Trollope's dozens of immense novels take place in London and all over the English provinces, but they never so much as mention industrialization. Only the fact that his characters travel by train demonstrates that the world has been changing recently, and because his mother had written a book condemning factory life, we know that he knew all about it. He just decided not to talk about it. George Eliot just once, in her novel *Felix Holt*, creates a politically engaged working man, whereas William Thackeray has none at all. That's a reminder, I think, that in large parts of Britain, particularly in the south, industrialization didn't make a very deep mark. It affected particularly the Lancashire, Yorkshire, Staffordshire, and Warwickshire areas much more emphatically.

Of course, the industry is always there in the background, creating fortunes for some people, making others poor, sharpening social class distinctions, but also challenging them as nouveau riche. Nouveau riche, newly rich people rise up in business and start marrying up into the older upper classes. You see an echo in these novels, but it's not there front and center.

In the late 19th and early 20th centuries, a new generation of novelists with working class backgrounds achieved success. I earlier mentioned Arnold Bennett from the five towns writing about the potteries, and also D. H. Lawrence. Bennett's novels are all set in the "five towns," the potteries district where Wedgwood had created the first modern factories for ceramics. D. H. Lawrence came from the Nottinghamshire coalfield. His autobiographical novel *Sons and Lovers*, published in 1913, describes his early life growing up as a coal miner's son. The father in *Sons and Lovers* is a tyrannical, hard-drinking man made coarse and desperate by his life underground, and the hero's mother, who's come to hate her husband, is determined that her son shall not suffer the same fate. It's a novel that's utterly unsentimental about the coarsening effect of endless hard and dangerous work, and the son Paul's avoidance of the mines is shown as his mother's small victory over fate.

Certain themes recur far into the 20th century. One of these tropes is that most writers and readers are middle class, and are constantly rediscovering the working class. For example, George Orwell's book *The Road to Wigan Pier*, a fabulous book written in the mid-1930s when Orwell, himself a middle class man, goes to investigate what living conditions and working conditions are like up in Yorkshire and Lancashire in his own day in the midst of the Great Depression. Another recurring theme is that new generations of genuinely working class novelists are always coming along. One group was the "Angry Young Men" of the 1950s and 1960s, like Alan Sillitoe, who wrote the wonderful novel *Saturday Night and Sunday Morning* about a bicycle factory worker. Or John Osborne, the playwright, author of *Look Back in Anger*.

Industrialization is an inexhaustible topic for poetry and literature, and there's no better way to get the feeling of it than through poems and novels. They're not literally true, but figuratively and symbolically they're richer, more emotionally intense than economic, technical, or political writing on the same topics could ever be.

From here, I'll turn in the next lecture to the political implications of industrialization and the way it redrew the political landscape of Britain, changing the balance of power between the old upper classes and the rising commercial and industrial middle class.

How Industry Changed Politics
Lecture 17

B ritain has always had social classes, but they were never as rigid or impermeable as those of Spain and Prussia, for example. Aristocrats were sometimes willing to involve themselves in industrial affairs. This flexibility in social structure meant that, as the first generation of industrialists became wealthy in the late 1700s and early 1800s, they were able to gain political power and influence national policy.

Political Representation for Industrialists

- Ever since the English civil wars of the 1600s, Parliament had been the center of power; but the king still remained influential. He could often buy the compliance of important figures with patronage.

- The political system in the late 1700s and early 1800s gave the strongest representation to the aristocracy and landed gentry, whose income came from the sale of crops and the rental of farmland. They had a strong presence in the House of Commons and an even stronger one in the House of Lords.

- The industrialists' first objective was to get political representation for the new industrial cities they had built. Manchester, Liverpool, and Birmingham had no seats in Parliament, and by end of the Napoleonic Wars in 1815, when these cities housed tens of thousands of people, there was no correlation between population and seats in Parliament.

- There was also no regular process of redistricting; thus, only an act of Parliament could effect change. The landed classes had an obvious incentive to discourage redistricting, fearing that it would lessen their influence.

A Corrupt System

- One nickname for the traditional political system was "Old Corruption," given by an influential journalist named William Cobbett. He meant that it was an elaborate system of special privilege, bribery, and the artful exclusion of the majority—a system that could not possibly be defended on principle.

- Britain had a representative government, but it was not a democracy. Less than five percent of the men could vote. In constituencies where there was a genuine choice, candidates had to bribe voters with dinners, gin, and straight offers of money, making a campaign expensive and highly uncertain.

- Many places whose population had been in decline for centuries still had seats in Parliament—the so-called "rotten boroughs." Others were "pocket boroughs," in which the local landowner was able to choose whom he wanted as the Member of Parliament, with no possibility of a challenge.

- One possible response to this system was for manufacturers to buy landed estates and join the traditional upper class. Men who became rich enough through trade or business could buy access to pocket boroughs.

A Wave of Reform

- One response to the corrupt political system was to provoke public discussion of the inequities of the current system and agitate for reform. At end of the Napoleonic Wars, a wave of reform agitation, strikes, and food riots swept through Britain, especially in the manufacturing areas. The end of the war had created a recession and widespread unemployment.

- The government responded with repression, notoriously, the Peterloo Massacre of 1819, when a massive demonstration in favor of political reform was attacked by soldiers, killing 15 demonstrators and injuring nearly 500.

- The situation reached a crisis point in 1832. The Reform Act of 1832 passed the House of Commons but was rejected by the House of Lords, who stood to lose by the changes. That led to rioting in the major cities, even an attack on the home of the duke of Wellington, hero of Waterloo. Finally, the legislation passed.

- The clutter of anomalous methods was now replaced by uniform rules for voting in every constituency. There was new representation of industrial towns, with 50 or 60 new seats. Successful factory owners began to campaign for seats and to represent their own interests in Parliament.

The Peterloo Massacre of 1819 become a defining event in British history—a symbol of the brutality of the old regime and the need for transformation.

Free-Trade Movement

- The industrialists, once they had more access, wanted British economic policy oriented in their interest rather than in the interest of the landowners. The main issues were free trade and political regulation of industry.

- First, industrialists wanted a reduction in tariffs. They believed in free trade—the idea that they should be able to import raw materials cheaply, without paying import duty, and export finished goods cheaply, without paying export duty. Reduced tariffs would enable them to sell their goods all over the world, expanding their markets and stimulating productivity at home.

- The industrialists also believed that free trade would generate peace—that is, everyone involved in trade arrangements would have an incentive to keep them going and to solve disagreements peacefully. They depicted themselves as men of peace, as opposed to the traditional aristocrats, for whom war was a way of life.

- Another benefit of free trade, from the employers' point of view, was that if food imports came in cheaply, they would be able to pay lower wages to their employees and, thus, enhance profits. The argument was self-interested, but its advocates were confident that workers' standard of living would also improve from sustained economic growth.

- Landowners, by contrast, wanted high tariffs on imported food because it enabled them to sell food at a higher price than if they had to compete with cheap imports. They had secured passage of the Corn Laws in 1815 to guarantee this principle.

The Anti-Corn Law League
- Once the manufacturing interest became more prominent in Parliament, the case for free trade grew stronger. Two Members of Parliament, Richard Cobden and John Bright, founded the Anti-Corn Law League in 1839 to campaign for free trade.

- The league held mass meetings, arguing that free trade was equally good for manufacturers and working people, bringing prosperity to all. It built Free Trade Hall in 1842, on the site of the Peterloo Massacre, which had become hallowed ground in Manchester.

- In 1842, the Tory government responded with many reductions of tariffs.

- Finally, the crisis of the Irish famine in 1846 prompted repeal of the Corn Laws. From then on, cheap food could enter Britain. Tariffs on most other goods were also ratcheted down to create a condition of near free trade.

Regulation of Industry
- A second issue was the political regulation of industry. Manufacturers argued that regulation should be left to individuals.

All men had the right to enter into contracts or not to enter into them, as they saw fit. This was the most fundamental freedom of all, and to legislate it was to limit freedom.

- Advocates of regulation argued that contracts were not being made by equally powerful people; thus, workers were at a disadvantage. They had to take what work they could get, even at near-starvation wages, and lack of political support exposed them to exploitation.

- Widespread use of women and children in the workforce strengthened the argument for intervention. Parliamentary commissions encountered dismaying cases of overwork, brutalization in the workplace, industrial disease, accidents, and premature death.

- This ushered in an era of growing statistical studies, sociological research, and public health campaigns. The argument was made on utilitarian grounds that regulation benefits even the employers by creating a healthier and less turbulent workforce.

- The outcome of these debates was a succession of factory acts and mine acts regulating the number of hours women and children could work and establishing baseline conditions for work.
  - The first of these was the Cotton Mills Act of 1819, prohibiting the employment of children in textile factories. It was strengthened in 1833 by the creation of factory inspectors and by specifying that children under 13 should be given some elementary schooling.

  - In 1842, after sensational revelations in public hearings, the Mines and Collieries Act banned the employment of women and girls in coal mines. In 1845, the first safety legislation regulating fencing of dangerous machinery was passed.

Trade Unions
- Industrial workers did not benefit from the Reform Act 1832. Only property owners could vote, and most workers owned no property.

- Some responded by joining movements for political reform in the 1830s and 1840s—notably the Chartists, who favored an extension of the franchise to all adult men. They wrote the "People's Charter," whose six points were designed to make it possible for ordinary working men to participate in politics.

- Other workers began to create trade unions. Although the Combination Acts were repealed in 1824, unions were still prohibited from picketing and intimidation and were still vulnerable to prosecution for conspiracy.

- Unions became steadily more powerful, especially among skilled workers, in the mid-19th century. Unions emphasized respectability, decency, and middle-class values as a way of allaying old fears but insisted on their right to participate in the benefits of industrialization.

- The Trades Union Congress (TUC), founded in 1868, debated common concerns. In the late 19th century, it began to explore the possibility of establishing a political party of its own—plans that eventually resulted in the creation of the Labour Party in Britain.

Karl Marx

- Meanwhile, a small minority of workers was attracted to the theories of Karl Marx. In Marx's view, industrialization was desirable but not so long as it was organized on capitalist principles. In his view, capitalism was always exploitative.

- Marx favored collective ownership of the means of production and believed that socialist revolution was inevitable. As the working class grew larger and the bourgeoisie grew smaller, there would be a transformation of quantity into quality, and the proletariat would become revolutionary and overthrow the capitalists.

- Marx expected the revolution to happen first in England, the United States, and Germany as those countries became industrial leaders—

but certainly not Russia, which was still overwhelmingly a peasant society.

- Industrialists were, of course, aware of the existence of Marxism and of the appeal it might have for disgruntled workers. One of the arguments for paying better wages and for permitting political regulation of industry later in the 19th century was to forestall the danger that Marxist prophecies might come true.

Suggested Reading

Pelling, *The Origins of the Labour Party*.

Royle, *Chartism*.

Rubinstein, *Britain's Century*.

Schonhardt-Bailey, *From the Corn Laws to Free Trade*.

Questions to Consider

1. Why was the political conflict between industrialists and landowners so sharp in the early 19th century?

2. Which was more useful from the perspective of working men in the 1830s and 1840s: the vote or better working conditions and wages?

How Industry Changed Politics
Lecture 17—Transcript

Britain has always had social classes, but they've never been impermeable; never as rigid as those of Spain or Prussia, for example, and certainly not as rigid as the caste systems of India. This means that aristocrats were sometimes willing to involve themselves in industrial affairs. It also means that as the first generation of industrialists became wealthy in the late 1700s and early 1800s, moving up from the middle class, they were able to gain political power and to influence national policy.

As we saw in Lecture 2, ever since the civil wars of the 1600s, Parliament had been the center of power. But the king remained influential; he could often buy the compliance of important figures with patronage positions. The political system of Britain in the late 1700s and the early 1800s gave the strongest representation to the aristocracy and the landed gentry, whose income came from the sale of crops and the rental of farmland. They were strong in the House of Commons, and even stronger in the House of Lords.

The industrialists' first objective was to get political representation for the new industrial cities they'd built. Manchester, Liverpool, and Birmingham had no seats in Parliament, and by end of the Napoleonic Wars in 1815, when these cities housed tens of thousands of people, there was no correlation between population and parliamentary seats. There was also no regular process of redistricting, so only an Act of Parliament could create a change. The landed classes had an obvious incentive to discourage the change, especially if they feared that it would lessen their influence.

One nickname of the old political system was "Old Corruption," given by influential journalist William Cobbett. What he meant by that phrase, "old corruption," was that British politics was an elaborate system of special privilege, bribery, and the artful exclusion of the majority of British people, a system that couldn't possibly be defended on principle.

Different towns around the kingdom and different counties had different rules about voting, a cockeyed collection of historical traditions. But although Cobbett claimed that this was an indefensible system, a theoretical defense of it was, in fact, made by Edmund Burke. His view was that each place has lived through the generations and has gradually developed a way of doing things, and when something is tried and tested by tradition and is found to work, it's that much more reason that it should be kept on. The Burkian view that the most reliable guide we've got is tradition is bumping into the new utilitarian view of rationality, the view that we should look at everything anew, we should give equal representation to all places, and that we should create uniform rules for everyone; two theories about how the political system should work, bumping into each other.

Britain did have a representative government, but it certainly wasn't a democracy. Less than five percent even of the men could vote, and voting was by public ballot. In fact, the opposition to the idea of a secret ballot was very strong. Politicians used to say, "I'm not going to sneak up to the ballot box as though I'm ashamed of whom I'm voting for, I'm going to do it publicly." In constituencies where there was a genuine choice between candidates, very often the candidates themselves had to bribe the voters by buying them dinners, giving them drinks of gin, or sometimes straight offers of money, which, of course, made a campaign very expensive and highly uncertain.

Many other places, whose population had been in decline for centuries, still had seats in Parliament. One of the most famous examples was Old Sarum in the southwest of England, whose population was zero by 1830. Nobody lived there at all, but it still had seats in Parliament. These were the so-called "rotten boroughs," boroughs that had once been populated and had gradually decayed down to nothing. Others again were called "pocket boroughs," in which the local land owner was able to choose whom he wanted as the MP for that district, with no possibility of a challenge. It was very common for members of Parliament or for local landowners to choose their own sons or sometimes a picked man whom they knew for certain would do their bidding in Parliament.

This was the system as the 19th century opened. One possible response to it was for manufacturers who wanted political representation to buy landed estates and to join the traditional upper class. For example, the Prime Minister Robert Peel, of the 1840s, was himself the son of a successful manufacturer who'd bought an estate and become a major landowner, buying his way into the old upper class. Men who became rich enough through trade or business could buy access to a pocket borough, and this was particularly true of a group called the "nabobs." Britain was the overlord of India by the late 18th century, and the nabobs were men who'd gone out with the East India Company and made great fortunes in India. Once Britain became the dominant power there, the opportunities for corruption, bribery, and self-enrichment were enormously strong, so men would bring great fortunes back from India and buy their way into the political system back in Britain itself.

One way was to buy your way into the system. Another possible response was to provoke public discussion of the inequities of the current system and then agitate for reform. At end of the Napoleonic Wars in 1815, a wave of reform agitation, strikes, and food riots swept through Britain, particularly in the manufacturing areas, which were the most underrepresented. The end of the Napoleonic Wars had created a recession and widespread unemployment, made worse by the fact that so many soldiers were coming back from the army. The government responded to this wave of unrest with repression, notoriously in an incident that's remembered in British history as the Peterloo Massacre of 1819. A giant demonstration took place in favor of political reform on St. Peter's fields in Manchester, and it was attacked by soldiers, killing 15 of the demonstrators and injuring another 500. It was called Peterloo as a mocking reference to the battle of Waterloo, which had taken place four years earlier; Waterloo a great and distinguished British victory, and Peterloo, on St. Peter's fields, a humiliating attack by the British army on its own subjects. Peterloo became a defining event in the history of British radicalism, a symbol of the brutality of the old regime and of the intensified need for transformation.

Britain did already have a degree of press freedom, and through the 1820s intense press campaigns emphasized the need for parliamentary reform. The situation finally came to a crisis in 1832. A reform act passed through the House of Commons; it undertook to reform itself and to get rid of many of these strange anomalies. But it was rejected by the House of Lords, whose members thought that they stood to lose by the changes, which was probably true. The fact that the Lords had rejected it led to rioting in the major cities.

There was even an attack on the home of the Duke of Wellington, the Prime Minister, and the great hero of the battle of Waterloo.

The Duke of Wellington was very shrewd. He finally persuaded enough of the Lords either to abstain or to vote yes so that the legislation could pass, because he understood that if that didn't happen they were going to have to create many more Lords in order to create a majority who'd then pass the legislation. But this expansion of the aristocracy for the sake of the act would have the effect of diluting the exclusivity of the peerage itself. The Duke was finally able to persuade the Lords to go along, albeit grudgingly, with what's called the Great Reform Act of 1832. This is one of the many occasions in British political history where the system learned how to bend so that it didn't have to break. It's another tribute to the political stability that was so important in nourishing Britain's Industrial Revolution. It certainly wasn't frictionless; there was a great deal of rioting and upheaval preceding it. But nevertheless, in the end, Parliament was willing to reform itself.

At this point, the great clutter of anomalous old methods was replaced by uniform rules for voting in every constituency throughout the nation. For the first time, the industrial towns were now given representation. Seats in Parliament were allocated, 50 or 60 new ones were created. This meant that for the first time the successful factory owners could campaign in their towns for seats in Parliament, and then they could begin to represent their own interests directly in parliament.

The historian W. D. Rubinstein writes about Parliament after the Great Reform Act. He says after 1832:

> [Into Parliament] came a new type of middle-class MP, the businessman, often a manufacturer, who was firmly rooted in the seat which returned him to Parliament. These men were often seen as indeed their town's "representative" in Parliament, being closely associated with local prosperity and often being major employers of labour in their constituencies. Very few manufacturers entered Parliament before 1832. After 1832 their number grew consistently.

The industrialists, once they had more access, wanted British economic policy oriented in their interest rather than in the interest of the landowners, as it clearly had been up to that point. The main issues they were interested in were free trade and the political regulation of industry.

First of all, they wanted a reduction in tariffs. They believed in free trade; the idea that they should be able to import raw materials cheaply from anywhere in the world without paying import duty, and then that they should be allowed to export their finished goods cheaply without paying export duty. Because Britain was then the world's leader in industrialization, that would mean that Britain would have an enormous competitive advantage, enabling them to sell their goods all over the world, expanding their market and stimulating more productivity at home by raising demand. They also believed that free trade would induce peace. In other words, that everyone involved in trade arrangements has an incentive to keep them going and to solve disagreements peacefully. The manufacturers depicted themselves as men of peace, as opposed to the older aristocrats for whom war was the great purpose of life; so it's a peaceful middle class displacing an old warrior aristocracy.

There was some merit to this point of view, and it's very striking to compare the 1800s with the 1700s. All through the 1700s, Britain was constantly at war, mainly with France but also sometimes with Spain. By contrast, there was a 99 years' peace between Britain's victory at Waterloo in 1815 and the outbreak of the First World War in 1914, 99 years later. This is a period of almost uninterrupted peace; not completely, but mainly. As the business middle classes rise to political dominance, this is the kind of conditions they want and they work for.

Another benefit of free trade from the employers' point of view was that if food imports came in cheaply, if food imports didn't have to pay an import duty, they, the manufacturers, would be able to pay lower wages to their employees, and thus enhance their own profits. Think about it this way: The workers, no matter how badly they're paid, have to eat, so there has to be a close correlation between food prices and wages. If the boss were to pay wages so low that the workers simply still couldn't afford to feed themselves, they'd simply stop working. So food prices do represent an absolute minimum beneath which wages can't fall.

These arguments being made by the manufacturers were clearly self-interested, but still their advocates were confident that the workers' standard of living would, in fact, improve from sustained economic growth. If there's lots of work, they can keep coming to the factory. Everyone is going to benefit.

By contrast, the landowners, whose position in politics is beginning to weaken slightly, wanted high tariffs on imported food because it enabled them to sell food that they were growing at higher prices than if they had to compete with cheap imports. The landowners had secured the passage of legislation called the Corn Laws in 1815 to guarantee exactly this principle. The Corn Laws were designed to keep food prices high inside Britain.

Once the manufacturing interests became more dominant in Parliament, the case for free trade grew stronger. Two Members of Parliament, Richard Cobden and John Bright, founded an organization called the Anti-Corn Law League in 1839 to campaign for free trade. They brought an almost evangelical zeal to this campaign, expressing arguments for free trade in terms of happiness for working people and world peace. But they didn't make it sound like a narrowly commercial matter; they made it sound like an enormous issue of principle on which the welfare of everyone in Britain depended. The Anti-Corn Law League was very good at publicity. It held mass meetings, arguing that free trade was equally good for manufacturers and working people, bringing prosperity to them all and harming only the selfish idle aristocrats. The Anti-Corn Law League built Free Trade Hall in Manchester in 1842, a great brick auditorium for mass meetings of this kind. It was deliberately placed on the site of the Peterloo Massacre of 1819, which had become hallowed ground in Manchester. St. Peter's field, Peterloo, was very much like England's equivalent of Ground Zero, especially for English radicals, manufacturers, and working groups.

The conservative government responded to this agitation in 1842 with many reductions in tariffs. Finally, the crisis of the Irish famine in 1846—this was the time when the potato harvest failed, when the Irish population was overwhelmingly dependent on potatoes as its basic subsistence, leading to the deaths of perhaps as many as a million Irish people and the emigration of more than a million more—finally prompted the repeal of the Corn Laws so that cheaper food could come in, partly to alleviate the famine. The repeal of the laws caused a split in the Tory Party, whose landed gentlemen—this was their party—felt betrayed by their own leader, Peel. Their view had been "We must keep the Corn Laws at all costs." When their own leader said "No, we're going to get rid of them," they felt that their leader had betrayed them.

From then on, it did mean that cheaper food could enter Britain. Tariffs on most other goods also ratcheted down to create a condition of near-free trade in the middle and late decades of the 19th century.

A second question that confronted the modified political system was the question of the political regulation of industry. Should Parliament have the right to specify how many hours people went to work, the age at which they could work, minimum standards of safety, and minimum rates of pay? The manufacturers, now better represented than before, said no; leave it to individuals contracting freely. Everyone has the right to enter into contracts or to not enter into them as they see fit. If a man decides to work at the factory and the boss agrees to pay him a certain amount, they're two freely-contracting individuals. This is the most fundamental freedom of all, so that to legislate it is to limit men's freedom. Of course, this is an argument that's still made right up to the present by libertarians. The advocates of regulation retorted that contracts weren't being made by equally powerful people, so that the workers were actually at an appalling disadvantage. They had to take whatever work they could get, even if it was at near-starvation wages, and the lack of political support exposed them to exploitation. The argument there is that government needs to defend the more powerless side of these negotiations to create a more level playing field.

The widespread use of women and children in the workforce strengthened the argument for political intervention. Parliamentary commissions investigating what was going on in the new industrial towns encountered dismaying cases of overwork, very, very long hours, brutalization in the workplace, industrial disease, accidents, and premature death. Propaganda in favor of political intervention in the system came from Charles Dickens in novels like *Hard Times* and *Oliver Twist*, from Charles Kingsley, and from many other writers.

The conservative tradition of noblesse oblige, the idea that the upper classes have a duty to the lower classes to take care of their interests, which is a central issue in hierarchical societies, led many conservatives to take the view "Of course we should be intervening. Our position has historically been to take care of members of the lower classes." The central figure representative of this point of view is Lord Shaftesbury, a conservative who was horrified at what he saw as the manufacturers' cynical exploitation of their workers.

The mid-19th century was an era of growing statistical sophistication. More sociological research was being done; more things were being quantified systematically. These are the decades in which there's the beginning of a public health movement, responding particularly to cholera epidemics in the cities. It became possible to make the argument on utilitarian grounds that regulation benefited everyone, even the employers, even though they were very reluctant to be interfered with or disturbed. The argument was: If we have regulation of hours and conditions in the factories, we'll create a healthier workforce, and they'll be less turbulent if they perceive that their interests are being properly taken care of. This is an argument to which some manufacturers responded favorably.

The outcome of the great debate of the 1830s and '40s was a succession of "factory acts" and "mine acts" regulating the number of hours women and children could work and establishing baseline conditions for industrial work everywhere. The very first of these acts had been the Cotton Mills Act of 1819, coming a little bit earlier, which prohibited the employment of children under the age of 9 in textile factories, and limiting the work of 9- to 18-year-olds to 12 hours per day. It still sounds like an extraordinarily long and hard day by our standards, but was a response to the fact that very young children until then were working 12, 14, and 15 hours in the factories. The act was strengthened in 1833 by the creation of factory inspectors to make sure that the law was being carried out, and by specifying that children under the age of 13 should be given some elementary schooling. Until then, many of them had none at all and were completely illiterate.

In 1842, the Mines and Collieries Act was passed by Parliament. It banned the employment of women and girls in coal mines after sensational revelations in public hearings. Lord Shaftesbury had published his commission's report with engraved pictures, and had emphasized the moral affront of having half-naked girls in the heat of the mines working alongside the boys. It was a response also to the Huskar Colliery disaster of 1838, when a large group of children working in the mine, boys and girls together, were drowned in a terrible flooding accident. During the lecture on coal mining, I read to you a section from Benjamin Disraeli's book *Sybil*, which also protests against the idea that the aspiring mothers of England should be working half naked in the mines. In 1845, for the first time, parliamentary legislation specified fencing off dangerous machinery to cut down on the number of industrial accidents that were dismayingly common inside the factories.

Manufacturers responded to legislation like this by warning that their costs would rise and that they'd become uncompetitive. Of course, comparable complaints about regulation have been made ever since, not only in Britain, but all over the world. In fact, the factory acts were often violated in practice, and they didn't cover all workers; farm laborers and domestic servants were outside the purview of the legislation. But this was at least the tentative beginnings of industrial regulation, which in Britain has gradually been consolidated in the century and a half since then.

Industrial workers didn't benefit from the Great Reform Act of 1832. For them, there was a bitter sense of continuing exclusion. Only property owners were allowed to vote, and most workers owned no property. Today, we assume that the sheer fact of being an adult citizen gives you membership in the political community, but not then. Property ownership was regarded by most political theorists as essential.

Some workers responded by joining movements for political reform in the 1830s and 1840s, notably the Chartists, who favored an extension of the franchise to all adult men. They wrote "The People's Charter," whose six points were designed to make it possible for ordinary working men to participate in politics, first as voters and then potentially as Members of Parliament as well. The six principles were these: universal manhood suffrage; every adult man should vote. Second: Payment of Members of

Parliament so that they could afford to become MPs. In those days, the tradition was that being a Member of Parliament was service. You shouldn't want to be paid. Third: They favored equal-sized electoral districts to make it more representative. Fourth: Annual Parliaments, so that it could be as representative as possible and changes in national mood could be reflected in the new makeup of the body. Fifth: A secret ballot to prevent intimidation and bribery of voters. Sixth: No property qualification for Members of Parliament. You shouldn't have to be the owner of any property in order to be eligible to run.

All these reforms have now been achieved, all except annual parliaments, but it was then regarded as a dangerously radical movement. Big demonstrations were held by the chartists in London and the provincial cities, and petitions were presented to Parliament in the late 1830s and again in the late '40s. But again, the Members of Parliament had no incentive to weaken their own power and strengthen that of the workers, whose intentions they feared. The manufacturers had enlisted the workmen's aid in agitating for the Reform Act, but they didn't intend to share their newly acquired power, and they feared that if the non-property-holding workers gained political power, the first thing they'd do would be legislate to end to private property itself.

Other workers began to create trade unions. The principle of a trade union is that one worker confronting the boss is virtually powerless—he can be fired—but that the whole workforce confronting him together can bargain for better hours, better wages, and safer working conditions. In 1799 and 1800, the era of the Napoleonic Wars, Parliament had passed the Combination Acts, forbidding men to create unions or gather together to plan strikes. I mentioned this in an earlier lecture. Their motive was fear of the terror in the French Revolution. Of course, we know that the terror didn't spread to England and that England didn't have a revolution, but the English upper classes were acutely afraid of it. The repeal of the Combination Acts in 1824 meant that unions were now allowed to operate, but they were still prohibited from picketing and from intimidation, and they were still vulnerable to prosecution for conspiracy. That meant, of course, that it was relatively easy for the employer to bring in strike breakers.

In the nature of things, trade unions are most effective when the workers are skilled, because if they're skilled workers they can't simply be quickly replaced by a group of unskilled strike breakers. When a group of skilled men threaten to withhold their labor, the manufacturer is much more likely to have to come to terms with them, because he can't do without the skills that they possess. That's one of the reasons why industrial employers were so eager to deskill the laborers, to make it easier to replace them. Skilled workers became steadily more powerful, and the unions they created, especially in the middle of the 19th century, but they weren't radicals. They emphasized their own respectability, their decency, their middle class values. They wanted to allay the fears of the manufacturers, but they wanted the manufacturers to feel "We have the same values you do. We believe in the system in which we're working, we simply want to be remunerated better within it." They insisted on their rights to participate in the benefits of industrialization. The unions, particularly the unions of skilled workmen, were very ceremonious. They'd dress up, they'd have special costumes, they'd have great banners, they'd sing Christian hymns. Some of them would take the pledge of temperance and sobriety and express extravagant loyalty to their crafts. It was demonstrative.

The Trades Union Congress, the TUC, was founded in 1868, an organization to bring together union members from many parts of the kingdom to debate common concerns. In the late 19th century, in the 1890s, it began to explore the possibility of creating a political party of its own, plans that eventuated in the creation of the Labour Party. The great difference between the TUC in Britain and the American Federation of Labor, the AFof L, is over this decision. The AF of L never did create a political party, whereas the TUC did.

A small minority of workers, meanwhile, was attracted to the theories of Karl Marx, a German revolutionary exile hard at work in the British Museum library. In Marx's view, industrialization itself is desirable, but not so long as it's organized on capitalist principles. In Marx's view, capitalism is always exploitative. He favored the collective ownership of the means of production and believed that socialist revolution was inevitable. He theorized like this: As the working class gets bigger and bigger, and as bourgeoisie, the employing class, grows smaller from consolidation and competition, there's eventually going to be what he called a transformation of quantity into quality. The proletariat, the working class, will become revolutionary and will overthrow the capitalists, at which point the exploitation will end. Marx expected it to happen first in England, in the United States, and in Germany as they became the industrial leaders. Certainly not in Russia, which was still overwhelmingly a peasant society. Marx had hardly anything to say about Russia. He would've been amazed to learn that after his death the first Marxist revolution took place there.

The industrialists were, of course, aware of the existence of Marxism and of the appeal it might make to disgruntled workers. One of the arguments for paying better wages and for permitting political regulation of industry later in the 19th century was to forestall the danger of Marxist prophecies coming true. In other words, if Marx said the proletariat was destined to become ever bigger and ever more impoverished, the manufacturers could counter by making it less impoverished, with improved wages and conditions.

From these political debates, we'll move in the next lecture to questions of economic theory. Economics as a discipline came of age along with industrialization as intellectuals struggled to understand why Britain had become so dynamic, why it was so quickly growing richer, and why its political and social structure were changing.

Dismal Science—The Economists
Lecture 18

E conomics as a discipline came of age along with industrialization as intellectuals struggled to understand why Britain had become so dynamic, why it was so quickly growing richer, and why its political social structure was changing. Now, a system was beginning to develop in which great rewards went to people who broke with tradition and tried something new. By the early 1800s, the continuous improvement of machinery, the growing scale of factories, the increased movement of people into factories, and the social dislocations that went with these changes helped give rise to the discipline of economics.

Mercantilism

- In the 18th century, the prevailing economic theory was mercantilism, based on the idea of a zero-sum game: One nation's gain must be another nation's loss. Therefore, according to the theory, a nation must bring in more gold and silver than it exported and try to keep as much trade as possible for itself.

- This theory motivated the acquisition and jealous preservation of colonies by Britain and other European powers. It justified high tariffs, to make it difficult for other nations' goods to sell in Britain. It inspired the notorious Navigation Acts, which mandated that all of Britain's colonial trade must come via England and must be in British or British colonial ships.

- Mercantilism presupposed that a nation's strength required close political regulation of economic activities—a claim that the theorists of the industrial age were about to challenge.

Adam Smith

- Adam Smith's *The Wealth of Nations*, published in 1776, is often regarded as the first modern study of economics. A philosopher and moralist during the Scottish Enlightenment, Smith was a professor at Glasgow University.

- In the book, Smith offered a sequence of fascinating and influential ideas, one of which was that self-interest can have positive social outcomes. In other words, a baker provides bread not because he is concerned about the welfare of others, but because he is concerned about his own welfare.

- Smith believed that wealth was based on labor, not on the possession of money. Nations were wealthy to the degree that they improved their efficiency in employing labor.

- An important point Smith made is that the division of labor increases efficiency to an astonishing degree. Therefore, three factors become important: workers' dexterity, their ability not to waste time, and the invention of machines to do specialized work even faster. Smith realized that there was an immense amount of cooperation and division of labor already.

- Smith argued that the "invisible hand" of the market was extremely good at organizing economic affairs. Individuals respond to a new demand by providing the required goods or services. Government does not need to specify that someone should do it—and is likely to make mistakes in trying. This attitude was in strict contradiction to the position of the mercantilists.

- Smith also argued that there is a human propensity to trade. This was itself related to the division of labor—because it makes it reasonable for individuals not to try to do everything for themselves but to exchange parts of their labor in trade.

- Importantly, Smith reasoned that economic growth is real—not a zero-sum game. As people get wealthier, they are not necessarily taking wealth away from someone else. What's more, consumers will benefit as producers compete to provide better-quality goods at lower cost. As successful businesspeople accumulate money, they will reinvest it in new factories, creating new employment for more people.

David Ricardo

- Smith's ideas were refined by David Ricardo in his 1817 book, *Principles of Political Economy and Taxation*. Ricardo, the son of a Jewish banker who had emigrated to England from Holland, was respected in Parliament for his understanding of complex economic issues.

- Ricardo witnessed the conflict between two groups of the wealthy—the landowners and the rising industrialists. Landowners wanted food to be expensive; industrialists wanted it to be cheap. Landowners were dominant in Parliament well into the 19th century and were eager to preserve their situation.

- Ricardo argued that as industrial progress continues, more workers are needed, and thus, wages will rise. Because workers have to be fed, food production increases. More and more marginal land will be used, and overall food prices will rise. Workers may get more money, but they are no better off because they have to pay more for food.

- The losers in the situation are the capitalists because they are forced to pay higher wages to keep their workforce. Landowners come out on top because they can charge high rent for land and get high prices for food.

- Ricardo became a great advocate of abolishing protectionist laws and allowing cheap imports of food into the country. He was more generally in favor of free trade to prevent unproductive landlords from profiting.

The Business Cycle

- Thomas Malthus, like Ricardo, assumed that even as national wealth increased, the poor would remain poor, because the ability to reproduce was so much greater than the ability to increase food production. Only voluntary self-restraint could reduce population—Malthus favored delaying marriage or not marrying at all as a way of reducing the size of the population.

- The next generation of economists took up the question of the business cycle. Malthus had glimpsed it but had never developed it fully.

- By the early 1800s, it was clear that booms and busts alternated in the business cycle. For example, individual manufacturers hear of rising demand for a product. That gives them a logical reason for trying to meet the demand. Many enter the trade until the demand is satisfied. Now, so many are in the trade that they create a glut. Demand and, therefore, prices fall; workers are laid off; and some businesses go bankrupt.

- This pattern was first theorized systematically by Swiss historian and economist Jean Charles Léonard de Sismondi in 1819 in his *New Principles of Political Economy*. Although Ricardo had doubted that cycles and crises could happen, Sismondi saw the evidence. He observed that employers don't have perfect knowledge of what's happening, and everyone is acting in the dark. He favored government intervention to support the unemployed.

- Sismondi also observed the tendency of capitalists to pay excessively low wages, which led to periodic phases of overproduction and under-consumption. This idea was later picked up by Karl Marx, who predicted that crises would become ever more catastrophic and eventually provoke revolution.

Robert Owen
- Economists also involved themselves in the question of social justice. They asked whether exploitation was central to industrial capitalism or whether workers and employers have a shared set of concerns and goals.

- The utopian socialists denied that class conflict was inevitable. For example, Robert Owen, who ran textile mills outside Glasgow, was a benevolent employer, who provided decent workers' housing, fair wages, and a school for the children, yet his business was still profitable.

- Owen's 1813 book, *A New View of Society*, advanced an environmental theory of human development. He favored a kind of humane social engineering to create suitable industrial-era people. He argued that the factory was a social system, as well as a place of production, and could be run so as to create a form of cooperative sharing socialism.

In addition to the New Lanark Mills outside Glasgow, the utopian socialist Robert Owen also attempted to establish an industrial commune in New Harmony, Indiana.

John Stuart Mill

- Ricardo and Malthus were also friends of Jeremy Bentham and James Mill, the utilitarians. They brought philosophy down to earth, insisting that the greatest good for the greatest number, rather than some religious principle, should guide human conduct.

- John Stuart Mill, James's son, tried to apply the utilitarian principle to economics. His *Principles of Political Economy*, published in 1848, became the great textbook of 19th-century economics and was widely read, translated, and reprinted.

- Mill pointed out that the laws relating to production that Smith and Ricardo had discovered were not matched by the laws of distribution; here, moral principles and community decisions must apply. He argued that if the community favored principles of equality, it could arrange distribution along those lines. No system of distribution was actually "natural" at all.

- Mill was not a socialist, but many socialists and trade unionists found him sympathetic for such insights. He knew that in contemporary Britain, the lowest incomes went to the people who labored the most and the highest incomes went to those who did almost nothing. Abandonment or transformation of such a system was not necessarily unjust.

- Mill believed in the value of private property and hard work. Mill also tried to turn economics into a rigorous academic discipline, modeled on the physical sciences. But he realized that prediction is always uncertain and that the complexity of human life makes accurate anticipation of the future impossible.

Shift to Mathematical Economics

- Already by the mid-19th century, some economists wondered whether the fundamental basis on which the Industrial Revolution was built would keep it going. William Stanley Jevons, a brilliant mathematical economist, wrote *The Coal Question* in 1865, arguing that Britain would soon run out of coal and the Industrial Revolution would end.

- The book also introduced the "Jevons paradox," which argued that as fuel use increases in efficiency, we don't use less of it but more. For example, after Watt improved Newcomen steam engines by making them more efficient, the number in use and total coal consumption went sharply up, not down.

- Jevons's work also demonstrated a shift to mathematical economics, which has been a trend ever since. Although Adam Smith was purely descriptive, by the late 19th century, statistics and equations were becoming all the more important as economics became more detailed and precise.

Suggested Reading

Heilbroner, *The Worldly Philosophers*.

Schumpeter and Schumpeter, *History of Economic Analysis*.

Smith, *An Inquiry into the Nature and Causes of the Wealth of Nations*.

Strathern, *A Brief History of Economic Genius*.

Questions to Consider

1. What was so revolutionary about Adam Smith's ideas, and what made them so difficult to grasp among his contemporaries?

2. Was John Stuart Mill justified in his claim that questions of distribution are not governed by natural laws and should be disconnected from questions of production?

Dismal Science—The Economists
Lecture 18—Transcript

As industrialization began to change the world, interested observers began to comment on what was happening and to ask why. Throughout most of world history, tradition and custom had been extremely powerful. People did what they'd always done. But now, a system was beginning to develop in which great rewards went to men who broke with tradition and tried something new. By the early 1800s, the continuous improvement of machinery, the growing scale of factories, the increased movement of people into the factories, and the social dislocations that went with these changes helped to give birth to the discipline of economics.

The great questions asked by economists are: Why does industrialization make people rich? Why are the rewards so unevenly distributed? What is the connection between individual wealth and national welfare? Is industrial society compatible with human ideas about justice and morality? As the industrial revolution continued, economists also began to ask: Why is there a combination of boom times and recessions, and can this fluctuation be influenced by government or prevented altogether?

The prevailing economic theory in the 18th century was mercantilism. Mercantilism was based on the idea of a zero-sum game: that one nation's gain must be another nation's loss; that there's only a fixed amount of goods in the world, and so if one nation's getting wealthier, it must be because another is getting poorer. Therefore, according to the theory, the nation must bring in as much money as possible, gold and silver in particular. It must bring in more than it exports, and try to keep as much trade as possible for itself. Mercantilist theory motivated the acquisition and jealous preservation of colonies by Britain and by the other European powers who shared the same essential theory. This was one of the sources of the recurrent 18th-century wars. It was also the justification for high tariffs, to make it difficult for other nations' goods to sell inside Britain. Hence the notorious Navigation Acts, which were the political embodiment of mercantilist theory. They said that all Britain's colonial trade must come via England, and must come in British or British colonial ships. The Navigation Acts presupposed that the nation's strength required close political regulation of economic activities, and this was a claim that the theorists of the industrial age were going to challenge.

Adam Smith's famous book *Inquiry into the Causes of the Wealth of Nations* from 1776 is often regarded as the first modern study of economics. Adam Smith was a professor in Glasgow. He was part of the Scottish Enlightenment. He was a philosopher and a moralist, and incidentally a near contemporary at Glasgow of James Watt, the instrument maker who went on to make the crucial improvements to steam engines. Adam Smith was famously absentminded. He spent several years as a young aristocrat's tutor on the Grand Tour in France and Switzerland, which was then better paid than his professorship. While he was in Europe, he met Voltaire and many of the other great figures of the European Enlightenment. He was one of the most highly educated people in Europe, and in touch with many of the new currents in contemporary thought.

His book's title, *An Inquiring to the Causes of the Wealth of Nations*, discloses what he was thinking about: Why do some nations become wealthy? Poverty had always been normal; poverty never had to be explained. But widespread wealth was something new and something surprising. In this great book, Adam Smith offered a sequence of fascinating big ideas. The first one was: Self-interest can have positive social outcomes. Surprisingly, private vice might even contribute to public virtue. This idea had come up previously. A writer called Bernard de Mandeville in 1714 had written *The Fable of the Bees*, in which he pointed out that a wastrel, a profligate young man, although he's dissipated and dissolute, is actually creating work for laborers to supply his dissolute lifestyle, whereas, said Mandeville, the upright, penny pinching virtuous man doesn't create demand in the same way. Smith takes this idea and works with it more systematically. In one famous passage from *The Wealth of Nations*, he says:

> It is not from the benevolence of the butcher, the brewer, or the baker that we expect our dinner, but from their regard for their self-interest. We address ourselves not to their humanity, but to their self-love, and never talk to them of our necessities, but of their advantages.

In other words, the baker provides bread not because he's concerned about my welfare, but because he's concerned about his own. He understands that the best way to look after his own interests is by providing good quality bread so that I and all the other buyers will keep coming back to him.

Adam Smith also believed that wealth was based on labor, not on the possession of gold and silver money. He said it might be an understandable mistake to think that it matters that we have a lot of gold and silver in the kingdom, but that actually doesn't matter. What matters is the people in the kingdom are working, and that they're working well and efficiently. He noted that in other societies, in other times and places, cattle had been used as money, or salt, or seashells, or tobacco, or cod, or sugar. All these things can be used as currency. Money is just an exchange medium. He says metal is, in fact, very good, especially a durable metal like gold or silver, because you can carry it around and it doesn't deteriorate, it doesn't rust. But it only represents other things, chiefly labor. So, says Adam Smith, nations were wealthy to the degree that they improved their efficiency in employing labor.

He also wrote extensively about the division of labor, and he said that division of labor increases efficiency to an astonishing degree. The famous example he gives in one of the early chapters of *The Wealth of Nations* is that of the pin makers. He said the pin making business has already been broken down into lots of different simple operations. When that's happened, when each part of the job is being done by somebody different, collectively the group of pin makers becomes much more efficient: "Ten persons, therefore, could make among them upwards of 48,000 pins in a day. But if they had all wrought separately and independently, they certainly could not each of them make 20, perhaps not one pin in a day." So by bringing together 10 men, you don't get 10 times as many pins, you get thousands of times as many. That was a very striking discovery that, of course, many of the industrialists were recognizing at exactly that time.

Of course, to make this happen, the workers have to behave in a certain way. Three factors were important: the workers' dexterity, their skill at doing it; their ability not to waste time; and the invention of machines to do the specialized work even faster. This mention of the machines shows that Smith is right at the start of the mechanization of industry and can't yet foresee in the mid-1770s the degree to which the machines themselves are going to become central to the whole business. Smith noted that as labor is ever more divided, the workers themselves often see how the tiny little bit of work that they're doing could itself be accomplished by a machine. He quotes a couple of examples of hands-on workers inventing a mechanical way of doing their work.

Smith also points out in *The Wealth of Nations* that there's an immense amount of cooperation and division of labor already, even that we don't often realize it. He gives the example of a simple, poor man and the plain coat that he's wearing. He says "Think of how many peoples' labor has gone into the making of this coat," the sheep farmer, the shepherd who looked after the sheep, the sheep shearer who cut off its wool, the carder, the dyer, the spinner, the weaver, the fuller, the dresser, the various carriers who took the fabric and the yarn from place to place, the tailor who made it up, and the shopkeeper who eventually sold it. He says the same is true of the rest of this poor man's life: "Without the assistance and cooperation of many thousands, the very meanest person in a civilized country could not be provided, even according to what we very falsely imagine, the easy and simple manner in which he is commonly accommodated." So, says Smith, even though we don't always notice it, there's an incredible degree of division of labor already going on and a very, very high level of specialization already.

Another famous theme in Adam Smith is the idea of the invisible hand of the market. Markets operate well, and they operate so well, it's almost as though an invisible hand was placing everything in the right place. Of course, there isn't really a hand; really it's a self-operating mechanism. The invisible hand of the market is extremely good at organizing economic affairs. Individuals will respond to a new demand by providing goods or services. People see that the demand is there and they strive to fulfill it. The government doesn't need to specify that somebody should do it. In fact, the government is likely to make mistakes in trying, because it doesn't have quick enough and reliable enough information. This, of course, is a straight contradiction of the mercantilists who did believe that government must supervise the economic activities of the kingdom.

Smith also says that there's a human propensity to trade. It's intrinsic to humanity that we want to trade, and in this respect we're totally unlike all the other creatures in the world: "Nobody ever saw a dog make a fair and deliberate exchange of one bone for another with another dog. Nobody ever saw one animal, by its gestures and natural cries, signify to another, this is mine, that yours; I am willing to give you this for that." This propensity to trade is itself related to division of labor, because it makes it reasonable for individuals not to try to do everything for themselves, but to exchange parts of their labor in trade; to specialize.

Also crucial to Adam Smith's understanding of the world is that economic growth is real. Economic activity isn't a zero-sum game, and one nation can grow wealthier without another one becoming poorer. As one person gets wealthier, he's not necessarily taking this wealth away from someone else. Incidentally, there's a famous article by an anthropologist called George Foster called "The Concept of the Limited Good." Foster talks about how in many undeveloped, preindustrial societies there's a very, very strong belief that there's only a certain amount of good stuff in the world, and that if one person's got it, it's because they've taken it away from someone else. Foster shows how that's very often linked to gift giving. In other words, the person with wealth is constantly giving it away to confirm his position in society, and if the gift giving breaks down, a social crisis can begin.

Smith, already in the 1770s, refutes the whole concept that we can't have growth. He says consumers will benefit as producers compete to provide better-quality goods at lower cost. Then, successful businessmen—people who have worked out how to improve quality and reduce costs—will accumulate money. They reinvest it in new factories or new economic opportunities, and in doing so they create new employment for more people.

Smith wasn't a Pollyanna. He didn't try to argue that the system was completely free of costs. It did, in fact, have a downside. As labor is more subdivided, work becomes far less interesting than it was in the days of the old master craftsmen, when one man could aspire to learn one of the mysteries: "The man whose whole life is spent in performing a few simple operations generally becomes as stupid and ignorant as it is possible for a human creature to become, unless the government takes some pains to prevent it." He thought there was a role for government to play in, for example, creating schools to make sure that before they submitted to a life of narrowly specialized work, people would have the opportunity to learn to read and to look about themselves a little.

Adam Smith's ideas were refined and complexified by David Ricardo in a book called *The Principles of Political Economy and Taxation* from 1817. Despite the name Ricardo, which sounds Italian or Spanish, Ricardo was English. He was the son of a Jewish banker who'd immigrated to England from Holland, and he himself converted to Quakerism, joining the religion that was so common among the rising entrepreneurial class. Ricardo made a fortune on the stock market—he was an extremely shrewd investor— then retired from business to become a Member of Parliament and a writer on economics. He was greatly respected in Parliament because of his understanding of complex economic issues that most of the Members of Parliament simply couldn't grasp. As I mentioned last time, before 1832 the Members of Parliament were mainly landed gentlemen. They didn't really have much of a clue about economics. Ricardo was very talented at explaining to them in a straightforward way what was actually going on.

He was witnessing, living when he did, the conflict between two groups of wealthy people: the landowners and the rising industrialists. The landowners wanted food to be expensive; the industrialists wanted it to be cheap. The landlords were dominant in Parliament well into the 19th century and were, therefore, eager to preserve their situation. David Ricardo argued that as industrial progress continues, more workers are needed to do the industrial work, and that leads to a rise in wages. They have to be fed, so food production rises. That means that more and more marginal land is brought into cultivation, and overall food prices keep rising. The workers may get more money, they may be paid more, but they're not going to be better off because they have to pay more for food, which is now in limited supply. Ricardo says the losers from this situation are the capitalists, because they're forced to pay higher wages in order to keep their work force. Who comes out on top in this system? The landlords, because they can charge high rent for land and get high prices for the food that they produce, either they or their tenants.

Ricardo became a great advocate of abolishing the Corn Laws and allowing cheap imports of food to come into the country. He represented the point of view that eventually was going to prevail. More generally, Ricardo was in favor of free trade because he wanted to prevent the unproductive landlords from profiting the most. With the abolition of the Corn Laws in 1846, he did finally get his own way, although he didn't have the chance to live to see it.

One of Ricardo's friends was Thomas Malthus. Malthus, like Ricardo, assumed that even as national wealth increased, which it certainly was doing, the poor would always remain poor. Malthus's insight was this: The ability to reproduce is so much greater than ability to increase food production. Population can rise geometrically, food production can only at best increase arithmetically, so population pressure is always going to be pushing right up against subsistence levels. The only way out of this what's now called a Malthusian trap, the only way that Malthus could see to prevent this, was voluntary self-restraint. He favored delaying marriage or not marrying at all as a way of trying to reduce the number of people. Later on in the 20th century, advocates of contraception and population control have been known as Neo-Malthusians. There were new advocates of Malthus's ideas.

The next generation of economists took up the question of the business cycle. Malthus had glimpsed it, but never developed it fully. By the early 1800s, it was clear that booms and busts alternated. Economic growth was real, but it didn't happen in a smooth, upward line; it was a very jagged line. Why should that be? The economists started to speculate like this: Individual manufacturers, or people who could be manufacturers, hear of rising demand for a product. That gives them a logical reason for trying to meet that demand. Several of them or many of them enter that trade and make the commodity that's needed until the demand is satisfied. But once it's satisfied, there are so many of them busy in that trade that they create a glut. Demand therefore falls off, the price falls because there's plenty of this stuff on the market, then men are laid off, and some of the businesses go bankrupt. Again, you've had a sudden surge of growth, but now it goes down again. It's not linear growth.

This idea of what came to be called "the business cycle" was first theorized systematically by the Swiss historian and economist Sismondi in 1819 in a book called *New Principles of Political Economy*. Ricardo had doubted that business cycles and crises of this kind could happen, but Sismondi saw the evidence; it was irrefutable that this really was happening. He realized employers never have a perfect knowledge of what's happening. To some extent, everyone is acting in the dark. Although people who are investing their own money have the best possible motives to be shrewd about it, they still don't know exactly what's going to happen; they can't predict future demand perfectly. Sismondi writes against the idea that the invisible hand works perfectly by saying: "Let us beware of this dangerous theory of equilibrium which is supposed to be automatically established. A certain kind of equilibrium, it is true, is reestablished in the long run, but it is after a frightful amount of suffering." Sismondi favored government intervention to support the unemployed rather than simply letting market forces plunge these vulnerable workers into chaos and suffering.

He also believed that the business cycle was related to the tendency of capitalists to pay excessively low wages, which led to periodic phases of overproduction and under-consumption. This idea was later picked up by Karl Marx, who was himself an intense student of economics. Marx predicted that these crises would become ever more catastrophic and eventually that they'd provoke revolution.

The theory of the business cycle certainly has been borne out by much later experience. Recessions and depressions did appear to become ever more serious as more people were drawn into the industrial economy. The Great Depression of the 1930s was so severe as to cause a widespread challenge to the legitimacy of capitalism itself.

Economists also involved themselves with the question of social justice. Was exploitation central to industrial capitalism, or did workers and employers have a shared set of concerns as they worked together? Were they allies or were they antagonists? The Utopian Socialists denied that class conflict was inevitable. I mentioned earlier Robert Owen, the man who founded the New Lanark Mills outside of Glasgow in Scotland. He bought the mills from his father-in-law in 1799 and was determined to be a benevolent employer. He built decent workers' houses, he paid decent wages, he created a school for the children, and yet he was still able to turn a profit. He kept on his workers at full pay during an American cotton embargo in 1807, when suddenly there wasn't work to be had.

His book, *A New View of Society*, published in 1813, advanced an environmental theory of human development. Owen said, "Treat people kindly and educate them, and you can make them mild, humane, and generous. Vicious treatment makes people vicious. There's nothing natural about it. So don't leave people to be free." In other words, he favored a kind of humane social engineering to create suitable industrial-era people, and he dismissed the claim of many of his fellow industrialists that they were simply letting freedom operate.

Owen realized that the factory was a social system as well as a place of production. It could be run so as to create a form of cooperative sharing socialism. Owen was greatly vilified in his day by many of his opponents, partly because he was also an advocate of free love; a very unconventional thinker for his time. Later on, he tried to export his ideas to the United States and ran an unsuccessful industrial commune in America at New Harmony, Indiana. It wasn't harmonious, and he discovered that people's self-interests can be a very, very powerful force that's extremely difficult to overcome.

Ricardo and Malthus were also friends of Jeremy Bentham and James Mill, two names we usually associate with utilitarian philosophy. These men brought philosophy down to Earth, insisting that the greatest good for the greatest number was the criteria in a philosophy rather than some religious principle, and that the greatest good for the greatest number should guide human conduct. This is an ideal philosophy for industrialists, who justified themselves by producing things that people would buy; things that they buy in the here and now. There's no spiritual dimension to it at all; it's all very practical.

The obvious weakness of the utilitarian philosophy, which its critics picked up on almost at once, is that happiness or pleasure is very difficult to measure. What about the issue of desire, for example? Is desire painful, or is it pleasurable? Certainly, people talk about an agonizing desire. Does that mean they're really in pain, or do they really enjoy it? Some utilitarians said one thing, others said the opposite. A second obvious weakness with utilitarianism is that it has no moral absolutes. For example, if killing a scapegoat delights thousands of others, then it might be the right thing to do by utilitarian measurement. But, of course, then it's done at the expense of human rights, and we've got good reasons to think that basic human rights sometimes ought to overcome the utilitarian calculus.

Bentham and Mill are famous also for their experiment with James Mill's son, John Stuart Mill, whom they educated to an incredibly high standard when he was still in early childhood in classical languages, in mathematics, psychology, economics, politics, and philosophy, only to see him suffer a nervous breakdown at the age of 19. But John Stuart Mill, the son, accepted the utilitarian principle and, in fact, he tried to apply it to economics. His book, *The Principles of Political Economy*, published in 1848, became the great standard textbook of 19th-century economics, constantly read, translated, and reprinted.

John Stuart Mill pointed out that the laws Smith and Ricardo had discovered relating to production weren't matched by laws of distribution. Here, says John Stuart Mill, moral principles and community decisions must apply:

> The rules by which distribution is determined are what the opinions and feelings of the ruling portion of the community make them, and are very different in different ages and countries, and might be still more different if mankind so choose.

In other words, if the community favors principles of equality, it could arrange distribution along these lines. No system of distribution was actually "natural" at all.

John Stuart Mill wasn't a socialist, but many socialists and trade unionists found him sympathetic for such insights as those. He knew that in contemporary Britain—the Britain of the mid-19th century—the lowest incomes went to the people who labored the most, and that the very highest incomes often went to those who did almost nothing, the aristocracy. His view was that the abandonment or transformation of such a system was not necessarily unjust. But on the other hand, John Stuart Mill certainly believed in the value of private property and the virtue of hard work. He wrote:

That the energies of mankind should be kept in employment by the struggle for riches as they were formerly by the struggle for war, until better minds succeed in educating the others into better things, is undoubtedly better than that they should rust and stagnate. While minds are coarse, they require coarse stimuli, and let them have them.

John Stuart Mill also tried to turn economics into a rigorous academic discipline, modeled on the physical sciences. But he realized that prediction is always going to be uncertain, and that the complexity of human life makes accurate anticipation of the future impossible. Others denied the possibility of strife-free production, and again I need to come back here for a moment to Karl Marx and the Marxists, whose influence was so great. For them, capitalism was inherently exploitative. Industry was good, but not so long as it was run by capitalists. It must be overthrown by force, they said, as the proletariat got bigger and more miserable, and as business downturns, depressions, became more catastrophic.

In fact, the workers weren't getting poorer. Bit by bit, certainly after about 1840, they were getting richer very slowly through the 19th century as real wages gradually rose and the hours of work to which they were subjected gradually decreased. Already by the mid-19th century, some economists were beginning to wonder whether the raw materials on which the Industrial Revolution was built would keep going. William Stanley Jevons, a brilliant but depressive mathematical economist, wrote a book called *The Coal Question*, published in 1865, arguing that Britain would soon run out of coal, and then that the whole Industrial Revolution would come to an end. The book also introduced what's called the "Jevons paradox." He said "as fuel use increases in efficiency,"—that is, as we learn how to use less coal for the same amount of work—"we don't use less of it, but more." For example, after James Watt improved the Newcomen steam engines by making them more efficient, the number in use and the total coal consumption went up sharply, not down. He anticipated with great seriousness that there was going to be no more coal left. It was taken seriously at the time and, in fact, this was the father of constant subsequent alarms that we'll run out of resources. This was one of the great concerns of the 1970s. Actually, it hasn't happened because we're so good at increases in efficiency and increases in substitution using something else instead.

Jevons's work also showed the shift to mathematical economics that's been going on ever since. Adam Smith's book, *The Wealth of Nations*, is all descriptive, but by the late 19th century, the statistics and the equations were becoming more and more prominent in works of economics as it became more detailed and more precise.

There's always been a connection between economics and politics, as I hope the last two lectures have made clear, but rarely a linear one. Politicians usually only understood a radically simplified version of the economics, and they were more attentive to lobbyists than to logic.

At this point, we're halfway through this course of 36 lectures. So far, I've talked almost entirely about Britain, where the Industrial Revolution began. But now it's time for us to spread our wings and travel to some other parts of the world to see how they reacted to Britain's newfound power and wealth. We'll begin with a visit to the United States, which was destined not just to catch up with Britain, but to overtake it as the world's industrial leader.

Bibliography

Allen, Frederick Lewis. *Only Yesterday: An Informal History of the 1920s*. New York: Wiley, 1997.

Allen, Robert C. *The British Industrial Revolution in Global Perspective*. Cambridge; New York: Cambridge University Press, 2009.

Allitt, Patrick. *A Climate of Crisis: America in the Age of Environmentalism*. New York: Penguin, 2014. Industry creates pollution, but better industrial methods combine pollution reduction with more economic growth.

Andrews, Richard. *Managing the Environment, Managing Ourselves*. 2nd ed. New Haven, CT: Yale University Press, 2006. Authoritative account of American environmental progress since the 1960s.

Ashton, T. S. *Iron and Steel in the Industrial Revolution*. Manchester, UK: Manchester University Press, 1951. A no-nonsense account of the iron masters' accomplishments and their forbidding personalities.

Atkinson, Frank. *The Great Northern Coalfield, 1700–1900*. London: University Tutorial Press, 1968. Excellent introduction to mining history and technology.

Bagust, Harold. *The Greater Genius? A Biography of Marc Isambard Brunel*. Hersham, UK: Ian Allen, 2006.

Barman, Christian. *Early British Railways*. London: Penguin, 1950.

Barrett, Neil. *The Binary Revolution: The Development of the Computer*. London: Weidenfeld and Nicolson, 2006. Companion to Lecture 33.

Belchem, John. *Industrialization and the Working Class: The English Experience, 1750–1900*. Aldershot, UK: Scolar Press, 1990.

Bell, Daniel. *The Coming of Post-Industrial Society.* New York: Basic Books, 1973.

Bilstein, Roger. *Flight in America, 1900–1983: From the Wrights to the Astronauts.* Baltimore, MD: Johns Hopkins University Press, 1984.

Boot, Max. *War Made New: Weapons, Warriors, and the Making of the Modern World.* New York: Gotham Books, 2007.

Borsay, Peter. *The English Urban Renaissance: Culture and Society in the Provincial Town, 1660–1770.* New York: Oxford University Press, 1989. How England's towns and cities grew, energizing productivity at the dawn of the industrial age.

Brindle, Steven. *Brunel: The Man Who Built the World.* London: Weidenfeld and Nicolson, 2005. The best of many biographies of the railway and ship titan.

Bryson, Bill. *One Summer: America, 1927.* New York: Doubleday, 2013. Excellent on aviation history, electricity, and the American consumer revolution of the 1920s—fun, too.

Burk, Kathleen. *Old World, New World: The Story of Britain and America.* London: Little Brown, 2007. A terrific history of the great Anglo-American relationship, with plenty of insight into why America caught up industrially.

Burton, Anthony. *The Canal Builders.* London: Eyre Methuen, 1972.

———. *Josiah Wedgwood: A Biography.* London: Deutsch, 1976. One of Britain's best historians of industry, here at the height of his powers.

———. *The Railway Builders.* London: John Murray, 1992.

Carnegie, Andrew. *Autobiography.* Boston; New York: Houghton Mifflin, 1920.

Chalkin, Christopher. *The Rise of the English Town, 1650–1850.* Cambridge, UK: Cambridge University Press, 2001.

Chang, Ha-Joon. *The East Asian Development Experience: The Miracle, the Crisis, and the Future*. New York: Palgrave Macmillan, 2007. How the Asian Tigers industrialized after World War II and what remains for them to accomplish.

Chapman, S. D. *The Cotton Industry in the Industrial Revolution*. London: Macmillan, 1972. Good on the economic aspects of the textile revolution.

Chernow, Ron. *Titan: The Life of John D. Rockefeller, Sr.* New York: Vintage, 1998. Hefty at nearly 900 pages, but then Rockefeller did live a very long and full life!

Christopher, John. *Brunel's Kingdom: In the Footsteps of Britain's Greatest Engineer*. Stroud, UK: Tempus, 2006.

Cipolla, Carlo, ed. *The Fontana Economic History of Europe: The Emergence of Industrial Societies, Part 1*. London: Collins/Fontana, 1974. A good starting point for understanding the European situation in the early 1800s.

Clark, Peter, ed. *The Cambridge Urban History of Britain*. Vol. 2: *1540–1840*. Cambridge, UK: Cambridge University Press, 2008.

Coad, Jonathan. *Historic Architecture of the Royal Navy: An Introduction*. London: Victor Gollancz, 1983.

————. *The Royal Dockyards, 1690–1850: Architecture and Engineering Works of the Sailing Navy*. Aldershot, UK: Scolar Press, 1989. Coad loves details and brings to life the world of the old wooden-navy shipyards.

Coote, Stephen. *Samuel Pepys: A Life*. London: Hodder and Stoughton, 2000. Pepys is a biographer's dream, and Coote enjoys himself in every area of his subject's life, from shipyard management to politics to sexual infidelity.

Corble, Nick. *James Brindley: The First Canal Builder*. Stroud, UK: Tempus, 2005. Companion to Lecture 9.

Corfield, P. J. *The Impact of English Towns, 1700–1800*. New York: Oxford University Press, 1982.

Crowe, Nigel. *English Heritage Book of Canals*. London: Batsford, 1994.

David, Deirdre. *The Cambridge Companion to the Victorian Novel*. Cambridge, UK: Cambridge University Press, 2001.

Deane, Phyllis. *The First Industrial Revolution*. Cambridge, UK: Cambridge University Press, 1965. Aging but still widely admired general history of the whole phenomenon.

Denison, Merrill. *The Power to Go: The Story of the Automotive Industry*. New York: Doubleday, 1956.

Dickinson, H. W. *James Watt and the Industrial Revolution*. London: Longman's Green, 1948. Admiring biographer of the steam engine innovator.

Dodds, James, and James Moore. *Building the Wooden Fighting Ship*. London: Chatham Publishing, 2005. Includes magnificently detailed illustrations of every process in assembling the preindustrial Royal Navy.

Dolan, Brian. *Wedgwood: The First Tycoon*. New York: Viking, 2004. Fine biography, emphasizing Wedgwood's skill in marketing and publicity.

Douglas, George. *All Aboard: The Railroad in American Life*. New York: Paragon House, 1992. Explains how the United States borrowed from the English railway pioneers but went on to improve on their achievements.

Engels, Friedrich. *The Condition of the English Working Class in England*. David McLellan, ed. New York: Oxford University Press, 1993 (1845). Still the single best book to give a sense of why Marxism was so emotionally appealing to those who found capitalism disgusting. A harrowing account of the suffering poor in the great English industrial cities.

Evans, Chris, and Goran Ryden, eds. *The Industrial Revolution in Iron.* Burlington, VT: Ashgate, 2005. Essays on the way British iron-making innovations spread through continental Europe in the 19th century.

Fitton, R. S. *The Strutts and the Arkwrights, 1758–1830.* Manchester, UK: Manchester University Press, 1958. Group biography of the Derbyshire entrepreneurs who mechanized the early textile industry.

Floud, Roderick, and Paul Johnson, eds., *The Cambridge Economic History of Modern Britain*, vol. 1, *Industrialization, 1700–1860.* Cambridge, UK: Cambridge University Press, 2003.

Freeberg, Ernest. *The Age of Edison: Electric Light and the Invention of Modern America.* New York: Penguin, 2013. In this superb book, Freeberg reminds us not to take electricity for granted and recounts its heroic early era.

Gallagher, Catherine. *The Industrial Reformation of English Fiction: Social Discourse and Narrative Form, 1832–1867.* Chicago: University of Chicago Press, 1985.

Galloway, Robert L. *A History of Coal Mining in Great Britain.* New York: A. M. Kelley, 1969. Companion to Lecture 7.

Ganguly, Sumit, and Rahul Mukherji. *India Since 1980.* New York: Cambridge University Press, 2011. Unblinking account of the severe obstacles confronting India's industrial transformation in recent decades.

Gelderman, Carol. *Henry Ford: The Wayward Capitalist.* New York: Dial Press, 1981.

Gourvish, T. R. *Railways and the British Economy, 1830–1914.* London: Macmillan, 1980. Explains how railways accelerated economic growth and knit together disparate parts of the United Kingdom.

Greene, Victor. *The Slavic Community on Strike.* South Bend, IN: University of Notre Dame Press, 1968. Fascinating, detailed study of an American immigrant community at work and on strike—gruesome in places.

Griffin, A. R. *Mining in the East Midlands, 1550–1947*. London: Cass, 1971.

Gutman, Herbert. *Work, Culture and Society in Industrializing America*. New York: Vintage, 1977. Brilliantly perceptive account by one of the greatest recent American historians.

Hanson, Harry. *Canal People*. Newton Abbot, UK: David and Charles, 1978. The people who lived on and worked England's network of canals.

Harris, J. R. *The British Iron Industry, 1700–1850*. Basingstoke, UK: Macmillan Educational, 1988.

Hastings, Max. *Bomber Command*. New York: Dial Press, 1987. How the Royal Air Force used an industrial mass-produced product, the bomber, to destroy German industrial cities during World War II.

Heilbroner, Robert. *The Worldly Philosophers: The Lives, Times, and Ideas of the Great Economic Thinkers*. 5th ed. New York: Simon and Schuster, 1980. A perennial classic on the history of modern economics—readable and lucidly clear, unlike the work of most other economic historians.

Hobsbawm, Eric. *Industry and Empire: An Economic History of Britain Since 1750*. London: Weidenfeld and Nicolson, 1968. The ideal companion to the first 18 lectures of this course.

Hosking, Geoffrey. *A History of the Soviet Union*. London: Collins/Fontana, 1985. Good summary of the crash-course industrialization favored by Lenin and Stalin.

Hounshell, David. *From the American System to Mass Production: The Development of Manufacturing Technology in the United States*. Baltimore, MD: Johns Hopkins University Press, 1985. Splendid account of American technological accomplishments from Eli Whitney to Henry Ford, with excellent illustrations and photographs. This is the single best book ever written on the technical side of the American Industrial Revolution.

Hyde, Charles K. *Technological Change in the British Iron Industry, 1700–1870*. Princeton, NJ: Princeton University Press, 1977.

Israel, Paul. *Edison: A Life of Invention*. New York: John Wiley, 1998.

James, Harold. *Krupp: A History of the Legendary German Firm*. Princeton, NJ: Princeton University Press, 2012. Thorough account of the German munitions company.

Johnson, Paul. *A History of the English People*. London: Weidenfeld and Nicolson, 1985. A highly opinionated and always controversial historian explains, among many other things, the relatively low status of industry in British life and the elite's disinclination to pursue it.

Jonnes, Jill. *Eiffel's Tower and the World's Fair*. New York: Viking, 2009. A reminder that the Eiffel Tower was once regarded by influential people as an industrial eyesore rather than the perfect symbol of Paris.

Keegan, John. *The Second World War*. New York: Penguin, 1989. Persuasive analysis of how the great industrial societies fought one another in the 1940s.

Kerridge, Eric. *The Agricultural Revolution*. New York: A. M. Kelley, 1968. Companion to Lecture 3.

Kirby, M. W. *The Origins of Railway Enterprise: The Stockton and Darlington Railway, 1821–1863*. Cambridge; New York: Cambridge University Press, 1993.

Kitchen, Martin. *A History of Modern Germany, 1800 to the Present*. Malden, MA: Wiley Blackwell, 2012.

Lane, Peter. *The Industrial Revolution: The Birth of the Modern Age*. New York: Barnes and Noble, 1978.

Lemire, Beverly. *Cotton*. New York: Berg, 2011. Entertaining account of the early English textile industry and its riotous workers.

Lewin, H. G. *The Railway Mania and Its Aftermath, 1845–1852*. New York: A. M. Kelley, 1968. Overly exuberant investors deceived themselves over what, briefly, seemed like the infinite profitability of railways. Many were ruined.

Lewis, Brian. *Coal Mining in the 18th and 19th Centuries*. Harlow, UK: Longman, 1971.

Lind, Michael. *Land of Promise: An Economic History of the United States*. New York: Broadside Books, 2012.

Livesay, Harold. *Andrew Carnegie and the Rise of Big Business*. Boston: Little Brown, 1975. An ex-working man who got his history Ph.D. late in life, Livesay understands both sides of the controversies that characterized Carnegie's life.

————. *Samuel Gompers and Organized Labor in America*. Boston: Little Brown, 1978. Sympathetic account of the American trade union movement and its first great leader.

Lomborg, Bjorn. *The Skeptical Environmentalist*. New York: Cambridge University Press, 2001. Controversial but persuasive alternative view of how industry and environment interact. A cheering accompaniment to Lecture 35.

Lynd, Robert, and Helen Lynd. *Middletown: A Study in Modern American Culture*. New York: Harcourt Brace/Harvest, 1957 (1929). The sociological classic that gives us a window into everyday American life in the 1920s.

Marsh, Peter. *The New Industrial Revolution: Consumers, Globalization and the End of Mass Production*. New Haven, CT: Yale University Press, 2012. Where we stand now and what may be coming next for the industrial world.

Mathias, Peter. *The First Industrial Nation: An Economic History of Britain, 1700–1914*. London: Methuen, 1969.

McCullough, David. *The Path between the Seas: The Creation of the Panama Canal*. New York: Simon and Schuster, 1977. How tropical diseases destroyed the French effort and how the conquest of those diseases, along with more capital, machinery, and engineering savvy, made the American effort a success.

McKendrick, Neil, John Brewer, and J. H. Plumb. *The Birth of a Consumer Society: The Commercialization of Eighteenth-Century England.* Bloomington, IN: Indiana University Press, 1982. Fine introduction to the way upper-class English fashions stimulated productivity and innovation by Wedgwood and others.

Milward, Alan. *War, Economy, and Society, 1939–1945.* Berkeley: University of California Press, 1980.

Mingay, G. E. *Arthur Young and His Times.* London: Macmillan, 1975. The life and work of the great agricultural writer and innovator.

Mirsky, Jeanette, and Allan Nevins. *The World of Eli Whitney.* New York: Macmillan, 1952.

Mokyr, Joel. *The Enlightened Economy: An Economic History of Britain, 1700–1850.* New Haven, CT: Yale University Press, 2009. The best recent economic history of the whole British Industrial Revolution.

Morgan, John Smith. *Robert Fulton.* New York: Mason/Charter, 1977. Biography of the American steamboat inventor and entrepreneur.

Morris, Charles. *The Dawn of Innovation: The First American Industrial Revolution.* New York: Public Affairs, 2012.

Musson, A. E. *The Growth of British Industry.* New York: Holmes & Meier, 1978.

Musson, A. E., and Eric Robinson. *Science and Technology in the Industrial Revolution.* Toronto: University of Toronto Press, 1969.

Nevins, Allan, and Frank E. Hill. *Ford: The Times, the Man, the Company.* New York: Scribner, 1954. The authors juxtapose Ford's astonishing astuteness in mechanics and business with his cluelessness about most other aspects of the human condition.

Nye, David. *Electrifying America: The Social Meaning of a New Technology*. Cambridge, MA: MIT Press, 1992.

O'Brien, Patrick, ed. *Railways and the Economic Development of Western Europe, 1830–1914*. New York: St. Martin's Press, 1983.

Overton, Mark. *Agricultural Revolution in England: The Transformation of the Agrarian Economy, 1500–1850*. New York: Cambridge University Press, 1996.

Overy, Richard. *Why the Allies Won*. London: Jonathan Cape, 1995. Superb account of Soviet, American, and British mass production in the war years.

Pelling, Henry. *The Origins of the Labour Party*. New York: St. Martin's Press, 1954. Institutional history of the British trade union movement and its decision to create a political party in the late 19th century.

Pells, Richard. *Radical Visions and American Dreams*. New York: Harper and Row, 1973. Futurologists of the 1930s and the idea of technocracy.

Ponting, Clive. *A Green History of the World*. New York: St. Martin's Press, 1991. Environmental perspective on the damage wrought by dirty industrial processes, by an apocalyptically gloomy author.

Pope, Rex. *Atlas of British Social and Economic History Since c. 1700*. London: Routledge, 1989. Keep it beside you while watching or listening to this course to learn exactly where in Britain all the innovations took place.

Rogers, Robert P. *An Economic History of the American Steel Industry*. New York: Routledge, 2009.

Rolt, L. T. C. *George and Robert Stephenson: The Railway Revolution*. London: Longman, 1960. A famous historian of technology, at the height of his powers, follows the lives of the father-and-son team who founded modern railways. Very good but prone to hero worship.

Ropp, Theodore. *War in the Modern World*. Rev. ed. Baltimore: Johns Hopkins University Press, 2000.

Royle, Edward. *Chartism*. London; New York: Longman, 1996.

Rubinstein, W. D. *Britain's Century: A Political and Social History, 1815–1905*. New York: Arnold, 1998. Excellent general history of the era, explaining the context of the industrial changes.

Salvatore, Nick. *Eugene Debs: Citizen and Socialist*. Urbana, IL: University of Illinois Press, 1982. Life of the American union leader and perennial Socialist Party candidate.

Schonhardt-Bailey, Cheryl. *From the Corn Laws to Free Trade: Interests, Ideas, and Institutions in Historical Perspective*. Cambridge, MA: MIT Press, 2006.

Schumpeter, Joseph, and Elizabeth Schumpeter. *History of Economic Analysis*. Rev. ed. New York: Oxford University Press, 1996.

Shurkin, Joel. *Engines of the Mind: The Evolution of the Computer from Mainframes to Microprocessors*. New York: Norton, 1996.

Simmons, Jack, and Gordon Biddle, eds. *The Oxford Companion to British Railway History from 1603 to the 1990s*. New York: Oxford University Press, 1997. All you need to know, and occasionally rather than more than all, on the topic.

Smith, Adam. *An Inquiry into the Nature and Causes of the Wealth of Nations*. Chicago: University of Chicago Press, 1977 (1776).

Smith, David. *The Dragon and the Elephant: China, India, and the New World Order*. London: Profile Books, 2007. The ideal companion to Lecture 34.

Sobel, Dava. *Longitude: The True Story of a Lone Genius Who Solved the Greatest Scientific Problem of His Time*. New York: Walker, 1995. This book is singled out by name in Lecture 14 on "Longitude" Harrison and his work.

Standiford, Les. *Meet You in Hell: Andrew Carnegie, Henry Clay Frick, and the Bitter Partnership That Transformed America*. New York: Crown, 2005.

Stearns, Peter. *The Industrial Revolution in World History*. 4th ed. Boulder, CO: Westview, 2013. If you want to read just one book on the whole topic of this course, Stearns's is the obvious choice.

Stilgoe, John R. *Metropolitan Corridor: Railroads and the American Scene*. New Haven, CT: Yale University Press, 1983. Heavily illustrated book on the transformed landscape made by railways, factories, dockyards, ash heaps, and power stations.

Strathern, Paul. *A Brief History of Economic Genius*. New York: Texere, 2001.

Swedin, Eric, and David Ferro. *Computers: The Life Story of a Technology*. Westport, CT: Greenwood, 2005.

Sylla, Richard, ed., *Patterns of European Industrialization: The Nineteenth Century*. London; New York: Routledge, 1991.

Thompson, E. P. *The Making of the English Working Class*. London: Gollancz, 1964. A true classic, this is the book that almost singlehandedly created the modern study of labor history. Every British and American labor historian since Thompson has had to argue with, or borrow from, his insights.

Tise, Larry. *Conquering the Sky: The Secret Flights of the Wright Brothers at Kitty Hawk*. New York: Palgrave, 2009. On the two methodical aviation pioneers and their aversion to publicity.

Vaughan, Adrian. *Isambard Kingdom Brunel: Engineering Knight Errant*. London: John Murray, 1991.

Walker, Judith Linsley, Ellen Walker Rienstra, and Jo Ann Stiles. *Giant under the Hill: A History of the Spindletop Oil Discovery at Beaumont, Texas, in 1901*. Austin: Texas State Historical Association, 2002.

Warburg, Jeremy. *The Industrial Muse: The Industrial Revolution in Poetry*. New York: Oxford University Press, 1958. Source of the amusingly awful poems quoted in Lecture 16.

Webb, Igor. *From Custom to Capital: The English Novel and the Industrial Revolution*. Ithaca, NY: Cornell University Press, 1981. Intelligent explanation of how novelists worked out ways to include factory owners and workers among their characters and in their plots.

Weinberg, Steve. *Taking on the Trust: How Ida Tarbell Brought down John D. Rockefeller and Standard Oil*. New York: Norton, 2008. Maybe the pen is even mightier than the monopoly corporation.

Whitworth, Joseph. *On an Uniform System of Screw Threads*. London: J. Weale, 1841.

Woodbury, Robert S. *Studies in the History of Machine Tools*. Cambridge, MA: MIT Press, 1972. Bone-dry account of the machine tools revolution, but full of learning and accurate information for the sufficiently motivated reader.

Yergin, Daniel. *The Prize: The Epic Quest for Oil, Money, and Power*. New York: Simon and Schuster, 1991. A whopping 900-page book on the oil business but as readable in its way as *War and Peace* and full of equally vivid characters.

Zakaria, Fareed. *The Future of Freedom: Illiberal Democracy at Home and Abroad*. New York: W. W. Norton & Co., 2003.

Bibliography